THE POETRY OF CRITICISM

THE POETRY OF CRITICISM

ટ્રે ટ્રે

Horace, *Epistles* II and
Ars Poetica

ટ્રે ટ્રે

Ross S. Kilpatrick

THE UNIVERSITY OF ALBERTA PRESS

First published by
The University of Alberta Press
Athabasca Hall
Edmonton, Alberta
Canada T6G 2E8

Copyright © The University of Alberta Press 1990

Canadian Cataloguing in Publication Data

Kilpatrick, Ross S. (Ross Stuart), 1934-
The poetry of criticism

Bibliography: p.
Includes index.
ISBN 0-88864-145-7 (bound). — ISBN
0-88864-146-X (pbk.)

1. Horace. Epistulae.   2. Horace. Ars
poetica.   I. Title.
PA6393.E8K55 1990   871'.01   C89-091310-2

Typesetting by The Typeworks, Vancouver, British Columbia

Printed by Hignell Printing Ltd., Winnipeg, Manitoba, Canada

❦ ❦　FOR SUZANNE
❦ ❦

&a &a CONTENTS

🍂 🍂 PREFACE

THE ARS POETICA, or the *Epistle to the Pisos,* is Horace's longest poem by far: 476 lines. The *Epistle to Augustus* (270) and *Epistle to Florus* (216) both fall short of the lengthy *Satire* 2.3 (326), but are still long poems by Horace's standards. This makes a total of 962 lines or about the length of the *Aeneid's* longer books: a convenient length for a papyrus scroll.

The critical bibliography on these three poems is enormous. There are 23 pages of titles overall in Charles Brink's three volumes of *Horace on Poetry* (1963, 1971, 1982), which he describes as "selective." The survey by Walter Kissel of Heidelberg, "Horaz 1936–1975: Eine Gesamtbibliographie," *Aufstieg und Niedergang der römischen Welt* II, 31.3 (1981), 1403–1558, includes eight pages of titles on *Epistles* II (1521–28). The same volume also includes a new critical survey by Francesco Sbordone, "La poetica oraziana alla luce degli studi più ecenti" (1866–1920). Nor is interest waning in the probable sources of Horace's views on poetic criticism; see, for example, H.J. Mette, "Neoptolemus von Parion," *RM* CXIII (1980), 1–24. Kissel prints two pages of bibliographies alone (1411–12). Representative of earlier surveys are A. Viola's two volumes, *L'Arte Poetica di Orazio nella Critica Italiana e Straniera* (Napoli, 1901, 1906).

The appearance of Brink's third and final volume of *Horace on Poetry*

(1982), coupled with all this bibliographical activity, gives us not only a complete overview of the critical scholarship on *Epistles* II and the *Ars Poetica*, but a whole new basis for a critical rationale.

> Horace had been a poet-critic almost as long as he had been writing as a poet. His criticism was fragmentary, *critique d'occasion*. It was prompted by his experience as a craftsman, and limited by the restricted aims of each of his critical writings. At one point of his career however he produced a work with a larger critical purpose. The work was the *Ars Poetica*, and its purpose was to present a view of the whole of what he considered great poetry.[1]

Throughout his three volumes Brink has aimed at a synthesis of the conflicting claims of both poetry and literary criticism upon these three poems. His historical account of the work and polemics of scholars of the nineteenth and twentieth centuries who have tried to identify, trace, and evaluate Horace's use of Aristotle and the Alexandrian critics has lightened the burden for all subsequent writers on this complex subject. At the same time he has set out to demonstrate Horace's own poetic artistry in composing them.

Objections to Brink's analyses have sometimes run high. Gordon Williams's reviews of *Horace on Poetry*, I and II, and his own critical discussions of the poems (see *TORP*) reveal a strong personal opposition to Brink's perceived conservatism in the textual and literary aspects of his commentary. Williams insists that "the didactic setting is not to be taken at face value," and that the setting is a "reflection of [Horace's] own interests," detecting in the *Ars* an element of "parody" of the traditional *artes*.

Another source of major controversy has been the question of the "epistolary" nature of these poems, in both the formal and autobiographical senses. The enduring nature of this controversy can be traced back to Quintilian's first use of the title, *"de arte poetica"* (rather than *"epistula ad Pisones"*). In modern times such scholars as Wieland, Wickham, Wili, Saint Denis, Ramain, and Williams have emphasized the importance of reading the *Ars* as both an epistle and a poem. Others such as Rostagni, Becker, Grimal, and Russell are on the whole more interested in its content and its choice and exposition of critical theory. Brink has not limited his investigation to either.

Problems in dating the three longer epistles seem to be less urgent at present; only the *Ars* itself remains adrift on the tides of such controversy. The identity of the three Pisos, *pater filiique*, remains a puzzle, in spite of Porphyrio's certainty. An extension of the questions of chronology, of course, is that of Horace's intentions for the *Ars Poetica's* publication. The manuscripts group the *Ars* with the *Odes* in spite of the work's obvious affinities with *Epistles* II. Were the three poems *ever* published together *in antiquity*, with the *Ars* included as *Epistle* 2.3?

My own interest in the three literary epistles grew out of work on *Epistles* I, now published as *The Poetry of Friendship: Horace Epistles* I (Edmonton: University of Alberta Press, 1986). That earlier study explored to a positive conclusion the thesis that Horatian epistles should be read first as dramatic monologues, with both the dramatic situation and character of the addressee of prime importance. Their epistolary motive (and raison d'être of the genre) is friendship. Rhetorically, the usual purpose of an epistle is advice or information, and as in *Epistles I*, Horace assumes the role of an older, wiser, mellower man writing letters to his friends (contemporary and junior) from the perspective of a former poet, now retired to the country and devoting all his time, at last, to contemplating life's *summa bona*.

In extending this study to the three literary epistles, separate analyses were the first step; second, the establishment of any relationships between the three in content, form, and purpose. Might Horace have conceived and intended them as a coherent, unified group of poems? Whatever the history of their actual publication, I now believe that he did.

While insufficient attention has been paid in the past to the more dramatic or occasional aspects of the literary epistles, considerable effort has been expended to isolate and account for Horace's choice of sources for critical theory, especially the (for us) shadowy Neoptolemus of Parium. Brink has brought order out of the chaos (even though some, like Williams, have lamented that the "poet" has disappeared in the quest for that order). What Brink has really achieved, however, is to show, in so far as that is possible, what parts of the *Ars Poetica* are based upon Neoptolemus, what on Aristotle, and what the criteria for its structural analysis might be, without ignoring the question of the work as poetry in its own right. For him it remains "a work of the imagination that makes a poetic symbol of literary theory."

Besides both Brink and Williams, the third major stimulus to my approach to the *Ars* has been the late Professor H.L. Tracy, a former head of my own department at Queen's University, who died recently in retirement after a long and distinguished career of service to Classics. In a fresh and undeservedly overlooked article, "Horace's *Ars Poetica*: A systematic argument," *G&R* XVII (1948): 104–15, Tracy applied the simple criterion of Horace's "lyrical method," which he compared to an artist's rapid sketch. Horace lays down two important aesthetic principles, the "Canon of Truth" (*simplex*) and the "Canon of Correctness" (*unum*), according to which a work must be "natural" and "whole" and "faithful to real life," and show "effective use of customary techniques." In structure, Tracy saw three "panels" in the *Ars Poetica*: Horace's general reflections (1–152), their first application (153–294), and second application (295–445), followed by a dramatic epilogue (451–76). It was Tracy's work that confirmed my belief that simple and valid insights were still possible into the *Ars*.

Finally the question was to translate or not? My decision has been to provide close prose translations of all three long epistles rather than introductory summaries. We have been abundantly well-served with English translations of these epistles in recent years. Niall Rudd's verse translations of the *Satires* and *Epistles* (Penguin, 1979) are lucid and felicitous and the same can be said for those of Jacob Fuchs (New York, 1977). The edition of the *Art of Poetry*, Burton Raffel (Albany, 1974) offers a lively (à la Fitzgerald) verse translation as well as a literal prose version by James Hynd, with notes. These translations with brief notes by the late Colin Macleod (*Horace: The Epistles Translated into English Verse with Brief Comment*. Instrumentum Litterarum. Rome, 1986) are superb. These four, along with the old Loeb translation of H. Rushton Fairclough (1929) have enriched our Horatian resources greatly. The translations appended to this book have but one main purpose, however, to serve as an extension of the commentary, suggesting at least, my views on matters of interpretation not explicitly discussed, and attempting to convey the tone and emphasis that I perceive in the originals. They make no claims whatsoever for literary merit, but only to be a deductive reflection of my researches into Horace's Latin.

❧ ❧ ACKNOWLEDGMENTS

A BEGINNING OF this research and analysis of the literary epistles was made possible by a Leave Fellowship from the Canada Council in 1977–1978, two months of which were spent at the American Academy in Rome as a Visiting Scholar, and by similar visits in 1982 and 1985, with the assistance of the Advisory Research Committee of Queen's University and the Social Sciences and Humanities Research Council of Canada, respectively. My special thanks are due to Lucilla Marino, the director of the AAR Library, for her many kindnesses. Access in Rome to both that library and that of the Deutsches Archäologisches Institut is any classicist's highest good fortune. Opportunities to present my views in seminars and lectures (at the University of Ottawa, Memorial University of Newfoundland, McGill University, The Canadian Academic Centre in Italy and the American Academy in Rome) have also been invaluable. I am most grateful to the Classical Association of Canada, and to those colleagues who made such occasions possible.

I am especially indebted to the two anonymous "Quintilii" who read the manuscript for the University of Alberta Press and the Canadian Federation for the Humanities, contributing a mine of detailed suggestions and urgent reproofs. This generous encouragement was much appreciated. Alexandra Beal and Laura Slade laboured patiently and expertly on the word-processor to prepare and edit my drafts; graduate students Carol Merriam, John Geyssen and David Meadows at Queen's checked bibliographies and references and helped greatly with indices. (My thanks and best wishes go with them now to Ohio State, Duke and McMaster Universities.) Charles Beer pared away many infelicitous or obscure words or phrases. Mary Mahoney-Robson, editor at the University of Alberta Press, saw the manuscript through the press. To all these friends, GRATIAS MAXIMAS.

This book has been published with the help of a grant from the Canadian Federation for the Humanities, using funds provided by the Social Sciences and Humanities Research Council of Canada.

My very personal thanks, finally, to Professor C.O. Brink for his hospitality and advice in Cambridge in 1978 and to the late Professor E.T. Silk, whose unflagging enthusiasm for the *Ars Poetica* (and all of Horace) has left me forever in his debt.

PARUM CLARIS LUCEM DARE COGET

The Epistle to Augustus
Epistles 2.1

■ ■

AN APPEAL FOR IMPERIAL PATRONAGE
FOR RISING POETS

PROFESSOR CHARLES BRINK'S FINAL assessment of *Epistle* 2.1 may be summarized as follows:

1) This work with all its many motifs contributing to a celebration of Augustan poetry is itself a masterly Augustan performance.

2) . . . its unity must depend on the clarity of the tone struck with regard to the Augustus on whom Augustan poetry depends.

3) It may be that even this unequalled master of civilized tone could not overcome an imbalance that may be felt between the several personages that here appear under the name of Augustus. . . . [They are] not fully compatible.[1]

Of these assertions I can agree fully only with the first, for this epistle seems to have a unity that responds to the conflicting sides of Augustus himself as the addressee. "The number of recent Horaces is large and their diversities are bewildering," writes Brink himself: "Few, if any of them could have written the poems that are the subject of *Horace on Poetry*."

Brink finds Syme's division of the Augustan age into two "new and novel" periods unconvincing; i.e. 43–28 B.C. (Cicero to the return of normal government) and 28–13 B.C. (*Aeneid, Odes* I-IV, *Epistles* I; and possibly *Epistles* II and *Ars Poetica*), for they would put *Odes* I-III into the same period as IV, and would exclude *Epistle* 2.1 from it. The years

19–10 B.C. are for Brink "a period of consolidation"—the consolidation of the "'restored republic' of the twenties."[2] They are marked by a shift from the internal process of "adjustments, political, constitutional and legal, between the Princeps and the nobility" to a process involving "largely those of the imperial succession." The death of Marcus Agrippa heralds the second great shattering of these plans, succeeding that of Marcellus by a decade.

But that decade also saw the celebration of the *Ludi Saeculares* (17 B.C.) and the introduction of the four *Leges Iuliae* of 18 B.C., and *Odes* IV. (On a more private level, it saw *Epistles* I and *Epistle* 2.2, and possibly the *Ars Poetica* appear.) Brink sees a watershed between those two periods, created by the deaths of Vergil, Varius, and Tibullus, and the publication of Propertius III, *Odes* I-III, and *Epistles* I and *Epistle* 2.2. The panegyric of the later period is almost completely missing in the earlier. (But of course see *Odes* 1.2, 1.12, 3.4.) *Epistle* 2.2 and *Carmen Saeculare* mark "the beginning of the new period" (Brink)—the former, at least, then, being a great poem.[3] In Volume III Brink reviews his own earlier thoughts on dating, his revised order being: *Epistle* 2.2 (19 B.C.), *Epistle* 2.1 (12 B.C.), *Ars Poetica* (date uncertain, but *after Epistle* 2.1).

Brink's overall view of *Epistle* 2.1 is, that as the most characteristic epistle of the second period, it was written on request—but in fact tells Augustus what he did not wish to hear (32–33). As the addressee, Augustus appears in three roles: reader, patron, and subject for panegyric. "This letter, unlike the *Florus* and even the *Ars*, leaves a trace of bewilderment in the reader which may point to some unresolved disharmony of a kind I am not aware of in the poems of the first period. . . . It purports to debate three or four large subjects. But however judged, their polyphony is clearly not meant to be reduced to a simple conceptual scheme, though we have seen that the simple conceptual schemes abound in modern scholarship."[4]

Brink finally discusses the obvious critical antitheses of *Epistle* 2.1: stage vs. study, and old vs. new. Here his assumptions invite further examination. Brink takes what Horace refers to as contemporary reading-poetry to mean "of the most recent past": Horace's own, therefore (inter alia), and Vergil's and Varius'. The *nos* (as opposed to the *veteres*) represent "a great new literature to which one of its makers can cast a backward glance."[5] It may be, however, that to exclude or downplay the good poets who are actually writing now (as Augustus reads) is misleading; it weakens the case for a central rhetorical theme in the epistle. It would certainly steer us to Brink's conclusion that "there is, among the several subjects of the letter to Augustus, no single conceptual scheme to which the poem can be tied down. Horace's opinions come out only in the intricate network of three or four large topics and they are falsified if they are artificially reduced."[6]

The Augustus-epistle is rhetorically a *suasoria*, one which must take into account the social position and personality of the addressee. When the two individuals are personal friends the requirements of tact become particularly important, if the appeal is to be effective and the relationship enhanced.

Horace sets quite a new tone in *Epistles* II, for this collection shares with the rest of his late work the absence of dedications to Maecenas.[7] Of the earlier works, only *Satires* II do not begin with Maecenas, although the entire centre-piece (*Satire* 2.6) is devoted at him with unparalleled length and with undisguised feeling. Neither *Odes* IV nor *Epistles* II address him, in spite of their richness of allusion to poetry's current progress and practitioners, and the theory behind its creation.[8] Horace's public patron is now Augustus and we know from a fragment of a letter to Maecenas that he had wanted Horace on his personal staff *in epistulis scribendis*. The offer was declined without offence.[9] The loss of Horace's reply is much to be regretted for it would have been a fine exercise in tact.[10]

At the beginning of *Epistle* 1.1,[11] Horace had tactfully declined to accede to Maecenas' wish that he return to lyric. Yet he did return twice at Augustus' request, composing the *Carmen Saeculare* (17 B.C.) and publishing *Odes* IV (13 B.C.).[12] We are expressly told by Suetonius that *Epistle* 2.1 was composed at his urging, since Horace had not addressed him directly in previous *sermones*.[13] "Quod non in plerisque eius modi scriptis mecum potissimum loquaris" refers to some significant group of epistles; whether they are *Epistles* I, or *Epistle* 2.2 and *Ars Poetica* or others, has never been clear.[14] The phrase "post sermones vero quosdam lectos," does not make it clear whether Suetonius himself actually knew which were meant. If Augustus meant longer epistles on the subject of literature,[15] any of *Epistles* 1.1, 1.19, 2.2, 2.3 might qualify. *Epistle* 2.2 is certainly early,[16] while the date of *Ars Poetica* is unknown.[17] As *Epistle* 2.1 is likely datable to 14–12 B.C.,[18] Suetonius could have at least four longer literary epistles in mind. (*Pleraque scripta* and *sermones quidam* sound like more than just two.)[19] *Potissimum* could imply that in Augustus' opinion Maecenas has had enough of Horace's time and attention. In *Epistle* 2.1, at any rate, Augustus holds the centre stage.

In his analysis, Edward Fraenkel stresses the importance of Horace's tact in writing to Augustus and praises his modesty and sensitivity in addressing the correspondent's interests before his own.[20] (Horace makes no reference to any confidential invitation to him to write such a poem.)[21] Tact had been a major component of *Epistles* I, poetic correspondence with a wide range of friends, from Maecenas to his farm bailiff.[22] Sensitivity to the tact required in writing to the imperial family was foremost in *Epistle* 1.9 (to Tiberius) and *Epistle* 1.13 (for Augustus, although addressed to Vinnius): he clearly wanted to avoid any suggestion of overconfidence.[23] This caution was already in evidence in *Satire* 2.1, where he denies any talent for epic verse on imperial subjects, and shows he is aware of Octavian's impatience with over-zealous poets (*Satire* 2.1. 18–20):

> nisi dextro tempore Flacci
> verba per attentam non ibunt Caesaris aurem:
> cui male si palpere, recalcitrat undique tutus.

These suggestions of a joking relationship between Horace and Octavian are confirmed by Suetonius.[24] Horace later alludes twice more to the latter's reserve:

> Augusto reddes signata volumina, Vinni,
> si validus, si laetus erit, si denique poscet;
> ne studio nostri pecces odiumque libellis
> sedulus inportes opera vehemente minister.
> (*Epistle* 1.13.2–5)

> multa quidem nobis facimus mala saepe poetae
> (ut vineta egomet caedam mea), cum tibi librum
> sollicito damus aut fesso;. . . .
> (*Epistle* 2.1.219–21)

The *non dextrum tempus* formula is used here in Horace's salutation:

> in publica commoda peccem,
> si longo sermone morer tua tempora, Caesar.
>
> (*Epistle* 2.1.3b-4)

An awareness of the lonely burdens of empire (1–3a)[25] is heightened by Horace's delay in saluting Augustus by name, with anticipation of the *laudes Caesaris* to follow (5–17).[26]

Finally, *non dextrum tempus* is picked up again at the very end of this epistle, where bad poets and sculptors force their attentions on Horace himself (266–70):

> nec prave factis decorari versibus opto,
> ne rubeam pingui donatus munere, et una
> cum scriptore meo, capsa porrectus operta,
> deferar in vicum vendentem tus et odores
> et piper et quidquid chartis amicitur ineptis.

The second excerpt is also reminiscent of Horace's predicaments in *Satires* 1.9 and 2.6, and in *Epistle* 1.19. He was pressed for favours because he was now seen as part of some higher circles (*Satire* 2.6.32).

Lines 5–17 continue the eulogy to Caesar, who is compared with humanity's legendary benefactors: Romulus, Liber, and Hercules.[27] In a lofty style Horace extols their achievements, reminding Caesar that it was envy of their brilliance which withheld due recognition from them while they lived. By contrast, as their successor Caesar is already venerated by his grateful people as *praesens divus*,[28] receiving their homage and honours as a *numen* (16):[29] "nil oriturum alias, nil ortum tale fatentes."[30]

Such unparalleled public homage Horace then contrasts with the badly flawed attitude toward art in Rome (18–21):

> sed tuus hic populus, sapiens et iustus in uno[31]
> te nostris ducibus, te Grais anteferendo,
> cetera nequaquam simili ratione modoque
> aestimat.

The gross flaw in their good sense and judgement appears in the way the

Romans evaluate literature, condemning modern writers because they still breathe (21–22) and praising the XII *Tables*, ancient treaties, and oracles (23–27).[32] By a *reductio ad absurdum* Horace proves that "old is best" is mere cant (28–29): "Since Rome is at her height, ergo she is better at everything—even than the Greeks—the arts included."[33] Then he proves (50–89) that such a canon vitiates Roman taste in literature and in education. Ennius ("The second Homer"), Naevius, Plautus, Terence, Livius and the rest are thriving in public esteem because they are in their graves with their virtues all catalogued (50–59).[34] And despite all the true might and magnificence of the present age, *Roma potens* goes on learning them by heart and flocking to their revivals on stage (60–63). His irony is confirmed by *vulgus* (63).[35] Although the crowd can sometimes judge soundly (e.g. about Augustus), in being so enamoured of the old writers it is dead wrong (63): "interdum volgus rectum videt, est ubi peccat."

Horace's view here is a balanced one, as it was twenty years earlier during the Lucilian controversy.[36] Roman literary classics are flawed (their virtues notwithstanding) by a harshness and lack of real sophistication and bother, as even Jove would agree (68).[37] (Horace's own youthful introduction to Livius Andronicus had been a painful one.) Rare flashes of *decorum* (73) and *concinnitas* (74) are supposed to be sufficient, in the public view, for great art.[38]

Horace's irritation at such unfair condemnation of contemporary verse (76) stems from the lack of concern for workmanship and subtlety (76–77) it reveals. In his opinion, the old writers require allowances, not accolades! In the first of a series of mini-scenes, his outspoken criticism of a play by Atta meets with fierce indignation from the city fathers, whose views were set in stone at grammar school (79–85).[39] An encounter with a literary snob follows, who naively praises Numa's *Carmen Saliare* (Horace does not understand the work either) and grimly attacks "us" modern poets and "our" works (89).

Up to this point, Horace has dwelt on Rome, praising Caesar and then attacking public opinion about literature. Now the "old vs. new" criterion is applied to Greece (90–102).[40] If the Greeks had hallowed *vetustas*, would they ever have created anything worth admiring? Their great passion for art, made possible by victory in the Persian Wars (93), was excessive (94) and fickle, however (95–98), as the simile of the child with her nanny (99–100) suggests.[41] The blessings that flow to art from peace and prosperity are not unmixed.[42]

If Greece's more serious concerns lay in warfare, Rome's are now typified by an austere, old-fashioned patrician performing his duties as *pater familias* and *patronus* (103–7).[43] But the *Pax Augusta* has altered Rome's priorities and her fickle citizens now show a universal passion for composing verse (108–9a). Horace's caricature of all this unseemly behaviour includes himself (111–13):

> ipse ego, qui nullos me adfirmo scribere versus
> invenior Parthis mendacior, et prius orto
> sole vigil calamum et chartas et scrinia posco.[44]

The irony here is at his own expense (he is still writing to Augustus),[45] although his own *modus scribendi* (112–13) sounds not at all like that of a dilettante.[46] And when he observes that all workmen (except poets) stick to what they know, it seems that real professionals run the risk of being lumped with the rest (117):

> scribimus indocti doctique poemata passim.

The next section offers a positive defence of genuine poetic talent, even if it seems indulgent and condescending (118–19):

> hic error tamen et levis haec insania quantas
> virtutes habeat, sic collige.

The one real vice of poets is verse.[47] They are not naturally materialistic (119–21) or dishonest (122–23a). They get by on very little food (123). They make poor soldiers, of course (Augustus might smile here and think of Philippi), but they have *some* public uses (*utilis urbi*: 124), even if in the wider scheme of things those may seem slight (125).

Such modest claims for his colleagues lead to a firmer apologia (126–28).[48] It is a poet's task to shape the lips, ears, hearts, and feelings of the young to resist corruption (126–29). His examples teach and console. A reference to the *Carmen Saeculare* gives an example of how a poet teaches prayer for the welfare of the state (130–38), further undercutting some of Horace's earlier modesty. This might remind Augustus of his own concern for *mores* (2) and of Horace's earlier eulogy: *praesenti tibi... tuum per numen* (15–16). Such disclaimers seem intended to point out their own irony.

The next section (139–55)[49] takes us back to the humble origins of poetry in the primitive countryside. The picture of virtuous city life in the past (102–7) is balanced by that of simple country piety, evident in offerings to the gods of earth and forest (142–43) and to the guardian spirit (144).[50] There too, earlier virtues and practices were perverted into extremes: the affectionate licence and fun of Fescennine verses became harsh, attacking individuals and families until the community was forced to restrain it by law and turn it to constructive ends (145–55). That native Roman instinct for order was eventually reinforced by the good influence of Greek *artes*, but these reached rural Latium only after Greece was subdued in war.[51] The primitive Saturnian verse gave way and a new sense of decorum (154) chased the reek of sweat (*grave virus*: 158), even if Rome has not yet completely lost her rustic ways. The influence of Greek theatre was late in coming, however (161–63),[52] and the Romans have always retained their instinct for independence and forcefulness (165–66):

> et placuit sibi, natura sublimis et acer;
> nam spirat tragicum satis et feliciter audet.[53]

What actually was wrong with contemporary drama in Rome (167–213)? One symptom has been considered already: the uncritical passion for the revival of ancient plays (50–85). Contemporary playwriting is discussed, but again Rome's promise is not fulfilled, for Greece's stern conqueror will not blot a line (167).[54] The example of comedy (168–76) proves the absence of careful revision in Roman plays, for erasing and revising are abhorred (167) out of plain ignorance (*inscite*: 167). Because comedy is based on everyday situations Rome feels that no effort is involved (*sudoris minimum*: 169).[55] Plautus is Horace's example of inexcusable carelessness in composition (170–76); for his sole motivation in writing was *money*, not pride of workmanship (174–76).[56] Just as Horace had made fun earlier of one of Atta's productions (79), he now does the same with Plautus, who is in too much of a hurry even to do up his "sock" and thus doomed to stumble. Fame and fortune rule such poets, and make them sleek or slim. The games (*res ludicra*: 180) are not for Horace: writing for the theatre can only subject a poet to the agonies of hope and fear, and the wise poet will avoid it. Even the poet endowed with the most Roman of writing's virtues, *daring*, will lose his nerve when the crowd rejects proper standards and demands bears or boxers instead (182–86).[57] The *eques* he quotes represents a somewhat better critical standard for the stage, but his taste too is flawed, for he is concerned with spectacle alone, and the eye is much inferior to the ear as a critical sense (187–88). Horace gives a lively sketch of visual excess on the contemporary stage, with its sham-battles and staged triumphs (190–93). The laughing philosopher, Democritus, would be more convulsed by watching the audience shouting its approval than he would be by the actual play (194–200a). To end this section, he focuses upon a brief ironic encounter between one such knight and Horace, sitting side by side in the theatre (204b–7); the former appears too naive to realize that the thunderous applause is for the actor's costume alone—who has yet to deliver a single line! After the long double section cataloguing the ills of the Roman stage (176–86 & 187–207) Horace pauses to wonder whether, since *he* is not a dramatic poet, Augustus might suspect him of being niggardly in his praise of playwrights even when they *do* produce good plays (208–12). So he hastens to offer full credit to any one of them who can whirl him away in a flight of imagination like a tightrope walker or magician.[58]

The tact of the disclaimer becomes clear in what follows, for vv. 214–18 contain the real point of the epistle:

> verum age et his, qui se lectori credere malunt
> quam spectatoris fastidia ferre superbi,
> curam redde brevem, si munus Apolline dignum
> vis complere libris et vatibus addere calcar,
> ut studio maiore petant Helicona virentem.

Discussion of the contemporary theatre is finished,[59] which has actually been preparation for a modest request on behalf of poets who, for since they do not write for the stage, are being unfairly ignored (214–15): *curam redde brevem* (216).[60] Horace suggests to Augustus that there are advantages for him in such generosity, for his own votive monument, the Palatine Library, would be much enriched; if he offered such a spur to genuine poets, they would do the rest, and with much more will and effort (216–18).

Horace's ironic depreciation of poets in general (111–17) had been a preface to a warm eulogy of them (118–38). Here Horace disarmingly follows up his petition on behalf of particular poets with the acknowledgement that poets sometimes do jeopardize their own chances for such favours. They are (himself included) annoying, boring, complaining, thin-skinned, self-pitying, and unrealistic in expectations (219–28), especially in hoping Caesar will issue a call, support them (*et egere vetes*: 228), and urge them to write.[61] That request, however is followed by a caveat: *sed tamen* (229) warns Augustus against being as indiscriminate in his favours as Alexander, whose impeccable taste in sculptors and portrait painters did not extend to poets (229–44).[62] Augustus will not make the same mistake, to judge by his generosity in the past to Vergil and Varius, the two great epic poets of the time.[63] Their success in portraying his *vultus* and *virtus* in verse is a tribute that Alexander would have envied. Horace disqualifies himself from such praise (and such tasks), concluding in a grand archaic style and with an ironic disclaimer (256–59):

> et formidatam Parthis te principe Romam,[64]
> si quantum cuperem possem quoque. sed neque parvum
> carmen maiestas recipit tua, nec meus audet
> rem temptare pudor quam vires ferre recusent.

The irony is found partly in Horace's familiar device of declining in epic style to write epic,[65] and partly in the refusal of his own *pudor* to consent to address a small poem to Augustus.

Two reasons are offered for reneging on this refusal (260–63). The turnabout (*autem*) is explained by *sedulitas*, "persistence" (260), referring to the poets on whose behalf Horace is now writing. *Sedulitas* is a word already identified with poets by Cicero, with reference to a poetaster who tried to foist a bad poem on Sulla.[66] *Sedulitas autem stulte quem diligit* (260), however, refers ironically to the persistence of those poets (cf. 214) who esteem Horace; the stipulation *praecipue cum se numeris commendat et arte* (261) indicates that their poetic merits *justify* such persistence. Vv. 262–63 explain his use of *sermo repens per humum* to make this request:

discit enim citius meminitque libentius illud
quod quis deridet, quam quod probat et veneratur.

A laugh may make a point and hold it more readily than something solemn and serious. *Nil moror officium quod me gravat* (264) makes it plain that Horace's yielding to their *sedulitas* is not by any means a distasteful form of obligation. Unworthy artists, however, he does exclude (264b-66); to do otherwise would only embarrass him and give his own work a bad name. Could this apply to Augustus as well, then? Such a humorous conclusion to a serious poem recalls others in which Horace used humour to defuse a delicate situation and leave the poem's recipient with a smile.[67] The inevitable fate of bad verses—i.e., the fish market— is an echo of Catullus, which Persius would later pick up.[68] Horace here adds funeral imagery (270) in which the covered bookcase becomes the coffin of the wretch whose reputation could not survive association with incompetents.

The strategy may be compared with that of *Epistle* 1.9, a standard letter of introduction.[69] Horace there explains his dilemma in acceding to the wishes of one worthy friend by asking a favour of another: he must sacrifice his *pudor* (12) in order to do so, because he does not want to take advantage of the other friend who is a very busy man. (In the end, of course, he has no hesitation about the character of Septimius.)

To summarize, then, Horace's request in *Epistle* 2.1 for support of other worthy poets comes with tact and humour. Augustus is sincerely complimented for the love and respect his people give him. But that esteem does not reflect the poor taste they show when it comes to poetry. They have no regard for anything written in the last century, but uncritically revere all that is "ancient." Rome's upper classes seem to have abandoned their old austerity to compose poetry themselves and Horace is no exception. But Augustus has to remember that poets still have important roles in contemporary society, especially in education and worship. There is an inborn force in Roman poetry, but it has always been spoiled by a lack of concern for technique—for *ars*. Fame and profit are the criteria in the theatre, which means catering either to the mob or to theatre-goers who want spectacle. Although this does not in any way detract from Horace's personal view of drama as a worthy pursuit, it is still essential that Augustus support good poets in other fields as well. Naturally poets must be chosen with discretion. Certainly

Alexander did not receive value for the money he lavished on Choerilus. As in all other respects, however, Augustus' past judgement of writers has proven excellent, and his poets have served him as honourably as his sculptors. Horace too, were he competent, would rather glorify Rome and Augustus than write humble verse; but great themes suit great poets alone and discretion restrains him.

Certain other poets, however, will persist in demanding that Horace be their advocate and their merits match their demands. Perhaps a laughable poem (like this epistle) may serve where a serious one would fail. His obligations to those poets are not onerous (264), and since they are good poets they can only bring him credit. But failure of discrimination could bring disaster!

There is external evidence as well bearing on the background and purpose of *Epistle* 2.1. Suetonius tells us of Augustus' passion for the stage and his extravagant expenditures on *spectacula*. His shows at the *ludi* (twenty-three in total) exceeded those of all other magistrates in variety, magnificence, and frequency.[70] He gave presentations (*munera*) of every kind in all parts of the city, such as plays, athletics, sea fights, hunts, races, pageants (such as the *Troiae lusus*), gladiators, and displays of rare beasts and freaks. (He himself had a number of embarrassing experiences while in the theatre.) He was determined to segregate the classes from each other in the theatre,[71] reserving the first rows for senators, separating soldiers from civilians, and providing separate sections for *praetextati* with their tutors, plebeians who were married, and Vestal Virgins. He restricted the times of admittance and the seating of women. When he attended himself he gave full attention to the shows (unlike Julius Caesar) and frankly admitted his addiction to them. He loved fisticuffs in the ring or in the streets: "universum genus operas aliquas publico spectaculo praebentium etiam cura sua dignatus est" ("He deemed the entire range of those working to provide public shows as worthy of his concern").[72] While restricting the rights of magistrates to punish actors, he was himself rigorous in disciplining them. Particularly fond of old Roman comedy, he often had it produced for public performance. Among his own attempts at poetry were a hexameter poem, *Sicilia*, and a small book of epigrams. He began an *Ajax* tragedy, but destroyed it before it was finished. (To friends enquiring about its progress he replied, "My Ajax has fallen on his sponge!")[73] His rewards to Vergil, Varius, and Horace for their poems were well known.

Augustus' regard for Horace is well documented by Suetonius in Suetonius' *Vita Horati*. Whether the two had discussed such broader patronage of poets previously, we do not know, but an implicit message that the dramatic writers did not need more support from him than they were already receiving does fit with an appeal for renewed support of other genres.[74] Horace's tact in *Epistle* 2.1 shows that delicacy is needed: while Augustus did have taste (witness his support for Vergil and himself), he also shared some of the decided public preference for older writers which Horace faults, and he spent large sums on stage revivals of them. His request for a *sermo* certainly offered Horace the opportunity to air some of his own views on contemporary theatre which did not match those of Augustus.[75]

While Horace and Suetonius provide useful commentary on each other, a contemporary of the latter may shed additional light on Horace's intentions. Juvenal's Seventh Satire exposed the sad plight of struggling intellectuals in the fields of poetry, history, teaching and law, and attacked the whole system of patronage in Rome.[76] Juvenal addresses himself rhetorically not to the emperor, but to the worthy poets and writers themselves, tactfully warning them that Caesar is the only reliable and honest patron to be found, since other wealthy men are too stingy or too egocentric to help (Juv. *Satire* 7.20–21): "Hoc agite, o iuvenes. circumspicit et stimulat vos... ducis indulgentia. ... " This line of Juvenal is reminiscent of Horace's "vatibus addere calcar" (*Epistle* 2.1.217); "*in Caesare tantum. Solus enim. ...* " (Juv. *Satire* 7.1–2) echoes Horace's first line. In Juvenal the futility of hard work and long hours composing is a sad echo of Horace's sketch (*Epistle* 2.1.113) of the good poet: "frange miser calamum vigilataque proelia dele" (Juv. *Satire* 7.27). The hoped-for reward is a bust garlanded with ivy ("ut dignus venias hederis et imagine macra": Juv. *Satire* 7.29), but such hopes seem as meagre as the bust.[77] Horace can reject a hack-work portrait in wax as confidently as a poor laudatory poem (*Epistle* 2.1.265–66). For Juvenal, the patron who fancies himself a poet will be stingy, although he is willing to acknowledge the virtues of a Homer, *propter mille annos* (Juv. *Satire* 7.39), and therefore far more extreme in his views than even Horace's critics (*Epistle* 2.1.39). Such an indiscriminate, pathological urge to write pervaded Juvenal's Rome as well ("tenet insanabile multos/scribendi cacoethes et aegro in corde senescit": Juv. *Satire*

7.51b-52a), and he carefully distinguishes the uncommon poet from the rest (Juv. *Satire* 7.53–59a):

> sed vatem egregium, cui non sit publica vena,
> qui nihil expositum soleat deducere, nec qui
> communi feriat carmen triviale moneta,
> hunc, qualem nequeo monstrare et sentio tantum,
> anxietate carens animus facit, omnis acerbi
> inpatiens, cupidus silvarum aptusque bibendis
> fontibus Aonidum.

Those poets Horace had distinguished as genuine are also very different from the hordes of common scribblers, and have no concern for material things (*Epistle* 2.1.118–24). Juvenal's melancholy portrait of the impoverished poet (Juv. *Satire* 7.59b–62) points a direct contrast with a Horace who was *satur* when inspiration struck. Vergil had his own retainer and a nice place to live (Juv. *Satire* 7.69–70); Lucan had been rich and content with his *fama* (Juv. *Satire* 7.79–80a). But what of Serranus and Saleius Bassus (Juv. *Satire* 7.80)? What good did *gloria* do for them or for Statius (Juv. *Satire* 7.81–87)? Dramatic poets in Juvenal's day had no Maecenas, Proculeius, Cotta, or Lentulus. Talent used to be rewarded and devotion to writing had been worthwhile (Juv. *Satire* 7.94–97). Towards the end of the satire, Juvenal describes a happy pair of poets' busts blackened with soot (Juv. *Satire* 7.226–27):

> cum totus decolor esset
> Flaccus et haereret nigro fuligo Maroni.

Such thematic and verbal echoes point to *Epistle* 2.1 as the model for Juvenal's attack on the plight of talent in the Rome of his own day.[78] That indictment of contemporary patronage is more explicit than Horace's and may be explained by the difference in genre, age, and milieu, and by the relationships between the two poets and their sovereigns. The warmth, tact and fair-mindedness so evident between Augustus and Horace must have seemed to Juvenal joys of a Utopian past.

CHAPTER 2

The Epistle to Florus
Epistle 2.2

ঽঽ

SELF-CRITICISM IN LIFE AND ART

THE SECOND EPISTLE of Book II is rich in associations with Horace's earlier works,[1] being, for instance, the second poem addressed to Julius Florus (compare *Epistle* 1.3) while he was abroad on Tiberius' staff. As a *recusatio* it shares with *Epistle* 1.1 the affirmation that moral philosophy is more suited to a man of the poet's own age, training, and circumstances.[2] To the extent that it concerns itself with poetry in general as well as his own career and standards, it complements *Epistles* 1.1, 1.2, 1.3, 1.4, 1.7, 1.13, 1.19, 2.1 and the *Ars Poetica*,[3] poems whose aesthetic and ethical themes were already represented in the *Satires* and *Odes*.

The first 25 lines of the Epistle to Florus are full of information and gentle irony. The salutation (*Epistle* 2.1.1) suggests a postmark and contains another compliment to the young Tiberius (*bono claroque*) to match the one to Florus (*fidelis amice*). A plausible dramatic date for the poem would be 19 or 18 B.C., with Florus and Tiberius still serving in the East, the latter as Augustus' legate.[4] This praise of Tiberius in the context of the second book also complements the opening of *Epistle* 2.1, where his stepfather Augustus was praised for his selfless devotion to the state. The kind of sustained irony (occasionally quite trenchant) in *Epistle* 2.2 would not have been appropriate in a letter addressed to Tiberius. (In *Epistle* 1.9, the one brief epistle addressed directly to him, the irony is carefully deflected towards Septimius and himself.) As with *Epistle* 1.13, the third party, knowing the foibles of both correspondents, would enjoy the epistle all the more.[5] The impression given earlier in *Epistle* 1.20.23 ("me primis urbis belli placuisse domique") and *Epistle* 2.1 is being sustained.[6]

The significance of the lengthy analogy offered in lines 2–17 (the sale of a slave) is suspensefully withheld.[7] Its frame is a long conditional sentence (*siquis... ferat*: 2–17), which dramatizes the glowing description of a certain home-bred slave... (*verna*: 6) as if a confidential offer of sale were being made to Florus. (The analogy is based on a point of Roman law making the disclosure of a slave's faults mandatory at time of sale.)[8] The vendor is not immodest in his claims for the merchandise but does ask a fair price.[9] The slave is handsome, knows some Greek, and will repay further training;[10] he can sing, also, though he has never had lessons (9). The vendor appreciates the need for full disclosure (10–11) and he is not pressed for cash or in a hurry to sell, let alone overcharge (12). He prefers to pick his own buyer (13–14). The lad does have one fault, mind you: he did run away once and was strapped for it (14–15).[11] If that's his only defect, the customer should pay the seller a fair price.[12] Such is Horace's view.

At line 18, Horace breaks the suspense. If the "sale" was an honest one, then why the mischievous "suit" against him by Florus (18–19)? At long last the point of the analogy and the identities of the real-life vendor and the defective merchandise are revealed (20–22):

> dixi me pigrum proficiscenti tibi, dixi
> talibus officiis prope mancum, ne mea saevus
> iurgares ad te quod epistula nulla rediret.[13]

Florus had "purchased" Horace as his correspondent when he set off with Tiberius, but in full knowledge (*prudens*) of his flaws: *dixi me pigrum... dixi... prope mancum* (20–21). Horace does admit he has been lazy. *Caveat emptor!*

The first of Florus' two charges against Horace has been disclosed: Horace has not written. The second follows (24b–25):

> quereris super hoc etiam, quod
> exspectata tibi non mittam carmina mendax.[14]

Florus thought he had grounds for expecting some lyrics by post and is very annoyed by this second breach of promise!

These first 25 lines tell us much about Florus. He longs for some poems as well as news from Horace. Another facet of his personality implied by the language of the analogy is a familiarity with the language of law, business, and the courts.[15] The point of law on which the analogy hinges has been mentioned already, and a number of terms with a legal and commercial flavour highlight it: *fides* (10), *venalis merces* (11), *meo aere* (12), *cessavit* (14), *poenae securus, opinor* (17), *prudens, vitiosum, dicta tibi est lex* (18), *insequeris, lite iniqua* (19), *mancum* (21), *iurgares* (22), *facientia iura* (23), *attemptas* (24). These terms impart a court-room flavour to *quereris... quod exspectata... mendax* (24–25). This whimsical use of legal language is reminiscent of the *Epistle to Torquatus* (1.5),[16] and its use for characterization is paralleled by the military language in the *Epistle to Vinnius* (1.13).[17] The inference that Florus is sufficiently interested and competent in both law and poetry to appreciate all this is confirmed by that earlier epistle to him (*Epistle* 1.3.20–25):

> ipse quid audes?
> quae circumvolitas agilis thyma? non tibi parvum
> ingenium, non incultum est et turpiter hirtum:
> seu linguam *causis* acuis seu *civica iura*
> *respondere* paras seu *condis amabile carmen*,
> prima feres hederae victricis praemia.

These allusions leave no room for doubt that Florus is competent in those fields, but we may also infer from both epistles that Florus can be unreasonable, something Horace tried to handle earlier with philosophy; here with a principle of law. In other words, Florus' charge that Horace is in breach of promise will not stand up in a court of law. As for the complaint about expected poems, well, that seems to go rather more deeply into Horace's view of life;[18] so he follows up the mention of that charge of "mendacity" with a second analogy. This time we have a story about a soldier, a third profession with which Florus could identify.[19]

The anecdote (26–40) whisks us away from Rome (and the busy slave market) to the east: an old event from the campaign of L. Licinius Lucullus against Mithridates (74–67 B.C.). Lucullus' army had included

many blooded veterans of the campaigns of Valerius Flaccus (85 B.C.)
who had often changed loyalties during the civil wars. Lucullus himself
had a well-known reputation for greed and was not popular with these
veterans.[20] The point of this story is that a soldier, having lost all of his
savings one night to a thief, performed deeds of great heroism in battles
and for his efforts was rewarded with 20,000 sesterces (33).[21] Lucullus
naturally assumes that the soldier will repeat his epic exploits to gain
further riches and urges him on in the grand style (37–38a):

> 'i, bone, quo virtus tua te vocat, i pede fausto,
> grandia laturus meritorum praemia. quid stas?'[22]

Lucullus is taken aback by the refusal. The soldier is a sharp-witted
Italian farmer (catus... rusticus: 39), whose blunt refusal is reinforced
with a parody of Lucullus' exhortation, which is punctured by the
soldier's stubborn determination just to get back that money-belt and
then relax (39b-40):

> 'ibit,
> ibit eo quo vis qui zonam perdidit', inquit.

This contrast in tones occurs at the climax of a sustained tension between
the poetic and the mundane in the parable, and is achieved by a mixture
of epic language and effects, military jargon and common speech.[23] It is
framed by the idea of a loss of worldly goods, and the lengths one may
go to recover them (viatica... ad assem perdiderat: zonam perdidit:
26–40). It is an anecdote with a thoroughly Roman practical appeal,
capped by the "put-down" of a pompous self-assured Roman aristocrat
by a sturdy Italian peasant.[24]

The point of the anecdote (26–40), suspensefully withheld all this
while, unfolds in the following section (41–54). Lucullus' once-angry
soldier (vehemens lupus... iratus... acer) gives way to a more un-
relenting hero: iratus Achilles (42). The reference to the Iliad as a cautionary moral tale for the young echoes Epistle 1.2 (1–6), where Homer
provided an easy introduction to Horace's moral advice to young Lollius.[25] Here it makes an attractive bridge between the military exploits of
the sturdy peasant and those of Horace. His own interest in moral philosophy, begun when he was still reading Homer at grammar school,

had taken him to Athens for further training, where he developed the passion to learn how to distinguish logically between the false and the true, there in the "groves of Academus" (43–45).[26] Like the soldier, Horace had been robbed of his heart's desire, the peaceful pursuit of moral wisdom, by the civil war between the republicans (for whom he had fought) and the might of Augustus (46–48).[27] The disaster at Philippi had left him "with wings clipped" and with the subsequent loss of everything, including his father's farm. Lacking the means to support his continued studies in philosophy, Horace (to Florus' surprise), was driven by poverty to desperate means for survival in Rome—to writing poetry (50–52a):

> decisis humilem pennis inopemque paterni
> et laris et fundi, *paupertas impulit audax*
> ut versus facerem.[28]

But now that he is well-off, he would have to be incurably mad to prefer writing verse to a sleep in the shade (52b–54)!

This whole section (26–54) is moving and varied.[29] The rhetoric is appropriate to his role as defendant, developing into an *apologia pro sua vita* (41–54) with the battle of Philippi as its centrepiece, crowned by the heroic figure of Augustus. The quiet tone with which it concludes is reminiscent of the warm serenity of *Epistle* 1.20. It leaves Florus to grapple with the unsettling notion that Horace's whole poetic career has been nothing more than an "unfortunate episode."[30]

Whether or not Florus is supposed to believe such an amazing revelation, Horace follows it with his more familiar claim that he is too old to write poetry, just as he is too old to enjoy the other pleasures of youth (56–57).[31] A similar claim was made earlier to Maecenas in *Epistles* 1.1 and 1.7,[32] to which he now adds the difficulty of varying tastes in poetry (58): no three guests at dinner can ever agree in their preference for lyrics, iambics, and satire, and such disputes can become acrimonious (59–64).[33] Another familiar claim (65–86) concludes: it is quite impossible for Horace to write in Rome. He must appear in court, drop everything to attend a recitation (67), visit a sick friend somewhere else (68), all with no time in between (70).[34] Florus might recommend quiet byways of the city (71), but he should know the hazards: mules, contractors, machinery, funerals, wagons, rabid dogs, muddy pigs everywhere (72–75).[35] Let him try it! In this section Horace makes skilful use of vivid *evidentia* (anticipating the later practice of Juvenal) to impress the "court" with the obstacles to composing poetry in town. He reminds his accuser of how poets are naturally disposed to seek the grove and avoid the city, to prefer sleep and shade in deference to their patron Bacchus (77–80), and challenges him (*i nunc*) to persist in following the sequestered paths of the true poets (80): "vis canere et contracta sequi vestigia vatum?"[36]

The last six lines in this section (81–86) present difficulties of interpretation for which dire critical remedies have been urged.[37]

> ingenium sibi quod vacuas desumpsit Athenas,
> et studiis annos septem dedit insenuitque
> libris et curis, statua taciturnius exit
> plerumque et risu populum quatit; hic ego rerum
> fluctibus in mediis et tempestatibus urbis
> verba lyrae motura sonum conectere digner?

The identification of the eccentric *ingenium* (81) has ranged from "some rival poet" or known Athenian character to Horace himself. There is also a question of text in v. 83, giving a choice between *curis* and *Curii*; but either way changing Brink's punctuation (by inserting a comma after *libris*) gives the syntax a clearer link to Horace (*me*: 79).[38] The *ingenium* seems to be Horace himself, as he was when a student. His choice of peaceful Athens long ago for years of study, his devotion to books which has continued into these his grey years (*Epistle* 1.20.24), and the attention he attracts in the streets by his eccentric and silent preoccupation with philosophy all testify to his preference for quiet seclusion, something the city life of a poet makes impossible. He would be most unlikely to want to engage in such public activities as composing or performing lyric verse (84b-86).[39] Horace is simply repeating here a point raised earlier (41–54): his own choice would have been to remain in Athens to study at the Academy, and now that he has achieved his wish to leave poetry and public life behind he will not give it up.

The next section (87–105) is introduced by a brief *exemplum* which continues the sequence consisting of the sale (2–17), Lucullus' soldier (26–40), and Horace's own career (41–52a). It presents the parable of

two brothers in Rome (an attorney and a rhetorician), so devoted that
they praised each other without end or real discrimination (87–89).

> †frater erat Romae† consulti rhetor, ut alter
> alterius sermone meros audiret honores,
> Gracchus ut hic illi, foret huic ut Mucius ille.[40]

The setting and the characters are in keeping with the themes of the
preceding lines: the clamour of Rome, the analogies of Gracchus and
Mucius,[41] and the two brothers' indiscriminate and outspoken mutual
praise prepare us for another aspect of the poet's role which Horace finds
uncongenial. Poets can be quite as objectionable as these brothers, as
lavish in their praise, and demanding effusive praise in return. The
dramatic setting is the newly-built Palatine library, alluded to already in
Epistles 1.3 and 2.1 as lasting witness to Augustus' virtue and piety and
crying out to be filled (91b–94) by Roman poets:

> mirabile visu
> caelatumque novem Musis opus. aspice primum,
> quanto cum fastu, quanto molimine circum-
> spectemus vacuam Romanis vatibus aedem.[42]

Such a *furor* drove the two brothers to compete in mutual admiration.
The competition is compared to a duel between gladiators (97–101), not
the obvious image perhaps to convey the kind of life Horace cherishes
(77–78): the grove, sleep, and shade.[43] The rules demand a potlatch of
compliments. An unnamed elegist offers him the title of "Alcaeus," and
he must respond with "Callimachus" or even "Mimnermus" if he
desires to have it (99–101),[44] which all involves much unpleasant effort
(*multa fero*) to placate the temperamental bards (*genus irritabile
vatum*), and win public acclaim (102–3). If he could drop his pursuits
(*finitis studiis*) and recover his wits (*mente recepta*: 104), he would just
plug up his spreading ears rather than suffer these unchallenged recitations (105).[45] All this appears to be a most telling defence of his chosen
inactivity. But it is not without its irony. If we compare Horace's suffer-
ings with earlier claims of independence of popular favour—owing to his
secure reliance upon the appreciation of Augustus, Maecenas, and his

peers—we may appreciate the rhetorical bravado and exaggeration.[46] The last line of the passage contains a laugh at his own expense, and a possible allusion to his own cognomen, *Flaccus*, "flop-eared" (105):

> obturem *patulas* impune legentibus *aures*.[47]

With this amusing image the account of Horace's personal reasons for not continuing his poetic career ends. He then proceeds to a more detached discussion of poetry and poets (106–25). He has been implying that an active and publicly successful career entails praise of others' work, including much that is not very good (*multa fero . . . genus irritabile vatum . . . impune legentibus*: 102–5). Here he specifically singles out the bad poets, who may be laughed at, but cheerfully praise their own verses if no one else will (106–8). The obvious contrast to *mala carmina*[48] is the *legitimum poema* (109). The poet who strives to develop and employ true *ars* will bring to his work "the spirit of an incorruptible *censor*"; that is, of candid self-criticism (109–10). This involves particularly the creative "risk" (*audebit*) the poet takes in deleting words and expressions lacking weight or force, even though they claim all the sanctity of hoary traditions in Rome such as Vesta's temple would protect (111–14).[49] Here Horace warms to specific precepts on poetic diction. Age itself is no criterion: old words which are *speciosa* may be reclaimed (just as those with *parum splendoris* are to be rejected), even though they be "heavy with ugly mold and forlorn old age" (118). In the same way new words will be introduced on the basis of the *usus*, "utility," which "sires" them (119).[50] The rising style of vv. 115–25 culminates with a eulogy of the poet's role in enriching his native speech, using two powerful images of the countryside: the clear, powerful sweep of a river with its life-giving water (120–21) and the vine-dresser who skilfully prunes the excessive growth:

> vemens et liquidus puroque simillimus amni
> fundet opes Latiumque beabit divite lingua.
> luxuriantia compescet, nimis aspera sano
> levabit cultu, virtute carentia tollet.[51]

Among the virtues of poetic diction he includes force (*vemens*), clarity

(*liquidus, puro*), and wealth (*divite*). The poet, as his own critic, must remove words which are rank and overgrown (*luxuriantia*),[52] and harsh (*aspera*) to the ear, with *sanus cultus* ("intelligent cultivation") of his vocabulary. Up to this point Horace has stressed the great effort and training required to master the proper use of poetic diction. But that strenuous effort must be hidden from the reader or listener and made to seem like play, like the long-rehearsed satyr's dance performed by the same actor who but a moment ago was playing the ponderous role of the Cyclops (123–25):

> ludentis speciem dabit et torquebitur, ut qui
> nunc Satyrum, nunc agrestem Cyclopa movetur.

Here Horace moves to his personal convinction about excellence in poetry, a passage that makes good sense punctuated as a rhetorical question (126–28a):[53]

> praetulerim scriptor delirus inersque videri,
> dum mea delectent mala me vel denique fallant,
> quam sapere et ringi?

The image of the growl (*ringi*) combined with *sapere* seems to mean "exercise like Diogenes a fierce, uncompromising discernment."[54] Common sense (as well as the views Horace has already put forward about bad poets) makes it unreasonable to accept "scriptor delirus inersque videri,/dum mea delectent mala me vel denique fallant" as any choice for himself as either artist or critic. That is the picture of the narcissistic poet we have just rejected.[55] *Sapere et ringi* provides the bridge across the parable of the eccentric Argive (128b–40) by anticipating *sapere est abiectis utile nugis* (141) and exploiting the two senses of "discernment" (*sapere*): the aesthetic and the moral. The point of the parable is that even the most normal people can suffer from someone's eccentricity to the point where friends and relatives will take a hand in their cure. (Horace sometimes expected the same concern from Maecenas.)[56] When cured, the Argive was terribly crushed to find all his plays and his actors were imaginary (136–40). The parable also recalls the poets who imagined they were good and would not relinquish their bliss (90–108). It

might just have applied to Horace, too, if he had not already realized that poetry was for the young and should be left to them in favour of a study not of measured words, but of the measured life (141–44):

> nimirum *sapere* est abiectis utile nugis,
> et tempestivum pueris concedere ludum,
> ac non verba sequi fidibus modulanda Latinis,
> sed verae numerosque modosque ediscere vitae.

As he tells us in the *Ars Poetica* (301–2), he sees to the purging of his own *voluptas* and *gratissimus error* (the poetic frenzy):

> o ego laevus,
> qui purgor bilem sub verni temporis horam.[57]

He no longer writes poetry. Instead he coolly performs the more mature role of critic, the "whetstone of poets" (*Ars Poetica* 304). And earlier in this epistle the choice of such a purge was seen as seemly and rational (53–54).

Horace is now engaged in the real poetry of life, and if he has not produced the lyrics Florus had hoped for, he will let him listen in to a passage of the real stuff so that he may appreciate the urge that has called the poet away to eccentric pursuits ("quocirca mecum loquor haec tacitusque recordor": 145). The following sermon (146–216) comes from other and greater minds than his, and is therefore all the more worth hearing.

The content of this sermon is important to the whole, as its length suggests: seventy lines (or the final third). As Becker points out, two-thirds of the epistle are devoted to poetry (in contrast to one-third of *Epistle* 1.1, of which it is to some extent a variation).[58] And although the proportion of lines devoted to philosophy in *Epistle* 2.1 is smaller, the message is similar: Horace is through with the play exercises of youth and is now determined at last to devote his time and energies to collecting and using the rudiments of moral philosophy.[59] This diatribe begins (as did his satires) with *avarice*, using an analogy from medicine (145–204).[60] The failure of wealth to produce discernment (*nihilo sapientior*) is stressed (151–57)[61] and the impermanence of human life

which grants us only *usus* (enjoyment) of our possessions, not *mancipium* (outright ownership) (158–79). A famous line of Lucretius expresses it this way (3.971): "vitaque mancipio nulli datur, omnibus usu."[62]

The fact is *usus* is all we need. The lawyers maintain that enjoyment (*usus*) of property renders it our own after a set period (159): "quaedam, si credis consultis, mancipat usus."[63] This can be applied in the ethical sphere to land and the labour that works it (160–62a). As you buy produce, you are gradually buying the land itself, insists Horace (162b–65). Conversely, the man who thinks that he owns his property outright along with its produce is actually enjoying salad and firewood for which his cash has already been paid (166–71a). Outright ownership (*mancipium*) is too fleeting a thing, too subject to time and fortune's whims to be a valid principle upon which to order one's life. One generation succeeds another like waves on the shore and heirs succeed heirs. The vividness of this image here, in Horace's swan-song to philosophy, recalls the frequency with which he had evoked it in the *Odes*[64] and makes us aware of the irony of his claim below to have ever really abandoned the study of philosophy for poetry (175–77a):

> sic quia perpetuus nulli datur usus, et heres
> heredem alternis velut unda supervenit undam,
> quid vici prosunt aut horrea?

The passage goes on to v. 189 in a rich poetic vein still reminiscent of the *Odes* and *Epodes*, pointed with a glittering catalogue of the trinkets both Italian and exotic for which others sell their souls, and allusions to the roles played in our lives by dread Orcus (178) and by the *genius* or guardian spirit of man that controls his mortal nature from birth to death, making him greedy or content, "white or black" (187–89).[65] His own certainty of creed has already been suggested (182): "sunt qui non habeant, est qui non curat habere."[66] This assurance is picked up again with a return to the principle of *usus* (190–92),

> *utar*, et ex modico quantum res poscet acervo
> tollam, nec metuam quid de me iudicet heres,
> quod non plura datis invenerit.

Contentment with a modest store of material goods is proof against any greedy and resentful heir.[67] Always present in his mind will be the principle of the "mean" in behaviour (*modus in rebus*) that enables him to distinguish the light-hearted from the extravagant, the careful from the miserly (192b-98). The key is enjoyment of the brief opportunities life offers, something a schoolboy understands well but which is forgotten with the years (197–98). His one abiding wish is that his modest dwelling not be sordid and unsightly ("†pauperies immunda domus procul absit†": 199),[68] a familiar theme in the *Satires* and the *Odes*, and closely associated with that "golden mean" (*Ode* 2.10.5–8):

> aurean quisquis mediocritatem
> diligit, tutus caret obsoleti
> sordibus tecti, caret invidenda
>   sobrius aula.[69]

As in *Odes* 2.10 and 3.29, the "house" image of the mean is linked to that of the voyage. His style of living is independent of size of ship and direction of winds, and he is content to be in the rear of the foremost (but to the fore of the hindmost) in the race of life.[70]

From these familiar affirmations the diatribe turns to admonition, completing the digest of moral principles for a good and happy life (*Epistle* 2.2.205–216). *non es avarus; abi!* (205) moves us from the first and cardinal sin, greed, to a catechism of other sins and moral weaknesses that must not be ignored: fear of death, anger,[71] ambition, and ghosts,[72] resentment of the passing years, an unforgiving nature, and resistance to moral improvement (205–12). For avarice is but one of the many thorns that must be uprooted from the spirit (213).[73]

The conclusion of Horace's philosophy "sampler,"

> vivere si recte nescis, decede peritis.
> lusisti satis, edisti satis atque bibisti (213–14)

recalls Lucretius (3.961–62):

> nunc aliena tua tamen aetate, omnia mitte
> aequo animoque agedum magnis concede, necessest[74]

and Horace's own earlier statement (*Satire* 1.1.117–19):

> inde fit, ut raro, qui se vixisse beatum
> dicat et exacto contentus tempore vita
> cedat uti conviva satur, reperire queamus.

In that satire, the overture to all of Horace's formally published works (35 B.C.), he closed with a humorous caricature of himself "pillaging the boxes of blear-eyed Crispinus" for all the precepts regarding the vice of avarice. In the *Epistle to Florus* (the last of his philosophical *sermones* and his final statement on the subject) he returns to the familiar technique of concluding with some comic relief,[75] an extension of the same image of the *conviva satur* (215–16):

> tempus abire tibi est, ne potum largius aequo
> rideat et pulset lasciva decentius aetas.

Indulgence must be left behind with youth. To continue to linger at life's feast would ultimately lead to shame and disgrace. We are left with the picture of a drunken old man, ridiculed by "an age more seemly wanton" (*lasciva decentius aetas*: 216). Youth rightly resents the stupid refusal of age to give over such behaviour and may crown his humiliation with a sound cuff on his bald head.[76]

All through the epistle Horace has stressed (as he had done in *Epistles* 1.1, 1.7 and *Ode* 4.1) advancing years as the reason for his retirement as a poet:

> singula de nobis *anni* praedantur euntes;
> eripuere iocos, venerem, convivia, ludum;
> tendunt extorquere poemata. (55–57)

> et studiis annos septem dedit *insenuitque*
> libris. . . . (82–83a)

> et tempestivum pueris concedere ludum. (142)

The motif is maintained here as a diatribe, with allusions to dropsy

(146),[77] heirs and the inexorability of death (173–79, 191), the mortality of man's nature (187–88), the fear of death (207), abhorrence of birthdays (210),[78] the approach of old age (211), and finally in the image of the sated guest who should leave the banquet while he can still do so with dignity (213–16). Now more than ever Horace is relying upon philosophy and, if one is to guess from the anxieties listed and allusions to Lucretius in the epistle, most of all, perhaps, upon the kindlier doctrines of Epicurus.

Another interesting feature of this diatribe is the amount of legal language it incorporates. The lawyer's concerns with *ususfructus* and *usucapio* (*si credis consultis*: 159) and the theme of inheritance take up one-third of the lines,[79] and balance the legal language used in dramatizing the analogy of the sale of the slave (2–17) and Horace's application of it in his own defence. Even his reference to true poetry is made in legal terms: *legitimum poema* (109).[80]

Epistle 1.3 suggests that Florus would appreciate Horace's use of this terminology. He would never devote two-thirds of a long epistle to poetry if his addressee had no interest in or knowledge of it.[81] What he actually says about poetry falls under two headings: (A) why Florus is not to expect lyrics from him (1–105) and (B) why a poet needs frank self-criticism to be good, especially in choice of diction (106–28a). This exclusive concentration upon diction (the only aspect of good and bad poetry that Horace does discuss) is striking, as it flows evidently from his unhappy recollections of having to suffer mediocre recitations spoiled by bad diction (90–105). This *copia* of words that enriches the speech of Latium stems from a sense of both proper selection (*analogia*) and of usage (*consuetudo*) which Horace calls *usus*, and is made possible by *doctrina* and a wide knowledge of the rich traditions of Latin poetry (115–23). With it all, the good poet will make his skill and effort seem like play (124–25). These convictions leave two choices open to him (126–28a): that of appearing wild and unschooled as a poet (like others he knows) as long as he pleases or fools himself, or showing his discernment (*sapere*) in a frank way (*ringi*). The story of the Argive (128b–40) shows how such delusions can be bliss, and [so] painful to forgo.

Why this exclusive treatment of the proper choice of words, and this preference for "frank discernment" on the subject? They enhance our understanding of Horace's misery in the poetic exchanges he describes, of course; but they must also be intended to fulfil some special requirement of Florus. Florus has asked for lyrics which are not being delivered (25):

> exspectata tibi non mittam carmina mendax.

One important reason Horace has left poetry is that it forces him to listen to the work of those who refuse to suffer gladly either criticism or silence (106–8). The good poet will be self-critical and receptive to criticism from others (109–28a) just like the good man (150–216). In contrast to the false and foolish friends and critics who give lavish and indiscriminate praise like hired mourners (*Ars P.* 419 ff), Horace describes the attitude (akin to *sapere et ringi*) of his late friend Quintilius (438–52):

> Quintilio siquid recitares, 'corrige sodes
> hoc' aiebat 'et hoc'; melius te posse negares,
> bis terque expertum frustra, delere iubebat   440
> et male tornatos incudi reddere versus.
> si defendere delictum quam vertere malles,
> nullum ultra verbum aut operam insumebat inanem,
> quin sine rivali teque et tua solus amares.
> vir bonus et prudens versus reprehendet inertes,   445
> culpabit duros, incomptis allinet atrum
> transverso calamo signum, ambitiosa recidet
> ornamenta, parum claris lucem dare coget,
> arguet ambigue dictum, mutanda notabit;
> fiet Aristarchus, nec dicet 'cur ego amicum   450
> offendam in nugis?' hae nugae seria ducent
> in mala derisum semel exceptumque sinistre.

Quintilius is an example of the wise critic who, as *vir bonus et prudens* will be frank and uncompromising in his standards. As an "Aristarchus" (contrast *fit Mimnermus*: 2.2.101), he will neither spare his friends such criticism nor shirk his responsibility even in "trifles," in case minor faults unchecked lead to major ones and ultimately to ridicule (450–52).

Horace's description of the mutual admiration he dislikes and his concern for frank criticism and for apt poetic diction now seem dramatically to imply that Florus, in asking for poems from him, had also sent along some of his own, expecting favourable comment. Horace would be faced therefore with the problem of reproving him for this attitude and encouraging him to greater self-criticism in the area where his work shows the most weakness.[82]

The guiding principle behind Horace's method in epistolary admonitions is tact, something achieved here as elsewhere by making it appear that he is the one under criticism, first in a defence of his silence as both a correspondent and a poet (1–105), and then in a diatribe addressed to himself (to be conned by rote); but also in detailing his failure to achieve a happy and quiet mind (145–216). It is difficult to resent admonition from one who is so sincerely aware of his own faults, and who recognizes your abilities by appealing to you in terms of your own interests and skills. A similar kind of tact is to be seen in the first *Epistle to Florus* (1.3), where the admonition to heal a friendship is introduced only after a long series of questions regarding the activities of his friends and a cryptic reference to *caelestis sapientia* (1.3.27). In that epistle Horace shows considerable informed opinion about the poetry of Titius and of Celsus in particular. Titius will be showing his daring in Pindaric verse or in tragedy, Horace expects (1.3.9–14). Celsus (*monitus multumque monendus*: 1.3.15) has been much cautioned by Horace to avoid plagiarism or he will be laughed to scorn (1.3.15–20a). The actual admonition to Florus was there prefaced by a tactful (and sincere) compliment to his skill as a poet (1.3.20b–22):

> ipse quid audes?
> quae circumvolitas agilis thyma? non tibi parvum
> ingenium, non incultum est et turpiter hirtum.

He has talent to spare, and it is neither uncultivated nor foul with neglect. (The seeming restraint in this compliment to Florus' *ars* seems almost to border on "faint praise," but of course Horace would have something specific to say on his own poetry elsewhere. In *Epistle* 1.3 he had other fish to fry.) Horace had already demonstrated very clearly that he has a great interest in his young friends' poetry, and wants to give them the benefit of his own expertise. But his personal approach to criticizing their work is rather different from that of Quintilius, for all their similarity in standards and aims.

Viewed in the light of Horace's firm and tactful approach to the criticism of his young friends' work, *Epistle* 2.2 suggests a careful inter-relationship with *Epistle* 2.1, the *Epistle to Augustus*.[83] In the most sincere and tactful terms Horace there intimated to Augustus that the quality of contemporary drama (already well supported by him) was inconsistent with the public's enthusiasm for it, and he made a modest and delicate appeal for Augustus' support of other poetry (214–18) too by reminding him of his acumen in years gone by in supporting Vergil and Varius (245–50a). This was seasoned with a sharp reminder: Horace is only too aware that involvement with bad poets can bring ridicule and ruin reputations (264–79).

Epistle 2.2 gives further insight into Horace's intimate relationship with one such worthy poet. Florus may one day gain entrance to the Palatine library too, but for now he must work to perfect his technique and devote time and effort to his improvement. Horace is interested in his friend's career and prepared to advise and guide him. His own career as a poet is behind him. Now at last he can fulfil his own fondest desires for self-criticism and self-improvement in quiet ease.

CHAPTER 3

The Epistle to the Pisos
Ars Poetica

🕭 🕭

PROFESSOR BRINK'S MONUMENTAL work on the *Ars Poetica* was published over a decade and a half ago.[1] In his commentary and earlier *Prolegomena* (1963) he stressed an abiding determination to keep all windows open now that a complete cleaning and inventory had been done of the vast amount of data bearing on the poem. In the light of his exhaustive analysis of the ancient sources for the *Ars*, we now see much more clearly, for example, where and how Horace has made use of the poetic theory of the shadowy Neoptolemus of Parium as "a traditional system of reference in the intricate diversity of the poem."[2] But Brink also sees "a simpler scheme... within it, superimposed on that of the literary critics;[3] ... by avoiding tediousness and technicality and the schools' language." Horace thus prevents the flow of the poem from being disturbed.[4] With the conceptual triad of *poema* (style), *poesis* (content), *poeta* (poet) artfully blurred, technical divisions which would otherwise have seriously depressed the level of the poetry subtly serve to support it. Brink rightly refuses to join the controversy over allegedly exclusive principles of design and unity, insisting always that the answers we receive from our enquiries about this work will differ according to the questions we ask. (Since other great Augustan poems continue to reveal a "multiplicity of patterns," why not also the *Ars*?)[5] Various underlying bipartite, tripartite, and even quadripartite schemes may coexist as complementary structures.[6]

Structural iridescence within the *Ars* is reflected in the range of our perceptions of what the work's main or unifying theme may be. The terminology of *mores* (ethics), for instance, is found in four different contexts: style, content, drama, and the poet's training.[7] (Such "grouping" or stressing might reflect Neoptolemus' influence and Aristotle's *Rhetoric*.)[8] But Brink's chief candidate for the most pervasive principle in the *Ars* (outvoting even *decorum*) is "craft," a choice in which Horace has apparently claimed no precedent from Aristotle[9] or even from Callimachus.[10] There may be a hint of this in Neoptolemus; for in supporting the claims of epic in his prescriptions he seems to have demanded standards of craftsmanship analogous to those of the small highly-wrought poem.[11] Brink rightly observes that in all of Horace's critical writings the Romans' weakness in craftsmanship (i.e., *ars*) appears as their "besetting sin. . . the topic weaves its way in and out of the whole discourse unceasingly. It is present almost everywhere. For ubiquity it beats 'appropriateness' by a large margin."[12]

Convincingly as Brink has pointed out how "craft" colours the thematic plan of the *Ars Poetica*, much of importance still remains to be explored. For example, that theme also illuminates Quintilian's own subtitle for the poem (itself controversial), *Liber de arte poetica*.[13] Translated "On the poet's craft" (instead of "on the art of poetry") it becomes a more accurate description of the contents, one that weakens much of the literature aimed at showing how well or badly the poem functions as a general technical treatise (an *"Ars"* in the extended sense of the word). One hypothesis that needs to be tested against the text of the poem (especially those aspects of it which Brink has illuminated) is that Horace was dramatically engaging his addressees (here the three Pisos) in the argument of *Epistula ad Pisones* no less intimately than he had done in the rest of the *Epistles*. That was argued a century and a half ago, in fact, by Wieland.[14] Is there a dramatic situation that consistently suits both the role of the Pisos as addressees and the tact of Horace's argument? The controversy over the meanings of the poem has been a long one. But thanks to Brink's analysis it may be possible to proceed without violating our poet's own canon: *opus est brevitate*.

Difficulties arise with every question concerning the external origins and the internal purpose and structure of *The Epistle to the Pisos*. When was it written and published?[15] Who were those Pisos?[16] Is it a "treatise" or a "poem"—or both? How is it constructed? What did Horace call it?[17]

Brink concludes that it encourages "many approaches but not a final assessment."[18] For the most part, analysis of *The Epistle to the Pisos* has concentrated upon its anatomy or (to extend the metaphor) its genetics. Into what clearly definable parts does it fall under dissection? What are its literary ancestors and what traits does it inherit from each? As our information has increased, for example, with the discovery of fragments of Philodemus' commentary on the work of Neoptolemus of Parium, our understanding of the transmission and evolution of Aristotelean canons of poetic theory has been greatly enhanced; and a chance comment by Porphyrio about Horace's use of Neoptolemus' most significant ideas has been verified.[19] Although further revelations are not likely, there may be room still for fruitful exploration in two areas. One lies in the possibility of inference from Horace's other epistolary poems (Books I and II); the second, in adopting a more physiological approach to our tests; asking not, "What are its parts?" but rather, "How do its processes work and to what end?"[20]

There are two abiding characteristics of Horace's epistolary poems: they are intended to be dramatic (involving our powers of inference with respect to the situations and motives of both parties), and they reveal the influence of Cicero in their treatment of ethics, for instance in the exploration of the nature and duties of *amicitia*. These principles now appear to apply also to the two long epistles of Book II, as they do to the *Ars Poetica*.[21] Parallels to Ciceronian rhetorical theory, of course, have long been looked for, and discovered, in the poem.[22] The real importance of Horace's repeated addresses to the Pisos has not been assessed.[23] Also the epistolary form he uses in his longest poem never has been systematically explored.

It seems about as difficult to say anything original about the *Ars Poetica* as to write a new tragedy about "fleet-footed Achilles." Sources for some of the views in this study will inevitably be found in the works of many scholars, especially in borrowings from Wieland, Vahlen, Wickham, Williams, Boissier, Norden, Fiske, Klingner, Wili, Tracy,[24] and, of course, Brink.

Given the limited scope thus imposed upon this study, one is obliged at the outset to acknowledge anew the contributions of E.D. Wickham, whose views on the poem are as perceptive as they are disregarded. Wickham's "General introduction to the literary epistles" and his "Introduction to the *Ars Poetica*"[25] merit careful consideration by any critic, for they represent very accurately one level of intention in the poem:

> The address to the Pisones, father and sons, is not conventional or complimentary, but has a vital relation to the course of the poem. . . . The places. . . where a name or other personal appeal occurs are always. . . where the chief points of the Epistle are to be enforced. . . . We can distinguish the different relation which the three persons addressed hold towards the Epistle. The father figures rather as the critic on whom the young writer may lean, and who will enforce Horace's teaching, than as a poet or learner himself at the present time. The younger son is only included as making up the literary family. But as the poem goes on it becomes clear that the elder son is the person for whom the advice is intended. . . he is imagined as not only having literary ambitions, but definite poetical schemes. Horace is putting on paper an old poet's advice to a young aspirant. He does not discourage him, but he would enlist him, if he is to be a poet, as a recruit in the severe and classical school. In an age of scribblers he must give to me to accumulate materials, time to understand his business; he must subject his work to honest and rigorous criticism; he must be slow to give it to the world.
>
> We may distinguish perhaps three parts to the poem: but they pass naturally into one another, and a single thread binds them together in the repeated doctrine, that poetry is an art and as an art has rules, and supposes previous instruction and patient effort.[26]

Wickham would now have to modify his scepticism about Horace's debt to Neoptolemus; but his insistence upon treating the work *qua* epistle is as salutary today as it was a century ago. Unfortunately, the excitement produced by the discovery and publication of Philodemus' fragments has tended to distract attention from Wickham's good sense.

One point upon which most critics do seem to agree is that Horace is at pains here to avoid the appearance of composing a rigidly constructed textbook. Even D.A. Russell, one who sees it as "very much a treatise with a Dear so-and-so at the beginning," recognizes that Horace does not "submit his exposition to it (*res/verba*) as a principle of division as a text-book should."[27] W. Wili does not read it as a didactic poem or handbook but as "ein Kunstbrief," and he remarks on its "letter-like leaping transitions, imitative of easy conversation."[28] Such concealing of transitions is not unique to epistolary composition, of course. In the *De Oratore* Cicero's Antonius observes that the handling of arguments in a speech should be varied to prevent monotony and that intervals between proofs should be masked to prevent any possibility of a mechanical count: "Tractatio autem varia esse debet, ne aut cognoscat artem qui audiat aut defatigetur similitudinis satietate... *interpuncta argumentorum plerumque occulas*, ne quis ea numerare possit (like Catullus' kisses?), ut re distinguantur, verbis confusa esse videantur."[29] Eduard Norden offers the parallel of a good architect concealing the joints: "The structure of the Epistle is without break; every attempt to displace a stone spoils its completeness."[30]

There is a tension in the *Ars*, then, between Horace's desire to make the argument appear to flow spontaneously as in a letter to friends, while incorporating as well the kind of unity and coherence in structure that he demands. Rhetorically the work begins as a *thesis* (argument of a general proposition), and it concludes as a *hypothesis* (argument of a specific proposition).[31] Opening with an exposition of the universal importance for a poet of the acquisition of mastery of his craft (1–37), it proceeds through selective prescriptions on the techniques of drama to focus upon the special needs of the older Piso brother (366).[32] There have been interesting attempts to identify within the poem the four canonical parts of a rhetorical exercise: *exordium, narratio, confirmatio*, and *peroratio*.[33]

The *Ars* certainly has an exordium: the first 37 lines. Lines 1–23 of this introduction deal with failures in art: first in painting, then pottery (21b–22). The argument shifts to the subject of poetry (24), with a pointed address to all three Pisos. More analogies to painting follow (29–30), then to sculpture (32–37), before we hear any advice dealing exclusively with writing poetry. The address to the Pisos tells something about the writer as well (*maxima pars vatum... decipimur specie recti*: 24–25): he includes himself as a poet working within a poetry-conscious society. This exordium begins *in medias res* on the subject of art, with the depiction of one painter's monstrosity (1–4),[34] and concludes with a reference to a certain second-rate sculptor (32–37) well known in Rome. Clearly the Pisos are interested in poetry: Horace seems to take for granted that they will share his views. The good will of an audience is of prime importance to a speaker or writer; so sympathy and a favourable reaction must be cultivated as soon as possible by whatever rhetorical means are appropriate.[35] Horace's most effective *captatio benevolentiae* in this exordium comes with laughter, and the importance of laughter here cannot be overstated. The *Ars Poetica* begins and ends satirically.

An imaginary painter (1–5)[36] is set against some familiar local artisan, neither of whom has any sense of *total* composition (32–37). The productions of each are ridiculous. What each lacks is a discernment of unity, proportion, and appropriateness, the very principles an artist must master to compose correctly. A *sententia* focuses that concern for artistic unity and correctness inherent in all the analogies of painting, pottery, and sculpture (23):

> denique sit quidvis, simplex dumtaxat et unum.

This discussion is enlivened by the claims of poetic licence (9–13) and artistic digressions (14–19a); the first coming from an interlocutor (9–10), the second raised by Horace himself. The answer to these apparent conflicts of poetic purpose is given in a commonplace from ethics (31):

> in vitium ducit culpae fuga, si caret arte.

So far two principles have been invoked to guide the artist. *Unum* was clear enough; *arte* does not seem quite so precise.

Clarification of *ars* comes in part from the lines that follow in the next section, a transition passage in the guise of a general exhortation to all writers (38–44) which applies the examples of flawed sculpture to their own craft.[37]

> sumite materiam vestris, qui scribitis, aequam
> viribus, et versate diu, quid ferre recusent,
> quid valeant umeri. cui lecta potenter erit res,   40
> nec facundia deseret hunc nec lucidus ordo.
> ordinis haec virtus erit et venus, aut ego fallor,
> ut iam nunc dicat iam nunc debentia dici,
> pleraque differat et praesens in tempus omittat.

The foundation for all artistic composition then (whether painting, pottery, sculpture, or writing) lies in the powers, *vires*, of the artist (39), for they will determine (*umeri... potenter*) the selection of material (*materia... res*). Excellence in style (*facundia*) and clarity of plan (*lucidus ordo*) should follow *vires*.[38] The relationship between *vires/potentia* and *ars*, however, still requires explanation.

Ars to Horace conveys at least three ideas: the practised mastery of craft, the systematic knowledge of theory and technique, and the capacity for objective self-criticism. In athletics *vires* must be developed from natural strength and aptitude through practice, exercise, training, and discipline. Poets too must have aptitude, training, practice, and discipline in order to choose material and compose.[39] Quintilian's subtitle *Liber de arte poetica* might lead us to expect the coherent exposition of a systematic doctrine of poetic composition. Although we are not entirely disappointed, the treatment of aspect of the *Ars* seems far from comprehensive, concentrating on the *artes* of tragedy and of satyr-plays, but giving disproportionally less space to general theory. As an "*ars*" in the sense of treatise this poem does not even pretend to offer inexperienced writers all they need to know. But Horace's coverage of *ars poetica* makes every point required. The unified theme is not "WHAT is *ars poetica*?" but rather, "WHY is *ars poetica*, the craft of the poet, so important?" In other words, the *Ars* is not so much epideictic as protreptic.

That is the theme that unifies the entire epistle, a justification of the immense investment in time and labour such *ars* demands, just as it was the function of the exordium to enlist the support of Horace's three friends the Pisos for his views regarding a remedy for the ills of contemporary poetry.[40] He has impressed upon them one inevitable and disastrous consequence in particular of the failure to master poetic art. The absurd mermaid visualized in vv. 1–4 (a controlling image in the work) resulted from the painter's lack of discrimination (*varias... undique, turpiter*). Horace seems confident that the Pisos will be kindred spirits and he invites them to share in the uncontrollable laughter the monster deserves (5):

> spectatum admissi risum teneatis, amici?

That rhetorical question lays down the fundamental antithesis that drives the *Ars* and makes it work as a poem (*ARS-RISUS*),[41] as well as encouraging his friends' support for his views. Having once ensured that support, he may urge upon them how similar it is to compose a book (*credite, Pisones*). Excessive claims of poetic licence are just as damaging. *Quidlibet audendi* is here uncomfortably close in spirit to *varias. . . undique*. His own reply to the sceptical interlocutor (*scimus. . . sed*) enlists the Pisos' sentiments once more: "*some* licence, of course, but earned by restraint" (11–13).[42] The contentious issue of the "purple patch" (15–19a) heads off further discussion of concessions (*venia*): high standards are needed and always restraint. Horace is then ready for his famous maxim on unity (23).

Tactfully it was his own performance to which he has applied the stick of critical judgement (24–27a):

> maxima pars vatum, pater et iuvenes patre digni,
> decipimur specie recti. brevis esse laboro,
> obscurus fio; sectantem levia nervi
> deficiunt animique.

Such self-depreciation should be seen against his respectful inclusion of the Pisos in the ranks of poets. An earnest search for what was genuinely "right" produced something "wrong." "Brevity" became obscurity; "smoothness," nervelessness. The catalogue of extremes then continues: "grand" becomes turgid, "cautious," fearful, "variety," silliness. *Ars* is somehow the cure for it all.[43]

The exordium has aimed at the attentiveness, agreement, and good will of all three Pisos. By means of his humour (sometimes at his own expense), modesty, variety, and vividness of example, Horace has made a case for unity and decorum as paradigms of what *ars* entails. The "carrot" is success; the "stick," public ridicule. Whoever these Pisos may be, no patrician family would relish public ridicule and loss of *dignitas*; if Horace can impress this upon them as a real consequence, persuasion will be much simpler.[44]

The central and longest part of the *Ars Poetica* (38–365) comprises a persuasive exposition of how much *ars* really entails of work and self-sacrifice.[45] Its length, like the unusual length of the whole poem, seems to reinforce and reflect this stern view. Following a transitional appeal for self-criticism by poets he moves to the definitions of *facundia* and *ordo*, allowing the terse account of *ordo* ("plan") (42–43) to precede a much ampler account of *facundia* ("style" or "expression": 44–72). The stylistic criteria and principles of word choice and collocation (Horace's expression *verbis serendis* compares the Minervan craft of weaving: 46) are based on *ars: tenuis cautusque* (46), *amet... spernat* (45), *egregie* (47), *callida iunctura* (47–48), *pudenter* (51), *parce* (53).[46] *Callida*, for example, means "clever" in the sense of "practised," where the choice of familiar words in collocations born of practised skill makes for memorable expression.[47] The licence to coin new words where required is affirmed (55b–59) on the basis of restraint and of Greek precedent, with reference to the examples of Caecilius and Plautus (48b–54), Cato and Ennius (56), even though contemporary critics now deny such licence even to Vergil and Varius (54b–55a). That licence is eloquently defended on behalf of all poets, in a richly poetic passage allusive of Homer and Lucretius (60–72). Words sprout, to fall and be replaced like leaves on a tree and new ones are always needed. *Usus* (71) is the criterion by which words come and go; i.e., the "practice" as rationally established by poets through *ars*.[48]

Epic reminiscences offer a starting point for the next aspect of *ars*. Homer showed the way for all epic poets (74), and a real poet must be expected to know the originators and the characteristics of his own and other types and genres (75–85). But then Horace abruptly contrasts the wrong-headedness of his contemporaries (86–88):

> descriptas servare vices operumque colores
> cur ego si nequeo ignoroque poeta salutor?
> cur nescire pudens prave quam discere malo?

He cannot empathize with this group, for in their view scorn for *ars* (and ignorance of it) brings not disgrace and failure, but acclaim! Such perverse influences block any effort to learn and master the craft. For Horace, this is the vice that condemns Roman poetry so often to mediocrity.

The general discussion of the genres and styles of literature (*vices operumque colores*: 86) moves to the specifics of tragic style (89–118), first its differences from the comic (89–92) which stem from appropriateness (*decentem*: 92). Decorum may license a grander style in comedy from time to time, and a plainer one in tragedy (93–97), but the ultimate criterion is always dramatic *effectiveness* ("si curat cor spectantis tetigisse querela"). Decorum will also determine the sort of language a character uses on stage (*voltum verba decent*: 106), for on stage the tongue has to be the interpreter of one's real feelings (111). The Pisos are reminded again of the price of ignoring the guidance of *ars* in avoiding *absona dicta* (112), for the inept playwright will be ridiculed:

> aut dormitabo aut *ridebo*... (105)

> Romani tollent equites peditesque *cachinnum*. (113)

From the pitfalls of composing tragic verse, Horace moves to another aspect of composition which must be controlled by craft or ridicule will follow: plot (119–20). Whether you borrow a legendary plot or invent, consistency and appropriateness of character are crucial (119–27). To borrow with artistry and originality (131–35) requires knowledge and experience and is at least as difficult (128) as attempting complete originality (125–27). Horace's preference for traditional plots is clear (128–30):

> difficile est proprie communia dicere; tuque
> rectius Iliacum carmen deducis in actus,
> quam si proferres ignota indictaque primus.[49]

But one must understand the perils of slavish translation and of being tightly bound by an even stricter literary propriety (*pudor*: 135) and the tradition (*operis lex*). The practice of the cyclic poets provides the right cautionary note against too vast a plot (136–39). To attempt the entire sweep of the events of the Trojan War was beyond even Homer's powers, but he knew from experience what he *could* handle well (*qui nil molitur inepte*: 140) and selected his material for the *Iliad* and *Odyssey* accordingly (140–42). Horace's eloquent and famous tribute to Homer's virtues is actually a tribute to his planning (*cogitat*: 144) and selectivity (*nec orditur ab ovo*... : 147); that is, his conscious and experienced artistry, or his craft (148–52):

> semper ad eventum *festinat* et in medias res
> non secus ac notas auditorem *rapit*, et quae
> *desperat* tractata nitescere posse, *relinquit*,

atque ita *mentitur*, sic veris falsa *remiscet*,
primo *ne* medium, medio *ne discrepet* imum.

That such a familiar author's mastery of craft should account for his appeal is a telling argument for *ars* and the pains it may entail. It is in this light that the famous mountain-mouse *sententia* should be seen (*parturient montes, nascetur ridiculus mus*: 139). The cyclic poet constructs a poem *inepte* and the vast bulk of his material will yield results which are miserable and laughable.

This purple patch about Homer (140–52) gives way once more to the *artes* of the playwright. The discourse is still addressed to the typical *scriptor* (120, 128), who must study the *artes* of character portrayal, an area where Horace and the theatre public at large share similar critical standards (153): "tu quid age et populus mecum desideret, *audi.*"[50] Decorum must be *learned* ("aetatis cuiusque *notandi sunt* tibi mores": 156), so the four ages of the world stage may be rightly imitated in terms of their inherent qualities (*adiunctis aptis*: 178). Decorum must determine what actions are described, for a bad performance here incurs a response more hostile than just laughter (*incredulus odi*: 188).

The importance of understanding the dramatic rules governing the number of acts (189–90), the *deus ex machina* (191–92a), the number of actors (192b), and the proper function of the chorus (193–201) is rapidly sketched, and a fuller account of the history and *ars* of musical accompaniment in drama given (202–19). The historical background to the deplorable degeneration of this aspect of the dramatic art leads to a moral attack on the present age: pipes are now pierced with many holes and bound with gilded brass to compete with trumpets in their blare (202–7). The contrast to the chaste simplicity of the old-fashioned pipes reflects the moral corruption that the years have produced. Their audience was once modest in size and manner (*frugi castusque verecundusque*: 207), and their taste in music reflected that modesty. But as the population increased (along with the number of festivals celebrated), so did the licence allowed to the tragic metres and modes. In words, music, and instrumentation *prisca ars* gave way to *motus* and *luxuries* (214): restrained lyrics became wanton and overpowering, and whether the subject was humble or sacred, they sounded like obscure and tortured oracles (215–19). Only detailed knowledge of the historical evolution of drama can give a writer the perspective he needs to avoid excess and discover a true Augustan standard in the face of present lack of taste.[51]

The writer must likewise know the background and purpose of satyr-plays to compose them, and they too are subject to the demands of decorum in style (225–39).[52] Here also Horace espouses the principle of following a familiar plot (*ex noto dictum carmen sequar*: 240) in a style that is uncommon but suited to the genre (234–36):

> non ego *inornata* et *dominantia* nomina solum
> verbaque, Pisones, Satyrorum scriptor amabo;
> nec sic enitar *tragico* differre *colori*.

There is a special force to this exhortation because Horace uses the direct appeal again to the Pisos, rather than the flat conventional *tu*: the demands of *ars* for training and experience are clear. Such artistry must be so well concealed that anyone might fancy he too can manage it; familiar words win acclaim (240–43) by a clever order and collocation (*series iuncturaque*: 242). *Pison et fils* are all reminded that honour and a crown are to be won from the "right" segments of the audience, the knights, patricians, and well-to-do (248–50), all of whom balk at poor stuff (248): "Offenduntur enim, quibus est equus et pater et res." Satyr-plays provide a pleasing relief from the seriousness tragedy, without compromising the dignity of the latter (222–26). Here too resides the force of artistic decorum (*conveniet*: 226).

The account of the *artes* of the playwright turns to tragic metre (251), a topic anticipated in vv. 79–80. *Ars* teaches the skilful variation of iambi with spondees, a fine point Romans have mastered only recently. Even the noble verse of Ennius and Accius often failed, either because they were too fast and too careless, or simply deficient in *ars*, a shameful charge for a compatriot to have to level (260–62).

> in scaenam missos cum magno pondere versus
> aut operae celeris nimium curaque carentis
> aut ignoratae premit artis crimine turpi.

The discussion of *artes metricae* then brings to the fore for the first time the subject of literary critics.[53] Critics themselves do not always see faults in metre and are inclined, besides, to give undeserved licence to

Roman poets (263–64). How should Horace, as a Roman poet, respond? Err fully as far as such licence allows? Anticipate a bare minimum of criticism (270–74)? Neither.

> at vestri proavi Plautinos et numeros et
> laudavere sales: nimium patienter utrumque,
> ne dicam stulte, mirati, si modo ego et vos
> *scimus* inurbanum *lepido* seponere dicto
> *legitimumque* sonum digitis *callemus* et aure.

Tactfully he includes himself with the Pisos once more (*ego et vos*) in the circle of *docti iudices* whose powers of discrimination are based upon knowledge and experience (*scimus... callemus*).

The history of Greek drama is brought down from the original discovery of tragedy to the end of Old Comedy (275–84), when *vis* and *libertas* were suppressed by law. Greek drama was of course the inspiration for Roman, and Roman writers left nothing untried, and with much success (285–88). But whereas the Romans spared no effort to be the best in their military exploits, it was a different matter in poetry.[54] Yet even here they could have excelled, if patient and precise polish and craftsmanship had not seemed so repugnant (290b–91a):

> si non offenderet unum
> quemque poetarum limae labor et mora.

There is only one recourse for poets when sound criticism is wanting at home. They must constantly study Greek tragedians at first hand (268–69):

> *vos* exemplaria Graeca
> nocturna versate manu, versate diurna.

The tone of this injunction is sharpened by the reintroduction of the *vos*-address (are the *vos* aspiring writers at large, or the Pisos alone?) in contrast with the poet's *ego* (265–68, 272–79). The Romans' neglect of *ars* is exemplified by their own ancestors' tolerance (*vestri proavi*)—even fascination—for Plautus' metrics and jokes. That tolerance was excessive and by the correct standards of *ars*, foolish (272–74).

A return to the topic of the Romans' uncritical view of their own poetry, their abhorrence of the rigors of refinement, and their impatience brings with it once more an earnest appeal explicitly to the three Pisos (291–94):

> vos, o
> Pompilius sanguis, carmen reprehendite quod non
> multa dies et multa litura coercuit atque
> praesectum deciens non castigavit ad unguem.

This heroic allusion to the ancestry of the Calpurnii Pisones (Calpus was the son of Numa Pompilius) is intended to appeal to *noblesse oblige*. The appeal for self-criticism echoes vv. 263–74, where Horace had once more implicated himself in a national weakness. In retrospect, the *vos* of that earlier passage does appear intended to draw the three Pisos more personally into the problem in anticipation of this stronger and more direct injunction. The rot has set in among Roman writers and Horace wishes to spare his friends the ignominy inferior performance brings. And why are effort, polish, patience, erasure, and correction not highly esteemed? Horace relieves the stringency of his exhortation by putting the blame satirically on the philosopher Democritus (295–97):

> ingenium misera quia fortunatius arte
> credit et excludit sanos Helicone poetas
> Democritus, bona pars non ungues ponere curat,
> non barbam, secreta petit loca, balnea vitat.[55]

It was Democritus, then, who first devalued *ars*; a poet with raw *ingenium* was to him more fortunate than one who had merely mastered a craft. His devotees were still to be seen in Rome: unshaven, mysterious, unwashed, and unkempt. Avoiding any stigma of sanity, they refused doses of spring tonic for their frenzied melancholia—as if any quantity would have helped! (299–300a). Horace contrasts his own "perverse" position with contented irony (301b-2):

> o ego laevus,
> qui purgor bilem sub verni temporis horam.

He rejects Democritus' aesthetic doctrine of the supremacy of talent and inspiration with ironic regret over his own failure to write inspired poetry (303–4a), and claims the more modest role of a critical whetstone which cannot "cut," but can "sharpen." This new role is not creative but corrective, and since he is not now actually composing, he cannot be accused of speaking from self-interest or grinding his own axe (306–7):

> munus et officium, nil scribens ipse docebo,
> unde parentur opes, quid alat formetque poetam.

It is now his duty and obligation (*munus* et *officium*) to teach the poet where his material comes from and what will foster and shape his craftsmanship. These issues are expressed in ethical terms (*deceat, virtus, error*); accordingly, his use of the concept of *sapere* (to be discerning, wise, tasteful in art or philosophy) as the basis of correct writing is not surprising (309):

> Scribendi recte sapere est et principium et fons.[56]

Cicero had insisted upon a philosophical training for the orator as a training in logic and a store of moral maxims and examples,[57] a programme for which Horace makes a parallel claim (310–11):

> rem tibi Socraticae poterunt ostendere chartae,
> verbaque provisam rem non invita sequentur.

Specifically, it would seem, he is recommending the Academy, Lyceum, and Stoa as guides. *Qui didicit* reinforces the point, as does *scit convenientia* (316). *Res* is also part of the *ars poetica*. The model of life and morals that philosophy offers gives the *doctus imitator* the insights needed to imitate life truthfully (317–18). Horace concludes his case for making *sapientia* part of the poet's training by alluding to plays that have pleased and held their audiences despite a lack of serious ideas or great skill because they were *speciosa locis*, i.e., attractive because of their moral *sententiae* (319–23). Clearly this is not to recommend such limited scope to a writer, but rather to underscore the importance of this aspect of *ars* in the total effect of a play.

The following section (323–32: *Grais ingenium . . .*) takes up once more the theme of the poet's training and education. The Muse's "gifts" to the Greeks of talent (*ingenium*) and technique (*ore rotundo loqui*) were matched by their desire to excel (*praeter laudem nullius avaris*: 324). But young Romans (perhaps both father and sons will understand the point) spend their school days doing fractions and practical calculations (325–30a) and they are constantly reminded of the practical advantages. Such "corrosive concern" with accumulating money (*aerugo et cura peculi*: 330) inevitably puts them at a great disadvantage when it comes to appreciating what great poetry is (330–32). That practical disposition of Romans, in part a function of their education, leads them to judge poetry by its practical benefits, the next point raised for consideration by the Pisos (333–34):

> aut prodesse volunt aut delectare poetae
> aut simul et iucunda et idonea dicere vitae.

The writer actually has three choices: to give profit or pleasure, or both at once. But there is clearly a split vote on this choice, even in Rome, and a favourable decision demands an appeal to both sides (341–44):

> centuriae seniorum agitant expertia frugis,
> celsi praetereunt austera poemata Ramnes;
> omne tulit punctum qui miscuit utile dulci,
> lectorem delectando pariterque monendo.[58]

The winning poet will both delight and teach: a simple enough precept— but how much *ars* it implies! Without this no work can win profit or fame, or long endure (345–46):

> hic meret aera liber Sosiis, hic et mare transit
> et longum noto scriptori prorogat aevum.

Horace is now poised to give special advice to the elder son of Piso (366 ff), but first there is one more general point to make. A poet's reputation and prestige depend upon his mastery of the craft and a correct assessment of his own ability: in short, upon his conscious capacity to instruct and delight. Some offences (*delicta*) are minor (347–50) and mechanical, such as those produced by an out-of-tune string or a false bow stroke. As long as they are few, and stem from occasional carelessness or human weakness, the critic will not take exception (351–53). But they must be rare, not chronic (354–60). The scribe who blunders continually will not be forgiven, nor the citharist who repeatedly strikes the wrong string: he is laughed at (in Horace's view), just like Choerilus, Alexander's epic biographer, whose occasional lapses into good verse provoked laughter (354–58a).[59] How different it is with Homer! When he nods Horace is annoyed, even though he acknowledges the licence due the long epic, the most demanding of literary forms. Poetry (here the analogy returns us to the exordium of the epistle) is like a painting. One attracts close up, another from a distance; one in shade, another in daylight—without fearing even the most trenchant of judges. One bears viewing once, another a dozen times (362–65).

The most decisive break in the poem occurs at v. 366, marked by another vocative: *vos, o maior iuvenum.*[60] So far, the relationship between the poet (*ego*) and his friends (*vos*, sometimes conjoined as *nos*) has been kept a family affair. "vos o Pompilius sanguis, carmen reprehendite" (291b–92) links the three Pisos in the quest for standards of self-criticism; the sudden isolation of the older brother presents a logical step in a tactful conditioning of his response. If Horace has won and kept his interest and good will in demonstrating how difficult and complex *ars poetica* is, it is time to offer some very pointed advice which occupies the remaining lines of the poem (366–69a):

> o maior iuvenum, quamvis et voce paterna
> fingeris ad rectum et per te sapis, hoc tibi dictum
> tolle memor, certis medium et tolerabile rebus
> recte concedi.

The young man has had instruction from his father, and achieved some discernment through his own efforts. Horace will build on that in order to thrust home a new critical idea. Unlike orators, poets must either achieve excellence or utterly fail.[61] Something like poetry, which has pleasure as its purpose, he argues, must give pain when it fails (369b–79); that is, when it is less than excellent. The young man who stays away from the athletic ground from lack of training (*nescit... indoctus*) would of course deserve to be laughed at if he did not (379–81). Yet somehow when it comes to poetry that lesson seems lost (382–84):

qui nescit versus tamen audet fingere. quidni?
liber et ingenuus, praesertim census equestrem
summan nummorum, vitioque remotus ab omni.

To prove his point Horace again reduces himself to just one more member of the crowd of poets. *Satire* 1.6.8–18 ("dum ingenuus... quid oportet/nos facere a volgo longe longeque remotos") suggests parallels to *Epistles* 2.1, 2.2, and vv. 25–27, 263–68a above. (He is free-born with money enough—so why should he not write?) The whimsical jab at himself is followed by the hopeful expectation that the young Piso major has more discrimination, and will understand his own limitations (385–386a, *per te sapis*). But if he ever does write something (*si quid tamen olim/scripseris*: 386b)—that is the issue! Cultivation of his *ars* requires criticism from a Maecius Tarpa (Cicero knew him as a producer for Pompey's theatre),[62] and from his own father, and from Horace. Keep a composition in its wrapper for nine years and resist all urges to publish. Once published it will be completely beyond recall and correction (387–90).

Vv. 385–86a constitute a kind of motto or emblem that sums up the whole argument as well as anything else on the poem:

tu nihil *invita* dices faciesve *Minerva*:
id tibi iudicium est, ea mens.

Minerva is a metaphor for *ars*, which is clear from the context here and from similar expressions in Columella (*pref.* 33), in Cicero (*pingui Minerva*: *Amic.* 5.19), and elsewhere in Horace *crassa Minerva*: *Sat.* 2.2.3); she can also represent *natura* (Cic. *Off.* 1.31.103) in the ethical sense in which a man's *natura* determines his own decorum. *Nihil* here (385) means *nihil boni* or *nihil decori*. Horace's advice to Piso is that true poetry can be achieved only through the sense of decorum granted by Minerva to writers of both talent *and* careful craftsmanship. That uncompromising principle must rule his efforts.

Thus far (366–90) Horace's advice has been strongly cautionary. Now an encouraging eulogy of poetry follows, with an account of the historical role of the poet in civilized society (391–407). The magical legends attached to Orpheus and Amphion reflect the poet's prophetic and civilizing roles as a law-giver and public conscience: that discernment (*sapientia*: 396) brought him honour and reputation in former days as an inspired bard (*divinis vatibus*: 40). The contributions (401–6) of later poets such as Homer and Tyrtaeus give grounds for a firm confidence in the worth of the poet's craft (406b-7):

> ne forte pudori
> sit tibi Musa lyrae sollers et cantor Apollo.

This apology serves as a counterpoise to Horace's earlier cautions against mediocre verse: "Don't be ashamed of being a poet—but do have the pride to be a *good* one." The Muse and Apollo combine to represent controlled inspiration. The epithet *soll-ers* (407) is a synonym for *callida*, linked by Cicero with *ingeniosus, versutus, providus,* and *diligens,* and associated with skill in the criticism of diction: "quod [genus acuminis] erat in reprehendendis verbis versutum et sollers" (*Brut.* 236). The scholastic question of whether *natura* or *ars* produces excellence follows naturally enough (408–11):

> natura fieret laudabile carmen an arte
> quaesitum est. ego nec studium sine divite vena
> nec rude quid possit video ingenium; alterius sic
> altera poscit opem res et coniurat amice.

Horace's own opinion is emphatic (*ego*: 409): as with the question of *aut prodesse volunt aut delectare* (333), reason teaches that success requires both, for each needs the other (409b-11). The examples he gives are appropriate to the interests of a youthful pupil: the work and severe discipline a boy requires to become a competitive runner or oboist (412–15). But how different are the present attitudes among Roman writers! Just declare yourself a poet and of course you are one! A perverted sense of shame prevents contemporary poets from admitting they have not mastered their craft (416–18):

> nec satis est dixisse 'ego mira poemata pango,
> occupet extremum scabies; mihi turpe relinqui est,
> et quod *non didici* sane nescire fateri.'

His attack on contemporary writers who have no real knowledge of their craft but write simply because they do not want to be left out leads back to the subject of self-criticism. Rich dilettantes, like auctioneers, bring their claques with them. How can they know true friends from false (419–25)? Piso (*tu*: 426) should not expect candour from someone he has given a present to, any more than he would expect sincerity from hired mourners (426–33). Kings ply candidates for their *amicitia* with wine (435–36a). Young Piso must not ever fool himself about his verses, like the crow with the cheese in the fable (436b–37):

> si carmina condes,
> numquam te fallent animi sub vulpe latentes.[63]

Carmina condes refers to serious composition; if a poet is confident in the mastery of his craft it is unlikely that he will be attracted to or deceived by the flattery of false friends.

The importance to Piso of finding honest critics has already been mentioned (386–90): one of Maecius' stamp, and his own father, and Horace himself. The importance of true friendship is clear, and here Horace becomes explicit about true criticism (438–52). His late friend and *candidus iudex*, Quintilius, is the model; his standards of poetic craft (*ars*) were stringent and uncompromising.[64] With him no offence (*delictum*) could be allowed to remain. Inartistic verses (*inertes*) must go back to the anvil—and no "buts" about it (445–52):

> vir bonus et prudens versus reprehendet inertes,
> culpabit duros, incomptis allinet atrum
> transverso calamo signum, ambitiosa recidet
> ornamenta, parum claris lucem dare coget,
> arguet ambigue dictum, mutanda notabit;
> fiet Aristarchus, non dicet "cur ego amicum
> offendam in nugis?" hae nugae seria ducent
> in mala derisum semel exceptumque sinistre.

This idealization of the critic-friend is justly famous and deserves to be seen in its exact context. Quintilius had been true to the tradition of the famous Aristarchus. Horace is himself assuming that critic's mantle now to advise and warn his young friend; for it is the obligation of a friend to reprove, as Cicero has said, even at the risk of offending.[65] The motive is clear: to save him from a harsh reception for his verse, and ridicule for himself. The poet's two options remain: either ARS or RISUS.

Horace's tactful message should now be very clear to young Piso. He must labour to master the poet's craft and accept proper criticism or face disaster to his hopes of being a poet and the bleak prospect of becoming a laughing-stock. That is strong medicine. To make its after-taste sweeter, Horace concludes the poem as he began it, on a humorous note. Cicero had contrasted the mad orator to the good one.[66] Horace uses the frantic image of the *vesanus poeta* to illustrate what monsters a talent without craft might produce (453–76). Whether his madness stems from itch, or epilepsy, or plain lunacy, discerning folk (*qui sapiunt*: 456) will shun him, leaving him plagued by the young and the unwary. If, as he wanders about belching forth his "lofty" song, he stumbles into a pit like a fowler intent on his blackbirds, no one will help him out, assuming that he did it on purpose (*prudens*) and does not want to be saved at all (457–63a). Empedocles the poet-philosopher serves as an *exemplum*: his quest for immortality led him to leap in cold blood (and brass boots) (*frigidus*: 465) into Etna's flames. A clear moral emerges (466b-67):

> sit ius liceatque perire poetis;
> invitum qui servat, idem facit occidenti.

Poets bent on such distinction in their mad quest for fame should have that right. The causes of this madness may be sin against the gods (470–72a), impiety, or sacrilege (cf. vv. 453–54)—but madness it is! The *Ars* concludes with a vigorous simile: like the circus bear who smashes his cage, the reciting poet eventually routs his whole audience (*indoctum doctumque*: 474) with his savage onslaught (*acerbus*). Then follows a fine metaphor as the sting in the tail (476): he is a leech who kills his victim with reading, and will not let go till gorged with gore!

> non missura cutem nisi plena cruoris *hirudo*.

The Epistle to the Pisos, *Ars Poetica*, began in a bizarre art gallery and ended at a circus. In between those two spectacles, Horace has cultivated the confidence and agreement of a young friend (secure in the company of his father and younger brother) by discussing the importance to the poet of mastery of his art as the only alternative to ridicule and disgrace. After his exposition of the poetic art required to compose classical drama addressed to all three, Horace singles out the elder brother, exhorting him to avoid flatterers and to submit his work only to critics who are both discerning and honest. (Horace may already have seen his work.) The slapstick conclusion tempers the seriousness, and invites Piso to laugh with him.

In tone and purpose this longest of the epistles echoes *Epistles* 1.2, 1.3, 1.18, and 2.2, works in which the resources of poetic tact are brought to bear on the problem of reproving young men of poetic talent, and possibly some pride and resistance to correction. In the long *Epistle to Florus* (2.2) Horace also criticized those who (without any self-criticism on their part) insisted on reciting to him and having him flatter them in reply. They are laughed at (*Epistle* 2.2.106), but on they write with fiendish glee, supplying for themselves the praise withheld by others (108). Florus was perhaps too close to this group for comfort.

The amount of attention given to classical tragedy in the *Ars* (especially satyr-plays) resembles that given in *Epistles* 2.1 and 2.2. Both dramatic revivals and new works seem to have had a tremendous vogue during Augustus' principate, reflecting his own predisposition to spectacles of all kinds. But the emphasis here focuses on and properly reflects the concerns of Piso. The elder brother seems to have caught this current craze for writing drama, blithely supposing that he can succeed without the *labor* and *ars* this entails, and can avoid troublesome criticism. Horace is confronted with the task of impressing upon him, in the face of much ignorant and insincere flattery from other "friends," that the road to success as a playwright is long and hard, calling for much discipline and patience to achieve mastery of the craft. The very length and complexity of the poem deliberately represents this. The alternative is ridicule.

As Porphyrio saw, the fruits of Horace's own long labour to achieve that *ars* are displayed in the fabric of the poem. Peripatetic literary theory, including that of Aristotle and of Neoptolemus, provides much of the *res*, and this material is selected with specific attention to drama (which Piso apparently wants to write) and to Homer (whom both have read and love), with the intention of providing not a handbook but an engaging if sobering paradigm of how very very much there is to learn. The debate over mechanical divisions in the *Ars Poetica* and the efforts expended in discovering its rhetorical structure and headings and sub-headings (e.g., Neoptolemus' *poesis, poema, poeta*) are all of limited use as criticism unless we see how Horace has spun out his argument into a *sermo* that is long but deceptively informal; sometimes making points briefly and then returning to develop them, but always with the situation and appropriate reactions of his young friend in mind. There could not be a finer example than his own of the principle he espouses of letting art conceal the art.

That Horace has in fact made poetry out of this mass of material shows that he knew how much his shoulders would bear. That he wrote it at all is yet another visible testimony to his Ciceronian concern for the proper discharge of the *officia amicitiae*.

CHAPTER 4

The Literary Epistles

ঌ ঌ

Pattern and Coherence

If the preceding rationales for the epistles addressed to Augustus, Florus, and the Pisos are substantially correct, they hold further implications for understanding the poems as a group. The three persons addressed are all, presumably, vitally interested in poetry: Augustus as a patron, Julius Florus and the elder son of Piso or as aspiring practising poets. There is in each epistle a pervading emphasis on the crucial importance of self-criticism. As a group, the addressees represent a full spectrum of the Roman upper-class interested in literature: Augustus as one of Horace's own generation, and Florus a contemporary of his stepson, Tiberius; Piso seems younger yet, just becoming interested in writing drama. Florus, of course, has already reached the stage where Horace can be enthusiastic about some of his achievements: "prima feres hederae victricis praemia" (*Epistle* 1.3.25).

Augustus (*Epistle* 2.1) is tactfully petitioned to reassess his own standards as a patron of the arts and assist promising young poets once more, as Horace reminds him of his part in the success of Vergil and Varius, and the glories of their art. The rhetorical context of Horace's request is a shrewd analysis of the present literary scene in Rome, one in which we see everywhere a chaos of artistic standards and motivations. The universal infatuation with the stage was not something to which even

Augustus was immune, a point which required a lot of tact to make.

We have an artistic overview, then, of a whole society: old-fashioned, set in its ways, and reluctant to honour a new generation of able poets now writing and claiming recognition. Contemporary standards of poetic excellence in Rome recognize only drama and in doing so persist in giving Plautus the same esteem Lucilius had enjoyed twenty-one years before (*Satires* 1.4, 1.10). *Plus ça change!* Endless antique revivals, spectaculars, pageants, and gorgeous costumes are what win applause in the theatre. But why must good young poets who do not write for the theatre be neglected? Augustus has nothing to lose and much to gain from a renaissance of enlightened imperial patronage. Conversely, he must also consider the implications of Horace's conclud-ing exemplum (given at his own expense, as usual): the celebrity who accepts poems of praise from unworthy poets. Never forget the fish-market!

Florus is probably a representative of that fresh, eager generation of talents for whom Horace is speaking. Like his contemporaries, however, Florus has his own foibles, notably a tendency to be unreceptive to con-structive criticism. He is able, but he must work to improve his verse, and must resist flattery and the seductions of mutual admiration. (He will get none from Horace!) Self-criticism is the key to excellence in art as it is in life and Horace is now concerned primarily with the latter. For the first time since his Athenian days he is doing what he truly loves and needs to do, and is living in perfect harmony with his own true nature.

The Epistle to the Pisos devotes itself to a still earlier stage of the poet's training, the learning of his "craft," or *ars*. There are really two stage: first mastering the details of technique (metre, character-drawing, genres, history of poetry's development, and so forth) and then cultivating judgement and self-criticism (*iudicare, castigare*). It is Horace's task (*munus et officium*) to teach the importance of *limae labor et mora*, polish and patience. His "carrot" is fame; his "sticks," ridicule, laughter and scorn, should the aspiring poet wilfully persist without first mastering *ars*. (Father Piso is described as a *doctus iudex*, and Horace most likely endorses his views on the matter.) Talent is not enough: in-spiration without *ars* is illustrated at the beginning by the mad painter, and at the end by Empedocles (who sprang in an inspired frenzy into the volcano), the bear in the cage, and the sucking leech. In other words, the road via *ars* to poetry is long and difficult, and lacks any instant gratification—even when the talent is there.

The bulk of the material in this poem is technical, ranging from simple definitions of the *iambus* to the complex schemata of Aristotle and Neoptolemus. It is this very bulk of detail that has attracted so much scholarly effort to extract Horace's own schematic synthesis. That synthesis, however, is there for another purpose. Young Piso must be made to see the vast *extent* of the technique he must learn, especially in the fields of history and theory, before he can ever become a poet. Horace is determined to make him see (by the very weight of the details of poetic doctrine) how much he must master before putting pen to paper. Horace's attention to the techniques of the satyr-play has always been a particular puzzle, and there can be only one reason for it. Piso wants to write dramatic poetry—perhaps even satyr-plays—now. We might even infer as background to this little drama that like Quintus Cicero (*Q.F.* 2.15.3), he had already experimented with such a work, and that his troubled father, seeking to influence him to learn the rudiments first, has shown it to Horace. *Hinc illa ars poetica!*

The obvious links in purpose between these three epistles, their scope and range, their pervading concern for the craft and its craftsmen suggest that, regardless of when each was written, Horace intended us to read them together in sequence: as a unified, coherent picture of the post-Vergilian world of letters in the second decade B.C. They offer together a consistent philosophy of literature for Rome, in a form that in its practical humanity is fully Horatian.

To Augustus
Horace, *Epistle* 2.1

BECAUSE YOU ARE performing all alone so many great tasks, defending Italy's interests with arms, morally enriching her and reforming her with laws, I should sin against the good of the state if I took up your time with a lengthy discourse, Caesar.

(5) When after their enormous achievements Romulus, Father Liber, and Pollux along with Castor were received into their temples as gods, they loudly lamented that during their sojourn on earth succouring mankind, settling bitter wars, assigning territories, and founding towns, their acclaim had not matched their hopes or their merits. He who crushed the dreaded Hydra and subdued infamous monsters with his fateful labour, found envy overcome only at the hour of death. One who soars above those talents that lie beneath his own scorches them with a brilliance all his own, but will be loved when dead and gone. Upon you do we heap timely honours while still among us, rearing altars to swear oaths upon by your divinity, acknowledging that nothing like yourself has arisen before, or ever shall again.

(18) But this very people of yours, wise and just on the one hand in extolling you above our leaders and those of the Greeks, reckons everything else by a completely different standard of measure and loathes and disdains things that have not departed the earth and had their day. Such devotees of antiquity are they, that they go on dictating the Tables that

forbid wrongdoing (laid down by the Board of Ten), royal treaties negotiated with Gabii and the stern Sabines, the scrolls of the Pontiffs, and
the Muses who inspired the aged volumes of the bards on the hill at
Alba!

(28) If, because the most ancient writings of the Greeks may invariably be called the best, Roman writings are to be weighed in the
same balance, not much more need be said: thus the olive has nothing
hard inside; the nut, outside. We have come to the pinnacle of fortune!
Our painting and singing to the lyre and our wrestling are much more
advanced than anything of the oiled Achaeans!

(34) If their date of production improves poems as it does wines, I
should like to know what year wins the prize for its scrolls? Should a
writer deceased a hundred years ago be classed with the flawless ancients, or among those who are worthless and new? We need some limit
to such contention. "A poet is old and beyond criticism who completes a
hundred years!" —What about one who perished a month younger, or a
year? Among whom should he be classed? Among the old poets, or those
our own generation (and the next) reject? (43) "The one you mean will
have a place of honour among the ancients whether he is short one
month or a full year." (45) I accept the year conceded and, like the hairs
from a horse's tail, I pull at the rest a little at a time, taking one away
and another one, till one who goes by the Fasti, and judges excellence by
years, and marvels at nothing not hallowed by Libitina herself is foiled
and put down by the analogy of the "diminishing heap."

(50) Ennius, the wise and brave—the second Homer of the critics!—
has little reason to be worried about what his claims and Pythagorean
dreams may achieve. Is Naevius not in our hands, fixed as securely in
our minds as if he wrote yesterday? So hallowed are all ancient poems!
Each time debate resumes about who is superior to whom, Pacuvius pre-
serves his reputation as the dean of sophisticated poets, Accius of the
sublime. Afranius' toga fits Menander, it is said; Plautus matches the
pace of his model Epicharmus; Caecilius wins on his gravity, Terence on
his art. Mighty Rome learns these by heart and flocks to see them,
packed into a crowded theatre; these poets she has held and counted as
her own from the age of the Livius to our own.

(63) Now and again public opinion is right; at times it is dead wrong.
If they so marvel at and praise the old poets that they give precedence to
nothing over them, compare nothing with them, they are wrong. If they

believe that some of those utterances are too antiquated, and many of them harsh, and admit that many passages are dull, they show sense and take my side, with Jove's approval of their judgement. (69) I am certainly not attacking the poems of Livius, nor do I think that we should consign them to oblivion (I remember old "Flogger" Orbilius dictating them to me when I was little!), but I am amazed that they should be viewed as "faultless" and "beautiful," or "little short of perfection!" (73) If by chance some *mot juste* flashes out, if one or two verses are slightly more harmonious, that unjustly serves to pass off the whole poem!

(76) I am outraged that anything should be faulted not for being coarse or unrefined in composition, but for being recent, and that no allowances are sought on the ancients' behalf, but honour and prizes! If I expressed a doubt whether or not Atta's play treads its way properly through the saffron and flowers, the patricians would shout, almost to a man, "For shame, Sir!" But I am just trying to fault something that the grave Aesopus or the learned Roscius acted in! (83) Either they hold that nothing they dislike is right, or they fancy that at their age it would be disgraceful to give in to their juniors and admit that what they learned in their beardless youth ought to be done away with. The one who now praises the *Carmen Saliare* of Numa, and wants to seem the sole repository of knowledge that (along with me) he does not have, does not favour talents dead and buried with applause (not he!), but assails our own with spiteful malice.

(90) But if "newness" had been loathed as much by the Greeks as we loath it, what would now be old? Or what would be publicly available for everyone in turn to handle and read?

(93) As soon as Greece put aside her wars and began to enjoy light diversion and to slip (with Fortune's blessing) into extremes, now burning with enthusiasm for athletes, now for horses, she developed a passion for artisans in marble, ivory, or bronze. She hung face and soul, upon the painted tablet; now revelling in pipers, now tragic actors. As with a baby girl playing under of her nurse's eye, the object of her desire was too soon possessed—and abandoned. [What like or dislike would you not regard as prone to change?] Such was the consequence of the good times brought by peace, and of favourable winds.

(103) In Rome, it has long been a pleasant, time-honoured practice to be up in the morning with house open, quoting laws to a client, paying

out secured cash loans (properly itemized), listening to elders, telling the young the means by which capital could grow and ruinous appetite be reduced. (108) The fickle populace has changed its mind, and is hot with the enthusiasm to write. Young men and solemn patricians dine with locks bound with greenery, dictating poems! (111) I myself, who insist I am not writing verse, show myself more treacherous than the Parthians, awake before sunrise and calling for pen, scrolls, and book-boxes! Those unfamiliar with ships are afraid to sail ships. Only one who has learned *how* risks giving wormwood to a patient. †Physicians† profess the business of †physicians†; carpenters handle carpentry. But here we are, unlearned and learned alike, writing continually.

(118) However, you may conclude as follows what great virtues accompany this aberration, this mild madness. The bard's mind is not naturally avaricious. It is verse he loves; that is his sole interest. He laughs at losses, runaway slaves, and fires. He does not think of defrauding an associate or a young ward. He lives on vegetables and coarse bread. He is lazy and cowardly in the field, admittedly, but is of some use to his city (if you grant that great ends are also served by little means). (126) The poet forms the young child's stammering mouth, and turns his ear at a timely hour from obscene discourse; next he also shapes his heart with friendly precepts, castigating harshness, resentment, and wrath. He tells of deeds honorably done, instructs rising generations by the examples of famous men, and consoles the sick and the helpless. (132) What of the unwed girl there with those chaste youths? From whom would she learn her prayers without the Muse's gift of the bard? The chorus asks and receives aid, and senses the divine presence. With the prayer he taught, they plead winningly for waters from heaven, avert plagues, drive away feared dangers, and call for peace and a year rich in fruitfulness. It is with song that the Gods above are placated, and the shades of the dead.

(139) At festival time farmers of old, doughty men and happy with little, having laid in their grain and endured their hardships in the expectation they would end, lifted up their limbs and their very hearts along with the companions of their labours (their children and faithful spouse), propitiating Tellus with a pig, Silvanus with milk, and their Genius, so mindful of the shortness of life's span, with flowers and wine. (145) Through this custom the Fescennine license was launched: pouring out rustic abuse in responsive lines. Such freedom was welcomed through the returning years, and its playfulness was affection-

ate—until fierce joking finally began to turn into unconcealed fury, threatening respectable households with impunity. Those assailed by its bloody fang felt the pain. Those untouched *were* concerned for the welfare of the community. Well, a law and a penalty were enacted which forbade abusing anyone with song. The poets were driven by fear of the rods to change their style, to speak fair and give delight.

(156) Captured Greece took captive her fierce captor and brought her arts into rustic Latium, so that the bristly Saturnian measure ebbed, and a concern for the proprieties routed oppressive rankness. Nonetheless, traces of the country have remained over a long period of time, and remain even today; for the Roman was late in applying his sharpness of wits to the scrolls of the Greeks, and in the peace following the Punic wars he began to find out what use Sophocles, Thespis, and Aeschylus might serve. He also experimented with adapting their material as it deserved, and was pleased with himself, being by naturally sublime and forceful, for he had a good deal of the tragic spirit and was fortunate in his daring. (167) But he was naively ashamed to erase, and abhorred doing so. It is common belief that comedy (because it gathers its material from common store) entails less sweat; but because a comic audience is less forgiving, the more effort is demanded of it. Just look at the way Plautus handles the roles of his amorous youth, his cautious father, and his treacherous pimp; at how huge his Dossennus appears among his gluttonous parasites; how he treads the boards, with sock falling off. You see, he loves to drop a coin into his pouch. (After that he does not care whether his play falls flat or keeps its feet on the ground.)

(177) The man brought to the stage by Fame in her airy car is shattered by a spectator's indifference, puffed up by his attention. Such a fleeting insignificant thing overthrows or restores the mind greedy for praise! Farewell, stage, whether losing the palm leaves me sickly thin, or *winning* it, sleek and fat! Often even a daring poet is routed in dismay because those whose numbers are greater but whose virtue and honour are less, who are unlearned, dull, and ready to fight it out if a knight disagrees, call (right in the midst of his poetry!) for a bear or boxers, for such things delight a crowd. (187) But even the knight's sense of pleasure has now moved entirely from the ear to the vain and dubious delights of the eyes. Four or more hours the curtains stay down while troops of cavalry and platoons of infantry are in retreat. Next the "Fortune of Kings" is dragged on, hands bound behind him; British

chariots gallop on, with carriages, wagons, ships. Captive ivory is paraded, and captive Corinth.

(194) Were he here on earth, Democritus would be laughing, whether a hybrid camelleopard were to catch the eyes of the crowd, or a white elephant. He would watch the people more intently than the games themselves, since they present many more attractions for him. He would fancy that the writers were telling their tale to a deaf donkey! (200b) For what voices have succeeded in drowning out the row echoing from our theatres? You would fancy that Garganum wood was lowing or the Tuscan Sea, there's so much din accompanying the games! And exotic works of art, and wealth! When an actor takes his stand on the stage decked out in all that finery, left hands rush to meet right:

— "Has he said anything yet?"

"Nothing at all."

— "So what *is* it that they like?"

"His cloak! It rivals violets with its Tarentine blend!"

(208) And do not suppose that my praise is niggardly when others handle well what I refuse to do myself. To me the poet who racks my heart with mere illusion, goading it, soothing it, and filling it with imagined fears, using his magic to put me down at one moment in Thebes, at another in Athens, seems able to walk along a tightrope.

(214) But please, do have a little concern as well for the poets who prefer to entrust themselves to a reader rather than put up with the distaste of an arrogant spectator, if you wish to fill your offering, worthy of Apollo, with books, and give a spur to bards to make for verdant Helicon with greater zeal.

(219) I know we often make a lot of trouble for ourselves as poets (let me hack at my own vineyards first) when we give you a book while you are preoccupied or weary, when we take offence if some friend dares to fault a line, when unasked we roll back to a passage already recited, when we lament that our efforts go unrecognized (our poems spun out like fine thread), when we hope that things will turn out well and that as soon as you are aware we are fashioning songs you will obligingly call us, bid us not deny ourselves, and constrain us to write.

(229) But just the same, it is worth finding out what kind of temple-attendants Virtue has, whether they appear in the field or at home, for she should not be entrusted to an unworthy poet. Choerilus, a favourite of Alexander the Great, showed a credit balance in "Philips," the coin of

the realm, for his careless and misbegotten lines. (235) But just as inks mark and stain when handled, writers tend to smudge brilliant deeds in a vile poem. That same king who bought such an absurd poem so dearly produced an edict forbidding anyone but Apelles to paint him, or anyone other than Lysippus to shape the likeness of valiant Alexander in bronze. But if you brought that nice discrimination in the visual arts to bear upon books and these gifts of the Muses you would swear he was born in the thick murk of Boeotia!

(245) But your judgements bring you honour, as do the gifts which your beloved poets Vergil and Varius won, along with the praises of the giver. Likenesses copied in images of bronze are no more recognizable than the minds and characters of illustrious men in the work of a bard. Nor would I choose to compose discourses which creep along the ground concerning great deeds, telling of the lie of lands and of rivers, of citadels perched on hills and of barbarian realms, of the worldwide struggle concluded under your auspices, of the bars confining Janus, our warder of peace, and of Rome, under your sway the terror, of the Parthians', even *if* my powers were equal to my desires! But your greatness does not lend itself to a little song, nor does my sense of propriety dare to attempt what lies beyond my powers.

(260) An individual's persistence, though, is annoying if he expresses his affection in a foolish way, and especially when he commends himself by his measures and his craft. For one learns to know and recall what one mocks more readily than what one truly reveres. I have no time for any favour that irks me; nor for that matter do I want to be displayed anywhere in wax with features fashioned for the worse or extolled in ill-made verses lest I blush when presented with so gross a gift and be laid out in a covered box and carried (author and all) down to the street where they sell incense, spices, pepper and all the things wrapped in inept scrolls.

To Florus
Horace, *Epistle* 2.2

SUPPOSE SOMEONE JUST wanted to sell you a slave
born at Tibur or Gabii and talked him up this way, "He's handsome and
fair from head to heel, and he'll be yours forever for eight thousand,
cash; he's homegrown, and ready to serve at his master's nod; he has
some Greek, and is ready to learn any skill you desire. You'll shape
whatever you like from his moist clay. Why, he'll even sing (not with a
trained voice, but one nice for drinking to). A raft of promises makes
you hesitate when a seller wants to unload merchandise and praises it
excessively. I'm not pressed for money: what cash I do have is in my
own name. No dealer would do this for you. Not just anybody would get
the same deal from me so easily! (This one did malinger once and, as will
happen, hid for fear of the strap hanging on the stairs.) Put down your
money, if it's just his running away that bothers you!" In my opinion,
he'd get his price without fear of penalty. You knew you bought a defective item. You were told the law. Are you still prosecuting this person,
and taking up his time with a suit you can't win?

(20) I told you when you set off that I was lazy. I told you that I was
almost useless when it came to such obligations, just so you wouldn't
wildly berate my behaviour because no letter of mine came back to you.
What good did it do then, if you insist upon suing me, though I have the

right on my side? And you complain about this as well: you allege that I have cheated your expectations in not sending you poems.

(26) One of Lucullus' soldiers had put together some savings through many a hardship. But one night while snoring away he had lost every last penny. A raging wolf after that, and angry at both himself and foe alike, with the ferocity of ravening teeth, he hurled the royal garrison with all its riches (so the story goes) down from its fortified heights. Renowned for this exploit he was heaped with honours and received twice ten thousand sesterces in cash. It happened about this time that his praetor was eager to raze some fortress or other, and began to urge the same fellow on with words that could have given even the craven the will: "Go, brave soldiers, where valour calls. Go with auspicious step, and win the great prizes you deserve!—Why are you standing there?" At this, that sharp fellow (very much the rustic) replied, "He'll go, go wherever you want him to, who has lost his money belt!"

(41) It was my good fortune to be reared in Rome and taught how great was the harm caused the Greeks by the angry Achilles. Noble Athens added a little more to my training; so of course I wanted to distinguish the "straight" from the "curved" and seek out the "true" amid the woods of Academus. But hard times dislodged me from my pleasant spot, and the tide of civil war bore me as a raw recruit to arms destined to be no match for the sinews of Caesar Augustus! From the moment that Philippi discharged me thence, humbled, wing-feathers clipped, and without the resources of my father's Lar and land, a daring bred of straitened circumstances drove me to making verse. But now that my possessions are not inadequate, what hemlock doses could purge me enough if I didn't think sleeping better than writing verses?

(55) The advancing years rob us of our possessions one by one. They've snatched away fun, love, banquets, play. They are determined to wrest poetry away. What do you want me to do?

(58) The point is, we don't all love and admire the same things. You rejoice in an ode, this man delights in iambics, that one in Bionean discourses with their black salt. I see three banqueters in some kind of disagreement, calling for very different things according to varying tastes. What do I give them? What not? What you decline, one of them calls for. What you ask for is utterly hateful and distasteful to the other two!

(65) Aside from everything else, do you think I can write poems at

Rome amid so many worries and so many labours? This man summons me to post a bond, this one to ignore all my duties and listen to what he's written. This one is sick in bed on Quirinus' hill, that one at the far side of the Aventine, and both need to be visited. (You see how such distances are not exactly convenient.)

"But the streets are clear, and won't interfere with your reflections."

A contractor is hot on the job with his mules and carriers; a crane is cranking up now a block, now a huge timber; dreary funeral processions wrestle with oaken wagons; a mad dog races this way, that way a muddy pig. Go on—just try now to rehearse some melodious verses!

(77) The whole chorus of writers loves the grove and shuns the city, ideal clients for Bacchus, who rejoices in sleep and shade. Do you want me to sing amid the din of nights and days and follow the narrow footsteps of the bards? A spirit that once chose leisurely Athens for itself, gave seven years to its studies, and has grown old with its books and preoccupations goes abroad more quietly than a statue, forever a source of trembling mirth to others? Would I deign here, in the midst of the tide of events and the storms of the city, to string words together to wake the sound of the lyre?

(87) There was a †rhetorician at Rome, brother† of an attorney: and matters were such that the one heard nothing but his honours on the other's tongue. The latter was a "Gracchus" to the former; to the latter, a "Mucius" he! Does such madness trouble our tuneful poets less in any way? I compose odes, he elegies: marvellous work to behold, and crafted by the nine Muses! First observe the great pride—the great self-importance—with which we gaze at the temple standing empty for the bards of Rome. And then, if you have the time, follow and hear at a distance what victories each wins while weaving a garland for himself. (96) We are battered, and wear out our foe stroke for stroke—Samnites we, in protracted duel till the first lamps! I come off "Alcaeus" by his reckoning. Who is he by mine? "Callimachus," of course! If he seems to require more, he becomes "Mimnermus" and swells with the title of his desire. I endure a lot to placate the irritable breed of bards when I write, pleading in my quest for popular suffrage. If I dropped my pursuits and regained my sanity, I would be the same one to plug up my spreading ears as others read on unrebuked!

(106) Those who compose bad poems are laughed at, but they exult in their writing, in awe of themselves. And if you are silent, they praise

what they have written without waiting to be asked, happy souls! But the one who wants to make a poem true to its own laws will take up the spirit of an honest censor along with his tablets. He will dare to remove from their places such words as are lack-lustre and lightweight and unworthy of the distinction they enjoy, no matter how unwillingly they may withdraw, lurking still in Vesta's inner shrine. The good poet will exhume terms for things long hidden to the people's view, and will bring attractive words forth to the light, those uttered by the Catos and Cetheguses of old, but now heavy with ugly mould and forlorn old age. He will admit new ones that usage has sired. Impetuous and clear, like an unsullied river will he pour out his riches and bless Latium with his wealth of tongue! He will cut down luxuriant growth, reduce by wholesome refinement what is rough and remove what lacks redeeming virtue. He will appear to be merely playing while torturing himself, like one who dances now the parts of a satyr, now the rustic Cyclops.

(126) Should I prefer the reputation of a wild and untrained writer (provided my bad work delights, or at least escapes me) to one of growling discernment? There lived an aristocrat in Argos who used to believe he was listening to superb tragic actors as he sat applauding happily in the empty theatre. He was always one to observe life's duties punctiliously: an excellent neighbour, affectionate host, kind to his wife, he could forgive his slaves and not go berserk over the broken seal on a wine-jar, and could avoid a rock or open well. When he had been cured with the helpful concern of his kin, had expelled his sickness and bile with full-strength hellebore and come back to himself, he cried: "Ye gods! You've killed me, my friends, not saved me! You've stripped me of my pleasure this way. You've deprived me against my will of the most blissful aberration!"

(141) The truth is, of course, that there is an advantage in putting aside trifles in favour of discernment, yielding to children the play seasonable for them, and, instead of pursuing the cadence of words for Latin lyres, learning by heart the numbers and measures of true living.

(145) This is the reason I talk with myself and repeat silently over and over: "If no amount of fluid satisfied your thirst, you'd be telling your doctors. Don't you dare to confess to anyone that the more you acquire the more you desire? If a wound did not become less serious by means of the root or herb prescribed for you, you'd shun further treatment with that ineffectual root or herb. Had you ever heard that when the gods

grant anyone something, perverse stupidity leaves him? And though you are no more discerning for all your wealth you'll still keep the same counsellors? No, if riches could make you wise, and less greedy and fearful—why, you'd blush to see anyone else in the world alive greedier than you!"

(158) If what you purchase with cash and balance is your property, there are some things over which *usus* confers ownership according to the lawyers. The plot of ground which feeds you is yours, and Orbius' bailiff senses you are his master when he hoes the growing crops to give you grain. The same applies to paying for grapes, chickens, eggs, and a keg of liquor. That way, you see, you are purchasing a little at a time a farm that was bought outright for perhaps three hundred thousand sesterces or more. What difference does it make whether you live on a sum made just recently or long ago, since the buyer of ploughland at Aricia or Veii dines on *bought* greens, though he doesn't think so? As the chill of the night sets in he heats his copper with *bought* wood; yet he still counts it his property all the way to where poplars planted along the boundaries prevent quarrels with his neighbour. (As if anything could be private property that changes owners by the shadow of the moving hour, now with a prayer, now at a price, now by force, and now by the finality of death, to fall into the control of a second party!) Thus, because *usus* is given in perpetuity to no one, and heir succeeds another's heir as wave succeeds wave, what's the good of hamlets and granaries, and tracts in Lucania merged with those in Calabria, if Orcus reaps the great with the small, deaf to gold's entreaty?

(180) Jewels, marble, ivory, Etruscan statuettes, pictures, silver, robes dyed with Gaetulian murex—there are some who do might not have them, and one at least who does not care to have them. Why one brother would prefer lounging, playing, and oiling himself to Herod's rich date groves, and the other one, wealthy and persistent, prefer cultivating his woodland field from first light to dark with fire and iron, only that guardian Genius knows who controls his birth star, the god of his mortal and human nature, changeable in countenance for each and every individual, white and black. I shall be a *user* and take from my modest heap as much as the situation demands, and not be afraid of how my heir may judge me because he has not found more than I was given. (192b) And I shall want just the same to know how much the simple, happy individual differs from the prodigal, how much the thrifty from

the miser. It does make a difference, you know, whether you scatter your wealth extravagantly or avoid stinginess in spending your money without toiling to make more; or instead, as you once did as a boy at the March break, snatch at the chance of some brief enjoyment. †May squalid poverty of house be far away!† As for me, whether sailing in large ship or small, I shall sail on as the very same person. We are not running with swelling sails before a favouring north wind; but neither are we beating all our life up-wind either. We're well behind the foremost in strength, talent, looks, virtue, station, and wealth, but ever ahead of the hindmost.

(205) You're not a miser? Good for you. But what of it? Have all other vices now departed along with that? Is your heart free of vain ambition? Of the fear of death? Of anger? Do you laugh at dreams, the terrors of magic, wonders, witches, ghosts by night, and Thessalian portents? Do you count birthdays gratefully? Forgive friends? Become milder and better as old age comes on? What relief is there in pulling out just one of many thorns? If you don't know how to live right, make room for those who do. You have played enough, eaten and drunk enough. The time has come for you to leave, lest when you've drunk more deeply than is sensible, an age more fitly wanton mock and cuff you!

To the Pisos
Horace, *De Arte Poetica*

IMAGINE A PAINTER wanting to attach a horse's neck to a human head, assemble limbs from everywhere, and add feathers of various colours, so that a woman beautiful above the waist tailed into a revolting black fish! Could you hold back your laughter, my friends, if admitted to view it? Believe me, Pisos, a book could be very like such a canvas, its images just empty inventions like a sick man's dreams: neither foot nor head would be rendered in a single form.—"Painters and poets alike have always had an equal prerogative to venture anything," you say?—We know. This is a concession we both ask for, and make in return. But not to the point where savage beasts mate with the meek, where serpents twin with birds and lambs with tigers! When weighty works professing greatness are under way, one or two purple patches are stitched in to give them far-seen brilliance, as when the grove and altar of Diana are described, and the windings of water rushing through pleasant fields, or the River Rhine, or a rainbow. (But this is not the place for such considerations). Perhaps you do know how to draw a cypress tree. What is the good of that, if what's wanted is a man (painted *ex voto* for a fee) swimming hopelessly away from his shattered ships? An amphora began to take shape. So why does a jug emerge as the wheel races on? The point is, whatever you're making, it should be unified and coherent.

(21) The majority of us bards, Father (and you, young men, so

worthy of your father), are taken in by what appear to be correct principles. I strive for brevity only to become obscure; I pursue smoothness
but nerve and spirit fail me. Aiming at grandeur, you become turgid;
over-cautious and fearful of the storm, you creep along the ground. One
who lavishes variety on a single subject paints a dolphin in the woods or
a boar in the waves. In avoiding blame you produce a flaw, if *ars* is lacking. Down near the school of Aemilius, one workman will mould fingernails and represent the softest hair, both in bronze. But the sum total
is unhappy, since he won't ever know how to lay out his entire work. As
for me, if I wanted to compose something I would no more desire to be
that man than go through life with a crooked nose—though I might at-
tract glances with my black eyes and hair!

(38) When you write, choose material to match your strengths, and
long consider what your shoulders refuse to bear and what they will.
The writer who selects according to his abilities will lack neither style
nor a clear arrangement. The virtue and charm of arrangement will be
found, if I'm not mistaken, here: in saying right now what ought to be
said right now, and deferring the rest for later. In weaving words together be sparing and careful. Let the author of a promised poem favour
one approach, and scorn another. You will have spoken in an uncommon
way if a clever collocation renders a familiar word new. Should it be necessary to explain obscure matters in fresh terms (and give shape to matters unheard of by the loinclad Cethegi!), such licence is available, and
will be given if exercised with restraint. New and recently fashioned
words will gain acceptance if they tumble from the well-spring of Greek
by judicious diversion. But why will a Roman grant Caecilius and
Plautus what he denies to Vergil and Varius? Why is it I am begrudged
the few words I can garner, when the tongue of Cato, and of Ennius, has
enriched our native speech and endowed it with new names for things? It
has always been permissible and always will be, to produce a word
stamped with today's date.

(60) Just as woods change their leaves in the †fullness† of the years,
falling one by one... so perish words with age, after flourishing and
thriving when newly born, like youths. We ourselves, and our works,
are debts owed to death. Whether Neptune protects the fleets in the
land's embrace from the North Winds, a †kingly† task, or the †marsh†,
long-unproductive and suitable for oars, sustains cities nearby and feels

the weight of a plough, or the stream (now taught a better course) has changed a course threatening crops, such things made by mortal men shall perish. Much less likely is it that the esteem and favour granted to modes of speech could live and endure (69). Many terms shall grow back which now have fallen away, and those now held in esteem shall fall, if our poetic practice so approves. Such is the criterion by which the judgement, rules, and standards for speech expression are to be discovered.

(73) The metre for handling the exploits of captains and kings and grim wars has been shown by Homer. Lamentation was the first to be couched in verses unequally linked, then afterward the expression of prayer as well. But as for who originated the slender elegy, well, the critics are debating this and the case is awaiting their judgement. Rage armed Archilochus with his characteristic iambus, the foot which comic socks and grand tragic buskins seized upon as suited to argument and the suppression of popular clamour. It was born to represent action. The Muse assigned the gods and sons of gods to the lyre, along with the victorious boxer, winning race-horse, youthful longings and wine's liberating power. If in producing my works I cannot observe (and don't know) the required genres and styles, why am I hailed as "Poet?" Why prefer wanton ignorance to learning?

(87) Comic material resists presentation in tragic verse. Likewise the "Feast of Thyestes" resents poetry that is conversational and worthy almost of the comic sock. Let each discrete detail keep the place allotted. From time to time, though, comedy does raise its voice too, as Chremes delivers accusations with his swollen mouth. A tragic actor frequently grieves in plain discourse; Telephus and Peleus, both poor and exiled, cast aside bombast and foot-and-a-half words if concerned to touch the heart of the spectator effectively with their lamentation.

(99) It is not enough that poetry be noble: it should impart delight, and transport the listener as it likes. As people's faces respond with laughter to those who laugh, so do they cry in response to those who cry. If you want me to cry, you must first cry yourself. Then, Telephus (or you, Peleus), will your misfortunes make me suffer. If you speak your assigned parts badly I shall either nod or laugh. Grim words are appropriate to a gloomy countenance; words full of threat, to the angry; wanton, to the playful; serious in delivery, to the severe. First, you see, Nature shapes us within for every aspect of life's fortunes. She gives us

pleasure, or drives us to wrath, or brings us to earth with the profound anguish of grief. Afterwards she brings out the heart's emotions with the tongue as their interpreter. If a speaker's words are not consonant with his fortunes, the people (both horse and foot) will burst out laughing!

(114) It will make a lot of difference whether a god is speaking or a hero; a mature old man or one still in flower of youth; a strong-minded dame or a busy nurse, a far-travelled merchant or a cultivator of a green farm, a Colchian or Assyrian, or someone reared at Thebes or Argos.

(119) Either follow a legend when writing, or make up details consistent with themselves. If, say, you are putting the †illustrious† Achilles back on stage, let him be unyielding, wrathful, inexorable, savage; have him say that by nature laws are not for him, never failing to appeal to a judgement of arms. Medea should be fierce and invincible, Ino tearful, Ixion faithless, Io wandery, Orestes grim. If you are putting something untried on stage, and trying to shape a new character, let him be the same from the beginning to the last detail, just as he was when he entered, and remain true to himself. (127) It is hard to make unique poetry out of the commonplace; you do better if you spin out a canto of the *Iliad* into episodes than be the first to present something unfamiliar and unworked.

(131) Public domain will become private right if you don't dally on the trivial and broad track, faithfully rendering word for word like a translator, leaping in your imitation into some narrow hole from which propriety or the law of the genre forbids you even to budge. You don't begin this way (as a cyclic writer once did): "Priam's fortune shall I sing, and a war far-famed." What will he produce by promising something worthy of so great an utterance? The mountains shall labour—a ridiculous mouse come forth! How much better did he begin who constructed nothing ineptly: "Tell me, O Muse, of the man who after the time of Troy's capture saw the manners of many men as well as their cities." His plan is not to give out smoke from the flash but light from the smoke, to produce striking tales of wonder from it: Antiphates, and Scylla and Charybdis along with the Cyclops! He doesn't begin "The Return of Diomede" with the death of Meleager, or "The Trojan War" with the twin egg! He is ever rushing towards the issue, carrying the listener into the midst of events as if they were known to him. He leaves

out what he despairs of handling with brilliance, telling his lies and mixing the true with the false in such a way that the middle harmonizes with the beginning, and the end with the middle.

(153) Listen to what I long for (and the public along with me), if you wish someone to stay in the hall to applaud, sitting till that moment when the piper says: "Applause, please!" You have to observe the characteristics of each age, and attribute proper behaviour to impulsive natures and years. The boy who now knows how to respond in words and press the earth with steady foot loves to play with his mates; he gathers his rage only to lay it aside again, and changes by the hour. The beardless youth, free from watchful eye at last, rejoices in horses and hounds and the sunny campus turf. He can be shaped to vice like wax; caustic with those who give him advice, slow to look ahead to future advantage, wasteful of money, high-spirited, passionate in his desires, and quick to abandon his fancies. When his pursuits change, the age and spirit of manhood seeks out wealth and friendships, pays service to honour, and is wary of doing what he may soon strive to change. Many handicaps swarm around an old man, whether he is seeking gain (but wretched even when he finds what he wants, for he shuns it and is afraid to enjoy it) or managing all his affairs with numbing fear—a †putter-off of hope,† tedious, helpless, fearful of the future, difficult, complaining, praising the good old days when he was a lad, correcting and censuring the young. The years bring many blessings with them as they come, and bear many away as they go. So don't let the part of an old man be assigned to a youth, and that of a man to a boy. A character will always dwell upon what is inseparable from, and suited to, his age.

(179) Action either takes place on stage or is narrated afterward. Those actions that reach us via the ear strike the mind less forcefully than what comes before our trusty eyes and what the spectator conveys to himself. But actions which ought to be performed off stage you must not bring on stage, and many you'll remove from view so that the full force of eloquence may relate them. Medea is not to slay her boys in public, nor the wicked Atreus cook human entrails in full view, nor Procne turn into a bird or Cadmus into a snake! Whatever you show me thus I view with disbelief and revulsion. (189) A play that really seeks to be in demand and then, once seen, revived, is not to be shorter or more extended than five acts. And a god is not to intervene unless a knot be

encountered worthy of such a deliverer. A fourth actor is not to attempt
to speak.

(193) Let the chorus preserve its role and forceful function as an actor,
and not break in between acts with a song contributing nothing to the
plot, nor fitting properly. Let it favour the good, and give friendly advice; control the angry and support those afraid to †hope.† Let it praise
the modest table, the benefits of justice and laws, and Peace with her
opened gates; let it conceal acts done, and pray to the gods that Fortune
may return to the wretched and depart from the proud. A simple,
slender pipe with only a few holes used to support choruses effectively,
accompanying them with its breath and filling the seats (not as yet too
crowded) with its blast. (It was not, as now, bound with orichalc, rival-
ing trumpets.) It was for that kind of performance, of course, that the
people would gather in manageable numbers (only a few, one might
guess), honest, righteous, and modest. After they began to extend their
domains victoriously, with a wider wall on the way to embracing the city
and their Genius lawfully placated with wine each day in daytime festivals, a greater licence was added to rhythms and modes. For what discernment would they, untaught, have had in their leisure, as rustic
mingled with urban, base with honourable? So the piper added movement (and decadence) to an ancient art, and he wandered over the stage
with his robe trailing behind. So also did notes increase on the austere
lyres, and forceful eloquence bring an unwonted style of delivery. And
keen on the scent of useful information, and prophetically inspired,
choral utterance rivaled that of Delphic oracles.

(220) Next, someone competing in tragic song for a paltry goat
stripped down his rustic satyrs, and in rough manner (but with some
dignity intact) tried some jokes. The reason was that the listener had to
be caught by enticements and novel delights when the rituals were over
and he was tipsy and free of the law's restraint. But it will be appropriate
to present your mocking chattering satyrs agreeably, and relieve the serious with the playful. Let no god or hero, once introduced in royal gold
and purple, move into shady taverns with vulgar speech. Nor is he to
grasp at clouds and nonsense in contempt for the earth. Tragedy despises
all chatter in light verses, and will be too ashamed (like a matron bidden
to dance on holidays) to mix with wanton satyrs! If I compose "Satyrs" I
won't be one to favour only unadorned and prevailing words and expres-

sions, Pisos. Nor will I so strive to avoid a tragic tone that it makes no difference whether Davus is speaking or bold Pythias (having bilked a talent out of the sharp-scented Simo) or Silenus, the guardian and personal servant of his divine charge. My object will be poetry so fashioned from the familiar that anyone may hope to achieve the same for himself—and in vain attempt waste much sweat and labour! This shows how important are poetic texture and combination, and how much honour accrues to material drawn from the common store. When Fauns are brought out from the woods they should, in my view, avoid acting as if born at some crossroads, regular denizens of the forum, or forever playing some adolescent part with vapid verses, or babbling in filthy and ignominious speech. For some people take offence at it (those with steed, ancestry and property). If some individual buying shelled peas and nuts expresses approval of a work, they don't just suffer it gladly and give it the crown!

(251) A long syllable following closely upon a short is called an iambus, a rapid foot; hence its name was also extended to iambic trimeters, though †for not that long a time.† It had been producing six pulses, each first to last like itself. To bring itself a little more slowly and sedately to the ear it admitted a steadying spondee with obliging tolerance to its adoptive rights, but not to the point of yielding the second and fourth place in the partnership. This foot rarely appears even in Accius' noble trimeters; and the verses of Ennius, when put ponderously upon the stage, are condemned on the serious charge of either too much hasty and careless work, or an ignorance of craft.

(263) Not every critic sees faulty rhythm in poetry, and favour has been given undeservedly to poets who are Roman. Am I therefore to hive off and write as I please? Or suppose that everyone will see my mistakes, but still be less watchful and cautious because they will (I hope) make allowances? In short, while avoiding censure, I earn no praise. You must unroll Greek originals in your hand night and day. (You say your forebears praised Plautine metres and wit? They admired both with an excess of tolerance, not to say foolishness, if you and I know how to separate coarseness from refinement in speech, and our fingers and ears are trained in the laws of sound!)

(275) They say the unknown genre of the tragic Muse was discovered by Thespis, who wheeled his poems about on wagons for men to sing and act, their faces well stained with lees. After him, as inventor of the

mask and the noble robe, Aeschylus laid out a stage with modest-sized beams, producing plays which resounded grandly and strode on the buskin. Old Comedy succeeded that, meeting with much approval. But excessive freedom led to abuse and a degree of violence that deserved to be curbed by law. The law was enforced, and the chorus fell basely silent, its right to injure removed.

(285) Our poets have left nothing untried, and not the least glory is due to those with the courage to abandon the Greeks' footsteps and celebrate things done at home, or produce either *praetextae* or *togatae*. Nor would Latium have greater might in virtue's field or arms' renown than with its tongue, if all our poets were not repelled by labour and patience with the file. As for you, O offspring of Pompilian blood, rebuke the poem not disciplined through many a day and many an erasure, and not trimmed off and ten times smoothed to the nail!

(295) Democritus believed that talent is a more fortunate thing than base craftsmanship, and because he excluded the "sane" from Helicon, a good part of our poets ignore fingernails and beard, heading for secret haunts and avoiding the baths. It seems that the prize and the name of "poet" will be gained by the one who does not entrust his head (three Anticyras full of hellebore could not cure it!) to Licinus the barber. (Oh how gauche am I then, purging *my* bile just before the spring season! No one else could have made better poetry—but it's not worth all that!) My function shall be that of a whetstone, therefore, able to render iron sharp, while not endowed itself for cutting. Though not engaged in writing myself, I shall teach its function and obligations; where its stores are secured, what fosters and shapes the poet; what is appropriate for him, what is not; where excellence takes him, where error.

(309) Correct writing finds its beginning and source in discernment. Socratic scrolls can show you your subject matter, and when that has been planned ahead, the words will follow without reluctance. The person who has learned what he owes to country and friends—what regard he should have for parent, brother, and guest, what a senator's duty is and a judge's, the role of a general sent into battle—certainly knows how to assign the appropriate qualities to each character. When he's trained in imitation I'll advise him to examine a pattern of life and mores, and draw living voices from this. From time to time a piece which has splendid maxims and a fine moral tone, even though lacking charm and without weight and craftsmanship, will give more pleasure and in-

terest to people than verses devoid of substance, and musical trifles. To the Greeks the Muse gave talent and a full-throated utterance. (The Greeks are a people greedy for nothing if not praise.) *Roman* children learn to divide a copper into a hundred parts with lengthy calculations: "Albinus Minor! Take one-twelfth from five-twelfths! What's the difference?—"One third."—"Très bien! You'll know how to preserve your capital. Now add one-twelfth. What's the answer?"—"One half!" When such corroding concern for private hoard has stained their hearts, can there be any hope of our fashioning poems worth dressing with cedar oil and storing in smooth cypress?

(333) Poets wish either to benefit or delight, or else say things at once pleasant and suited to life. Whatever your precepts, be brief, so that people's minds may grasp what you say quickly and easily and retain it faithfully. All excess overflows from a mind that's full. Things fashioned to give pleasure should be very close to reality. A story should not demand belief in absolutely anything, or draw a live boy out of a Lamia's belly after lunch! Our divisions of elder citizens condemn anything devoid of "profit"; the disdainful Ramnes pass rough poetry by. Mingling the "useful" with the "sweet" wins every point, by alike delighting and advising the reader. That is a book worth its price at the shop of the Sosii; there is the one to cross the sea too, and greatly prolong the life of its author's fame.

(347) Some offences, though, we are willing to forgive. For instance, a string does not render the sound wanted by hand and brain [and when you demand a flat it quite frequently gives a sharp]; nor will the bow always strike the target it points at. But when the bright places in a poem are more numerous I am not one to be offended by a few blemishes that carelessness has let in or human nature failed to avoid. What am I getting at? Just as a copyist is not to be excused if he persistently makes the same mistake in spite of being warned, and a lyrist is laughed to scorn if he makes a series of blunders on the same string, so, in my view, one who fails badly becomes a "Choerilus." I greet his one or two nice touches with laughter and astonishment! Yet I am the very one to resent it whenever good Homer nods. The fact remains, sleep is ordained to steal over a long work.

(361) A poem is like a picture. One will captivate you if you stand closer, one if you stand further away. This one favours shadow; that one

will want to be seen in daylight if it is not to dread the edge of a critic's tongue. This one pleased just once, this one will after ten visits.

(365b) O elder youth, though bred to the true by your father's words and possessing a natural sense of discernment, take hold of what I say to you here and remember it. An average and an adequate quality is rightly allowed in certain things. The average barrister and attorney is far removed from the force of Messalla's eloquence and lacks the knowledge of Cascellius Aulus—but he does have his value, nonetheless. That poets should ever be "average" is not a concession allowed by man, gods, or the stalls. As an out-of-tune orchestra, and gooey unguent, and poppy seed with Sardinian honey spoil the pleasure of banquet tables (the dinner could have gone on without them), so a poem, created and revealed to give our hearts delight, approaches the worst if it falls short of the best.

(379) A man who does not know how to compete stays clear of athletic gear, and if he has no training in ball, discus and hoop, stays on the sidelines, so the encircling crowd won't be entitled to break out laughing. Yet one who doesn't have the knowledge still has the audacity to fashion verses! (So what? you say? He is free—and free-born—and most of all, given equestrian rank by his cash. And he's far removed from every vice!)

(385) Don't utter or fashion anything over Minerva's objections. There's a criterion. There's an attitude of mind. But if you do write something, let it find the ears of Maecius to be judged, and your father's, and mine. And keep it shut up for nine years right inside its parchment wrapper. What you haven't published may be destroyed: the uttered word is beyond recall!

(391) Woodland folk were frightened away from their slaughtered fare by Orpheus, a holy man and a prophet of the gods. Hence his reputation for taming tigers and furious lions. So too was Amphion, founder of the city of Thebes, described as moving rocks by the sound of his tortoise and the charm of his entreaty, leading them wherever he wished. Once upon a time such things as these were counted for discernment: distinguishing public from private, sacred from profane; restraining promiscuity, giving rules for marriage, building towns, carving laws on wood. Honour and renown came thus to inspired bards and their

songs. After them came renowned Homer and Tyrtaeus, whetting manly hearts for martial wars with their verses. Oracles were told through poems; a way of life was shown, and the favour of kings sought through Pierian measures. And play was discovered, and an end to lengthy labours. So don't be ashamed of the lyre-skilled Muse and Apollo the singer!

(408) The question was raised whether a praiseworthy poem comes about by nature or by craft. For my part I don't see what dedication can achieve without a rich vein of talent—or, for that matter, untrained inspiration. The one calls for the resources of the other and makes a friendly collaboration with it. A youthful runner dedicated to touching the longed-for goal has endured and achieved much: sweating and shivering, abstaining from women and wine. Any piper who plays at the Pythian games first learned how, trembling in fear of his master. These days, it seems, one may just say, "I compose marvellous poetry. Let the devil take the hindmost! I would be ashamed to be left behind, and forced to admit complete ignorance of what I have not learned!"

(419) Like a hawker collecting a crowd to buy his wares, the poet for his own profit—though wealthy in property and capital put out at interest—orders his claques to show up. Even if he is one who can afford a rich spread (and do it right) and put up a bond for some poor nobody and rescue one entangled in an awkward court case, I'll be surprised if (for all his blessings) he knows how to distinguish a false friend from a true. So whether you've presented a gift to someone or will intend to give one, don't introduce him to your verses when he's sated with happiness. "Beautiful! Fine! Excellent!" he'll shout. He'll grow pale over them, and trickle dew from his dear eyes, leap up, thump the earth with his foot! Just as hired mourners at a funeral say and do more than those who are grieving from the heart, in the same way a mocker makes more of a show than the man whose praise is sincere. Kings are said to ply with many a goblet someone whose worthiness of their friendship they are striving to assess, and rack him with strong wine. If you compose poems, the sentiments that lurk beneath †the skin† should never deceive you.

(438) Whenever you recited something to Quintilius, he would say: "Correct this, please, and that." If, after two or three vain attempts you continued to insist that you could do no better, he would just tell you to delete it and put your ill-turned verses back on the anvil. If you

preferred to defend a mistake, rather than change it, he would not burden himself with any further word or useless effort to stop you being sole unchallenged lover of yourself and your work! The good and wise man will rebuke verses lacking craftsmanship, fault harsh ones, put a black oblique stroke of the pen next to your sloppy ones, cut back ambitious adornment, force you to illuminate what is unclear, reproach you for an ambiguous statement, censure what should be altered. He will become an "Aristarchus," and will not say, "Why offend a friend in trifles?" Such "trifles" will get that friend into serious trouble once he has been laughed at and unfavourably received!

(453) Like one attacked by a bad case of scabies, or the royal disease, or aberrant frenzy and a wrathful Diana, men of discernment are afraid to touch a "mad" poet and they avoid him. The young and impetuous flush him out and chase after him. If thus belching and raving sublime verses he falls down a well or pit like a fowler intent on blackbirds, let him long shout, "Help, Citizens! Save me!" But no one will be bothered to lift him out. If someone should be concerned enough to bring help and let down a rope, I would suggest that he just may have thrown himself down there on purpose, and not want to be saved!—and recount the demise of the poet of Sicily.

(464b) In the throes of passion for immortality, Empedocles leapt in cold blood into Aetna's flames. Poets should have that right—*let* them perish! To save someone against his will is like murder. Not just once has he done this, nor will he behave normally if he is restrained and lays aside his passion for a glorious death. Nor is it quite clear why he goes on scribbling verses. He may have pissed on his father's ashes or disturbed some grim enclosure in an unholy way! He is unquestionably mad, and like a bear whose might has smashed the confining bars of his cage he routs the unlearned and learned alike with fierce recitation! Anyone he seizes he grips and murders with his reading—a leech with no intention of letting go his skin, until he's full of gore!

Notes on the Text as Translated

The Latin text used in the above discussions and translations of *Epistles* 2.1, 2.2, and *Ars Poetica* is that of C.O. Brink, *Horace on Poetry* II (1971) and III (1982). The reader is referred generally to Brink's notes, including the "ADDENDA AND CORRIGENDA to VOLUME II, THE 'ARS POETICA'" in volume III, pp. 578–79. Other Horace citations are from F. Klingner's Teubner Text (3rd ed., 1959). Consonantal "v" is used in citations (a departure from Brink).

Brink's obelized words and phrases have been handled as follows:

Epistle 2.1
Line 115–116:   †*medicorum*†... †*medici*†: as printed.

Epistle 2.2
Line 87:   †*frater erat Romae*†... *rhetor*: transposed to *rhetor*... *frater*. (The result clause following will then follow from the general idea of brotherhood.)

199:     line as printed.

Ars Poetica
Line 60:   †*pronos*†: emended to *plenos* (after Funke, *H*, CIV [1976], 191–209).

65:     †*regis*†: as printed
†*diu palūs*†: absolutely unmetrical. See Brink on the history of this crux, and the special bibliography (pp. 115-16). An eventual solution may lie in emending *palus* to *Padus*. For the

84

image of the Po/Eridanus in poetry, cf. Verg. *G.* 1.482, 4.371–3; Lucan 6.278–9, 10.272–278; Sil. 8.600–601. *aptaque* would then be construed as a neuter plural substantive. Horace uses the neuter plural of adjectives substantively 29 times, and with a dependent dative in *Satires* 1.4.42, 2.2.111; *Epistle* 1.6.9; *Ars P.* 334. For *apta* + dative, see Mel. 3.19, Tac. *Ann.* 3.31. For a singular verb following a compound subject coupling a singular and plural substantive, cf. *ipse meique ante Larem proprium vescor* (*Satire* 2.6.65): "I myself, and my friends, feed:); cf. also *Ars P.* 153, ("quid ego populusque mecum desideret"), and Liv. 1.32.13 (*ego populusque Romanus indico*). Horace's *sterilisve diu Padus aptaque remis alit* might then be translated: "or the long-unyielding Po, including its navigable parts, sustains... " (62–69). The reference could then apply to Augustus' recent works at Ravenna, as well as older works along the Po valley, and *"sterilis"* could refer to its silt-choked marshes. Seneca seems to be thinking of brackish or muddy water (*sterili vado*: *Thy.* 173), and Silius describes a hungry sea monster who has long sought food unsuccessfully in the deep (*sterili profundo*: 15.785). Could *regis* (65) be the *rex fluviorum*, Vergil's Eridanus (*G.*1.482)?

120: †honoratum† as printed. As Wickham's and Brink's lengthy notes make clear, the meaning of this word (the reading offered by all the mss.) has occasioned a lot of debate since Bentley's emendation, *"Homereum"* after Acro's note. The range of possible interpretations is disconcerting. Is it playful or serious, representing a Homeric epithet, a dramatic event, or the popular view of the character? (To the epithets already compared one might add *aidoios nemesêtos* (Il.11.649); cf. *Aen.* 5.49–50.) Wickham suggests "time honoured," which does fit the context well: i.e., *qui semper est in honore* "Perennial favourite" might catch the sense here.

172: *dilator* †*spe longus*† *iners, avidusque futuri* repunctuated to construe *dilator spe*, (= genitive: cf. *Ode* 3.7.4; Pl. *Aul.* 617; Gell. 9.14) *longus*,—"tedious putter-off of hope," which seems closer to the Aristolelean notion of δύϲελπιϲ cited by Brink as: "slow to conceive hopes." For *longus* as "tedious," cf. Cic. *Fin.* 2.2785, *N.D.* 1.36.101; Quint. 10.1.18. See also now J.G.F. Powell (*CQ* XXXIV [1984], 240–41) who emends to *splenosus*.

197: †*peccare timentes*†. I have emended to *sperare timentes* "fearing to hope." Cf. Soph. *O.T.* 834–37 for a chorus so urging.

254:        †*non ita pridem*† as printed. A vexed passage.

437:        †*animi sub vulpe latentes*†. I have emended (after Ribbeck) to *animi sub pelle lantentes*. *vulpe* could result from an intrusive gloss (*"vulpis"*) on *pelle*.

❧ ❧ ABBREVIATIONS

AC	*L'Antiquité Classique*
ANRW	*Aufstieg und Niedergang der römischen Welt*
Athen	*Athenaeum*
BStdLat	*Bollettino di Studi Latini*
BVSA	*Berichte über die Verhandlungen der Sächsischen Akademie der Wissenschaften zu Leipzig*
CQ	*Classical Quarterly*
CR	*Classical Review*
G&R	*Greece and Rome*
H	*Hermes*
Hermath	*Hermathena*
HThR	*Harvard Theological Review*
JP	*Journal of Philology*
JRS	*Journal of Roman Studies*
KHB, Briefe	*Q. Horatius Flaccus Briefe* (Kiessling, Heinze, Burck)
Lat	*Latomus*
Mnem	*Mnemosyne*
Phil	*Philologus*
POF	*The Poetry of Friendship*
REL	*Révue des Etudes Latines*
RhM	*Rheinisches Museum für Philologie*
RPh	*Révue de Philologie*
SBBA	*Sitzungsberichte der Bayerischen Akademie der Wissenschaften*
SBPA	*Sitzungsberichte der Preüssischen Akademie der Wissenschaften*

SO	*Symbolae Osloenses*
Studien	*Studien zur griechischen und römischen Literatur*
TAPA	*Transactions & Proceedings of the American Philological Association*
TORP	*Tradition and Originality in Roman Poetry*
WS	*Wiener Studien*
YCS	*Yale Classical Studies*

Citations of secondary works will be given in full on first occurrence, subsequently by short title, author, or abbreviation. (See the Selected Bibliography.)

Preface

1. C.O. Brink, *Horace on Poetry*, Vol. I, *Prolegomena to the Literary Epistles* (Cambridge, 1963), p. 154.

1 The Epistle of Augustus

1. C.O. Brink, *Horace on Poetry*, Vol. III, *Epistles, Book II* (Cambridge, 1982), p. 495.
2. Brink, III, pp. 526 ff., 546; R. Syme, *History in Ovid* (Oxford, 1978), p. 3.
3. Brink, III, pp. 562–67.
4. Brink, III, pp. 563–64.
5. Brink, III, p. 565.
6. Brink, III, pp. 566–67.
7. Brink, III, p. 33, describes the opening tone as "respectful but cool and uninvolved. . . . It also suits the style of a real letter in prose. . . . "
8. Maecenas is mentioned in *Ode* 4.11.19, inviting Phyllis to a birthday party for him.

9. Suet. *Vit. Hor.* (p. 2.6–7 K1.)

10. E. Fraenkel, *Horace* (Oxford, 1957), pp. 386–87.

11. For the strategy of *Epist.* 1.1, see R. Kilpatrick, *The Poetry of Friendship. Horace, Epistles I* (Edmonton, 1986), pp. 1–7. (Hereafter cited as *POF.*)

12. Suet. *Vit. Hor.* (p. 2 K1.) and Porphyrio on *Ode.* 4.1.1. See Fraenkel, pp. 364–82, 400–410.

13. Suet. *ibid.*

14. See Fraenkel, *Horace*, p. 383. Fraenkel identifies the *pleraque eiusmodi scripta* as *Epp.* 2.2 and 2.3 (*Ars P.*). (Cf. A. Kiessling, R. Heinze, E. Burck, *Q. Horatius Flaccus, Briefe.* Erklärt von Adolf Kiessling, bearbeitet von Richard Heinze, 7th ed. (Berlin, 1961)(hereafter cited as "KHB, *Briefe*"); M. Schanz, C. Hosius, *Geschichte der römischen Literatur bis zum Gesetzgebungswerk des Kaiser* (München, 1927); and A. Rostagni, *Arte Poetica di Orazio* (Torino, 1930).) Mommsen preferred *Epp.* I; P. Giuffrida, "Horat. *Epist.* II i.118–138: Elogio o parodia?" in *Studi in onore di Gino Funaioli* (Roma, 1955), p. 114, argues unconvincingly that Augustus' letter (*vereri autem mihi videris. . . non deest* (p. 3 K1.)) is his reply to *Epist.* 2.1.

15. Fraenkel, *Horace*, p. 364.

16. E.g., Vahlen argued plausibly for 13 B.C. as the date for the composition of *Epist.* 2.1 (See Th. Mommsen, "Die Litteratur-briefe des Horaz," *H* XV (1880), pp. 103–10.) For Mommsen's own dating, see n. 18 below. C. Becker, *Das Spätwerk des Horaz* (Göttingen, 1963), p. 231, places *Epist.* 2.1 soon after *Epp.* I.

17. See P. Händel, "Zur Augustusepistel des Horaz," *WS* LXXIX (1966), pp. 395–96; and Brink, I, pp. 239–43; III, pp. 554–58.

18. Mommsen, p. 107 argued that *praesenti tibi* (v. 15) refers to Augustus' return from Gaul in July, 12 B.C., and that *Epist.* 2.1 should be dated in the same year. (The establishment of the worship of *genius Augusti* dates to this same year.) For the relationship between the terms *numen* and *genius* see D. Fishwick, "Genius and numen," *HThR* LXII (1969): 356–67, and his review of Dieter Heenig's monograph on *Sejanus* (*Phoenix*, XXXI (1977), p. 285): Fishwick's conclusion is that in *Carm.* 4.5.33, and *Epist.* 2.1.15, *numen* has the "developed sense of a divinity (cf. Ov. *Fast.* 5.14 f.) and hence is not an equivalent here to *numen Augusti.*" G. Williams (*Horace* (Oxford, 1972), p. 39) would place *Epist.* 2.1 soon after *C.S.* (17 B.C.); Syme (*History in Ovid*, pp. 176–77) places it after the death of Agrippa (12 B.C.). Brink dates it tentatively to 12 B.C. (III, pp. 553–54). See also A. Alföldi, *Die zwei Lorbeerbäume des Augustus* (Bonn, 1973), pp. 39–45.

19. Cf. A.Y. Sellar, *The Roman Poets of the Augustan Age: Horace and the Elegists* (Oxford, 1899), p. 104, who supposes that *Epist.* 2.2 and 2.3 may have been among the *plerisque*; and Becker, p. 231, n. 20.

20. Fraenkel, *Horace*, p. 386–87. F. Klingner, "Horazens Brief an Augustus," *SBBA* V (Munchen, 1950) cited from F. Klinger, *Studien zur Griechischen und Römischen Literatur* (Zürich und Stuttgart, 1964), p. 413 (hereafter cited as *Studien*), contrasts the oblique ("schrag") opening of *Epist.* 2.1 with those of *Epp.* 2.2 and 2.3 ("sokratisch").

21. Fraenkel, *Horace*, p. 387; *Studien*, p. 431.

22. *POF*, passim.

23. *POF*, pp. 14–18, 41–43.

24. E.g., Augustus' pet terms for Horace: "*purissimus penis*" and "*homuncio lepidissimus*" (Suet. *Vit. Hor.* p. 2 K1).

25. See Brink, III, p. 36, on *unus*. (Horace is *solus* also, as poet laureate.)

26. Fraenkel, *Horace*, p. 384. See K. Witte, "Der Literaturebrief des Horaz an Augustus," *Raccolta... in onore di F. Ramorino* (Milano, 1927), pp. 417–19, for his *schema*, who sees the poem's main charm in its composition; and Händel, p. 394. Brink divides the preamble into two sections: 1–4 (to Augustus) and 5–17 (deified benefactors, envy and posthumous deification, and Augustus' position).

27. See Fraenkel's analysis of this eulogy (pp. 383–87). For Hellenistic background of such "monarchic mystik" see E. Doblhofer, *Die Augustuspanegyrik des Horaz in formal historischer Sicht* (Heidelberg, 1966), pp. 127–41; D. Pietrusinski, "L'apothéose d'Auguste par rapport à Romulus-Quirinus dans la poésie de Virgile et d'Horace," *Eos* LX, III (1975): 273–96; and Brink, III, pp. 40–42.

28. Cf. *Odes*. 3.52, 4.14.43. See Brink, III, pp. 49–53, on *praesens*.

29. See Brink, III, pp. 55–56, on altars and oaths.

30. *Studien*, p. 386. The plight of unappreciated heroes actually anticipates that of the struggling poets in contemporary Rome. See Brink, III, pp. 56–57, on *orior*.

31. Whether or not there should be a comma after *uno* (18) has been in question at least since Bentley changed *hic* to *hoc* to balance *cetera* (20). Fraenkel, *Horace*, p. 387, n. 1, rejects the comma, as do Klingner (in his latest edition: see also his article, p. 9); KHB, *Briefe*; and F. Villeneuve, *Horace. Epîtres. Texte établi et traduit* (Paris, 1934). I would restore the comma because of the antithesis with *cetera* and because *uno te... anteferendo* "giving you sole preeminence" is a tautology. Still it is merely a matter of rhetorical emphasis which does not affect the sense of the passage. See I.G. Orelli, *Q. Horatius Flaccus*, 2 vols. (Turin, 1852), *ad loc*. Brink feels that Horace would be unlikely to maintain that the *populus* "shows insight only in one respect." (But either way *uno... cetera* does seem to maintain just that.)

32. The elevated style of vv. 23–27 seems intended to parody the solemnity of the claims of the *fautor veterum*.

33. *Achivis* (33) adds a mock-epic tone here along with its epithet (*unctis*). See Brink, III, p. 73.

34. See Brink, I, p. 194 and III, pp. 83–113, on Horace's classification and catalogue of Roman poets. On "Ennius... leviter curare videtur" (51) see now P. White, "Horace, *Epistles* 2.1.50–54," pp. 227–34, who renders: "Seems frivolous for worrying."

35. "Humorous surprise" (Brink, III, p. 114).

36. *Satires* 1.4, 1.10. See Fraenkel, *Horace*, p. 388.

37. Fraenkel, *Horace*, p. 388, n. 1, sees no allusion to Augustus here, in contrast to KHB *Briefe* who cite *Epist.* 1.19.43 (*Iovis auribus*) and Suet. *Aug.* 86. Suetonius describes Augustus as being vigorously critical of those writers who went to extremes in antiquarianism and preciosity (*cacozēlos*). Maecenas was a favorite target, nor did he spare his stepson Tiberius. Augustus himself might have wondered about Horace's intentions here. See Becker, p. 230, n. 17, on the possible extent of Augustus' literary patronage of Horace. Brink is skeptical (III, pp. 117–18).

38. Klingner, "Horazens Brief an Augustus," pp. 429–30, sees a strong Callimachean bias in *Epist.* 2.1; but Brink, I, p. 195, n. 3, believes that Horace is in "flagrant disagreement" with some Alexandrian principles. Such polemical terms as *dure, ignare* (66–67), *emendata, exacta* (71–72), *crasse, inlepide* (77), *pingui* (267), *chartis ineptis* (270), etc., set the tone. See also Fraenkel, *Horace*, p. 388. There is no mention of this passage in J.V. Cody's monograph, *Horace and Callimachean Aesthetics: Coll. Lat* CXLVII (Brussels, 1976).

39. Horace (born 65 B.C.) would be at least 47 and no impertinent youth.

40. Klingner, "Horazens Brief an Augustus," p. 413, is doubtful about the relationship of vv. 93–102 to the rest of the epistle. Händel, "Zur Augustusepistel," p. 386, runs the passage on to *Romae* (v. 103, with Vollmer). See Brink, III, pp. 132–33, on the content. Brink sees 90–92 as a "link passage"; and the common denominator of 93–176, as "society and poetry."

41. *Nugari* and *in vitium labier* are the keys to the sense here. Cf. Horace's famous dictum on moderation, *Sat.* 1.1.106, and his portrait of Tigellius, *Sat.* 1.3.1–8. See Brink on the simile of the girl (III, pp. 137–38).

42. The same moral for a nation is stated in the "Roman Odes" (*Odes.* 3.2 and 3.6). See Brink, III, pp. 142–43.

43. Cf. the conclusion of *Odes* 3.5, where Regulus is portrayed with the air of such a Roman.

44. Vv. 132–38 do not exclude the possibility that the *Carmen Saeculare* is (as Horace writes this epistle) being planned or composed. The following parallels are suggestive: *C.S.* 6: *Epist.* 2.1.132; *C.S.* 29: 2.1.143; *C.S.* 45: 2.1.2: *C.S.* 74–76: 2.1.134–38. The chorus in *C.S.* speaks of itself in the first person singular (73–76), while Horace speaks of his chorus in the third person singular (*Sat.* 2.1.134).

45. See KHB, *Briefe*; and Brink, III, pp. 150–51.

46. Contrast Persius' ironic portrait (*Sat.* 3), with Horace's (*Sat.* 2.3). Cf. Catullus (65).

47. Cf. *Satt.* 1.3.60, 1.4.140, 1.6.65; *Epist.* 1.1.41. Giuffrida, p. 107, argues unconvincingly that Horace is loading poetasters with virtues to make fun of them; i.e. *insania* is the mother of their virtues (113).

48. Cf. Cic. *Arch.* 15–19; *Ars P.* 391–407. W. Wili, *Horaz und die augusteische Kultur* (Basel, 1948), p. 339, compares Cicero's hymn to philosophy in the *Tusculans* (5.25).

49. Klingner, "Horazens Brief an Augustus," p. 413, is doubtful about the relationship of vv. 139–44 to the rest of the epistle. But see Brink, III, p. 184.

50. These references to old-fashioned country rites remind us of the earlier reference to Augustus' altars and *numen* (15–16). For the fescennine verses as the seeds of Roman drama, see Händel, "Zur Augustusepistel," I, p. 390, Brink, I, p. 205; Becker, p. 208.

51. Cf. *Ars P.* 265–69.

52. Händel, "Zur Augustusepistel," p. 390 refers *serus* (161) to *Graecia capta* (i.e. 240 B.C., Livius Andronicus' first production.) See also W. Hupperth, pp. 81–82, Becker, pp. 215–16, and Brink, III, pp. 204–5.

53. "Daring" (or "risk") is a poetic virtue. The expression *feliciter audet* (166) qualifies it more precisely. Cf. also *Sat.* 2.1.10; *Epp.* 1.3.20; 2.1.182, 258; 2.2.51, 111; *Ars P.* 10, 125, 382. See Brink, III, pp. 209–10.

54. Cf. *Ars P.* 289–94, 389; *Sat.* 1.10.72.

55. A clear distinction is made between the "reek of sweat" of the Saturnian (158) and "honest perspiration" of the conscientious artist. Perhaps the first is intended to recall the smell of goats (cf. *Epist.* 1.5.29; *Cat.* 69.5, 71.1; Ov. *A.A.* 3.193). See Klingner, "Horazens Brief an Augustus," p. 423.

56. See Sellar's comments on "rapid and careless composition" and "the uneducated taste of the audiences" (p. 107).

57. Such acts remind us of the premiere of Terence's *Hecyra* (*Prol.* 1.1–5; 2.25–34). Bears and boxers did appear at the games (A.S. Wilkins, *The Epistles of Horace. Edited with notes* (London, 1892), *ad loc.*), and Augustus himself was a boxing fan (Suet. *Aug.* 45). Brink here renders *res ludicra* (180) as "drama."

58. Horace credits the good dramatist with pulling his audience through the entire gamut of emotions, thinking perhaps of Aristotle's *catharsis*.

59. Klinger, "Horazens Brief an Augustus," p. 428 points out that Horace makes no reference to any genuine success(es) of Augustan drama, such as Varius' *Thyestes*.

60. Brink, III, p. 239, calls this "a weightier... and more courtly version of such transitions as *S.* 1.4.38. ... "

61. Brink, I, p. 191, n. 3, discusses the use of *cogere* of official patronage. He disagrees with Fraenkel, *Horace*, p. 386, regarding the sense of *exprimere* as used by Suetonius (*expressitque eclogam ad se*). See Brink, III, pp. 236–37, on the ancient theory of literature for private reading. In the expression *et egere vetes* (228) Brink recognizes an "official note."

62. Cicero speaks more favourably than Horace about Alexander's taste in writers (*Arch.* 24). Envying Achilles' good fortune in having Homer as his poet, Alexander gathered a great number of writers around him: Aristobulus, Ptolemy Lagi, Callisthenes, Anaximenes, Onesicritus, Clitarchus, and (on Horace's evidence) the poet Choerilus. (See Nall's commentary on *Pro Arch.* 24, London, 1901).

63. Vergil and Varius are said (*Comm. Cruq.*) to have each received one million sesterces from Augustus. Suetonius (p. 2 K1.) mentions great generosity to Horace on two occasions: "unaque et altera liberalitate locupletavit."

64. Juvenal makes fun of Cicero's line (*Sat.* 10.122); Quintilian comments (11.1) that it was criticised in his day by "*maligni*." See W. Allen, Jr., "'O fortunatam natam... '," *TAPA*, LXXXVII (1956), p. 141; and Brink, III, p. 257.

65. For a discussion of *recusatio* in Horace see now Cody, pp. 73–102.

66. Cic. *Arch.* 25. Sulla ordered a reward be given to him—but only on condition that he not write anything else! In this way he rewarded the *sedulitatem mali poetae*. Brink, III, pp. 253, 259, is sceptical about a direct allusion to Cicero: "accounted for by the genre of commemorative writing."

67. Cf. *Epp.* 1.1, 1.4, 1.7, 1.17, 1.19,; 2.2, *Ars. P.*

68. Cat. 95.7; Pers. 1.43.

69. *POF*, pp. 41–43.

70. Suet. *Aug.* 43.

71. Suet. *Aug.* 44

72. Suet. *Aug.* 45.

73. Suet. *Aug.* 85, 89.

74. Various views of Horace's purpose in *Epist.* 2.1 have been put forward. Wili, *Horaz*, p. 264: "... sein an Augustus gerichteter Brief ist die Bibel

der Literatur dieser Zeit." Brink, I, p. 191: "It is a command performance." Fraenkel, *Horace*, p. 388: "to overcome dull opposition to any fresh production; . . . In this epistle it is Horace's primary object to outline the character and the scope of that new poetry and to allot to it its proper place in the body politic. . . Fraenkel, *Horace*, p. 342. . . . . Horace is engaged in an embittered struggle for his own and his friend's artistic ideals. . . . " KHB, *Briefe*, p. 198: "Ein Bericht gleichsam, den H. an den princeps über die gegenwartige Lage der römischen Poesie als ihr berufener Fürsprecher erstattet. Nicht ihr Leistungen fuhrt er vor, sondern die Schwierigkeiten. . . . " Villeneuve, p. 146: "l'oraison funèbre de la génération de poètes dont Horace avait [*Sat.* 1.10] célébré l'épanouissement." Klingner, "Horazens Brief an Augustus," p. 432: "Aber in Wirklichkeit ist sein Brief eben doch das letzte Wort der grossen augusteishcen Dichtkunst geblieben." P. Gros, "Horace et la tentation du désert. Note sur *Epist.* I. II v. 7–10," *Mélanges P. Boyancé* (Rome, 1974), p. 374: "motive par l'amertume réelle d'un homme dont les allusions s'effritent." Witte, p. 413: "poetry's usefulness to the state." (Also Händel, "Zur Augustusepistel," p. 395, K. Bringmann, "Struktur und Absicht des horazischen Briefes an Kaiser Augustus" *Phil* CXVIII (1974): 236–56, and Sellar, p. 103: " 'a defence of poetry,' and especially a vindication of the poets of his own time against the criticism that ranked the older poets above them. . . combining with [Augustus'] praises a deserved eulogy on him as a patron of literature.") Brink's final judgement, III, p. 495, is: "This work with all its many motifs contributing to a celebration of Augustan poetry is itself a masterly Augustan performance. . . . I doubt. . . whether the unity of tone, and thus the resolution of its complex diversity of content and style, is so fully realized as it is in the other two great Epistles—the *Florus* and the *Ars*."

75. Augustus, Varius, Pollio (and later Ovid) had themselves all written tragedies. Klingner, "Horazens Brief an Augustus," p. 430, wonders whether Horace is trying to bring Augustus over to his side in respect to criticism of the contemporary stage. See also Bringmann, pp. 253–54.

76. See R.S. Kilpatrick, "Juvenal's 'patchwork' satires: 4 and 7," *YCS* XXIII (1973): 229–41.

77. Asinius Pollio had introduced the custom of placing poets' busts by their works in libraries. (Pliny, *N.H.* 8.31, and E.C. Wickham's note on *Sat.* 1.4.21, *The Works of Horace with a Commentary*, 2 vols. (Oxford, 1891).)

78. Cf. *largitur honorem* (Juv. 7.88) with *largimur honores* (*Epist.* 2.1.15) and *vendit* (Juv. 7.135, *Epist.* 2.1.75)

2 The Epistle to Florus

1. See G. Kettner, *Die Episteln des Horaz* (Berlin, 1900), p. 166; Becker, p. 54. Vahlen's impression of the clarity of thought in *Epist.* 2.2 is frequently

noted (e.g., M.J. McGann, "Horace's Epistle to Florus," *RhM* XCVII (1954): 343). This poem is similar in argumentation to *Epist.* 1.7 (See *POF*, pp. 7–14). Becker notes that Florus is not exhorted to philosophy here as he was in *Epist.* 1.3.

2. Brink appropriately cautions against applying the term *recusatio* to the *Florus* (*III*, p. 267).

3. See Wickham, II, p. 363. Brink correctly affirms that *Epist.* 2.2 is "not a literary treatise. It is a poetic epistle and it has the structure of a Horatian poem. . . . The literary criticism of the letter is fitted into this psychological setting with great skill" (I, pp. 184–85). However, the sense of "personal dissatisfaction" which Brink feels within the poem is much less tangible.

4. Vahlen's date of 18 B.C. has been generally accepted, putting Tiberius (and Florus) still in the east after Augustus' return to Rome (see KHB, *Briefe*, p. 244). Other views date it to 19 B.C. (Mommsen) or as late as the expedition to Dalmatia and Pannonia in 12–11 B.C. (Kruger, Lejay). Sellar, pp. 108–9, felt that the apparent reference to Propertius favoured an earlier date, but that the impression we get of Florus in *Epist.* 2.2 is more mature than in 1.3, and that *dixi*. . . suggests that he had returned to Rome since the time of *Epist.* 1.3. But none of these three premises is secure. See Brink, I, p. 184, n. 1; III, p. 552, for summaries.

5. Tiberius was born in October 42 B.C. during the campaign at Philippi (Suet. *Tib.* 5). By Vahlen's dating he would be 23 or just 24 years old. Wickham, II, p. 362, sees Horace as making his refusal through Florus to Tiberius.

6. Cf. *Epp.* 1.1, 1.3, 1.7, 1.8, 1.9, 1.13, 1.19, 1.20.

7. McGann, p. 344. See Brink, III, p. 266, on this fiction.

8. See Brink, III, pp. 274–77, on the Roman law of sale applying here.

9. Brink, III, p. 270, takes issue with the standard view that 8000 sesterces is a moderate price.

10. For *imbutus* in the sense of "having a little knowledge," cf. Cic. *Tusc.* 1.7.13, Tac. *Dial.* 19, Suet. *Gramm.* 4.

11. There could be some irony in this euphemistic disclosure. The verb describing the slave's faulty behaviour is *cessare* (14) "malinger," be away from house and work without the master's permission, a charge previously levelled at Davus by Horace (*Sat.* 2.7.100). That classes him not (*pace* Porph.) as a *fugitivus* (runaway) but rather as an *erro* (one who tends to wander off). See *Dig.* 21.1.17.14 and Brink, III, p. 273.

12. I construe (with Bentley, Wilkins, Kruger, Wickham, McGann, p. 345, Brink, III, pp. 274–75) *des* (16) as jussive, and therefore part of the *vendor's* remarks. This in turn urges the indicative, *si laedit*: "if that's all that's bothering you. . . . " For the contrary view (*des* as apodosis), see Wilkins, KHB, *Briefe*, and Klingner. A final appeal to price and payment is

quite consistent with salesmen's spiels even today. ("Now, what do you think it would cost to have this in your home?") According to McGann, p. 345, "The personality of the poet comes before us for the first time with *opinor.*"

13. Without pressing the intended analogies between the slave and Horace too far, we may note his training in Greek, his Italian birth, and his ability to please people (at least when in their cups) with his singing. Horace "ran away" from Maecenas (*Epist.* 1.7) and was scolded for it.

14. Horace imagines Maecenas to have labelled him *mendax*, too (*Epist.* 1.7.2), but there for a promise *actually* made and broken.

15. For *attemptare* (in legal sense) "discredit" cf. Val. Max. 7.8.3; Quint. 12.18.14; (Ulp.) *Dig.* 12.6.23.1; for *cessator* (= *erro*) cf. (Ulp.) *Dig.* 21.1.17.14. Cf. also; *fiet eritque* (5), *excepta* (16), *optivo* (101) [G. *Inst.* 1.154], *impune* (105), *Legitimum* (109), *movere loco* (113), *libra et aere* (158), etc. The real purpose of all this legal colour will be suggested below.

16. See *POF*, p. 64; e.g., *dissignat, recludit, iubet esse ratas, onus eximit, paupertate solutum, rescribe, inconsultus, inter amicos.*

17. *POF*, pp. 15–16.

18. See R.B. Rutherford, "Horace, *Epistles* 2.2: Introspection and Retrospective." *CQ* XXXI (1981): 375. *super hoc . . . mendax* puts the aspect of the undelivered *carmina* in a climactic position.

19. There are four such analogies in the epistle. For the function of such parables (αἶνοι) in Horace see E. Fraenkel, "Zur Form der αἶνοι," *RhM* LXXIII (1920): 366–70; McGann, p. 347, who compares Lucilius, Book XXX; Rutherford, p. 376; and Brink, III, pp. 277–89.

20. See KHB, *Briefe* and Brink, III, *ad loc.*; also Plut. *Lucull.* 33.3; Sall. *Hist.* 5, frag. 10M.

21. See Wilkins, Wickham, KHB, *Briefe*, Brink, III, *ad loc.* on Plutarch's data. The attitude toward Lucullus of his men is implied by Horace's anecdote.

22. See Brink, III, pp. 286–87, on the rhetoric of *i . . . i*, etc.

23. The high style of vv. 30–32 contrasts with *ob id factum* (33), *quid stas* (38: cf. *Sat.* 1.1.19), *quantumvis* (39), etc. See Brink, III, *ad loc.*

24. Cf. Cat. 53, Hor. *Sat.* 1.7, Juv. 2. *Catus* (sharp) is an old Sabine word (Varr. *L.L.* 7.46), used often by Ennius and Plautus. Cicero apologizes for it in prose (*Leg.* 1.16.45) but does use it in the *Aratea*. Horace uses it three times (twice in *Odes*: 1.10.3, 3.12.10). The effect here is archaically heroic, and clashes with *quantumvis*. Ulrich Knoche, "Betrachtungen über Horazens Kunst der satirischen Gesprachsführung," *Phil* XC (1935): 469–82, comments on the sequence of the serious (26–54) and ironic (55–57) sections here. See now Brink, III, 287–88.

25. *Epist.* 1.2.31. For the use of Homer as a school author, see also Quint. 1.8.5, Plin. *Epist.* 2.14.2.

26. Like W. Wili, I feel that Horace was heavily indebted to the Academy and Cicero in his formative years. See *POF*, pp. xvii-xviii; also M.N. Porter Packer, "Cicero, Horace and the New Academy," *TAPA* LXXX (1949): 430–31. The "shady groves of Academus" is an expression going back at least to Eupolis (frag. 32 M). Sulla had cut the trees down during the siege of Athens (88–87 B.C.) but thirty years had elapsed between then and Horace's sojourn. (Wilkins, *ad loc.* sees no Academic influence in Horace's works.) The usual reading of *vellem* (v. 44) makes the best sense in the context of Horace's affection for Athens and his reluctance to leave. (*possem* makes almost no sense of v. 45). The play on the geometrical and ethical senses of *curvo* is imitated by Persius (3.52, 4.11). See Brink, III, p. 291.

27. The image of wrestling is suggested by *lacertis* (48). Horace refers frequently to Philippi (and even to Brutus himself by name), invariably with self-depreciating irony, but never with disloyalty to his former political friends. The compliment to Augustus here is most significant, following as it does *Epist.* 2.1 (assuming the two to have been in fact so arranged by Horace). The metaphor *decisis pinnis* is reminiscent (in context) of Cic. *Att.* 4.2.5: "eidem illi, qui mihi inciderant, nolunt easdem renasci." (See Brink, III, pp. 293–94.)

28. The theme of *paupertas* with its positive and negative interventions in the lives of Poets is studied by W. Wimmel, in "Apollo-Paupertas. Zur Symbolik von Berufungsvorgängen bei Properz, Horaz und Calpurnius." *Festschrift Büchner* (Wiesbaden, 1970), pp. 291–97; and N. Rudd, "Horace's poverty" *Hermath* LXXXIV (1954): 16–25. Rudd interprets *paupertas* as the force which impelled Horace to seek patronage (22). See Brink, III, pp. 294–96.

29. Are we ironically reminded here again of Horace's past refusals to write epic on Augustus' exploits? See Brink, I, p. 170.

30. McGann, p. 348.

31. The vulnerability of *veritas* in forensic oratory is admitted even by Cicero (*de Or.* 3.56.215).

32. *Epp.* 1.1.1–6, 1.7.25–28; *Ode.* 4.1.

33. Knoche, p. 478, sees *sale nigro* (60) as related metaphorically with *palato* (62). See Brink, III, pp. 299–302, on these genres.

34. E.g., *Satt.* 1.6, 1.9, 2.6. In vv. 68–69, the Quirinal (NE) and Aventine (SW) must be understood as far apart, the forum in between. J. Vahlen, "Zu Horatius' Brief an Florus (II2)," *Zeit. f. öster. Gym.* XXV (1874): 112 (cited from *Gesammelte Philologeische Schriften* (Leipzig und Berlin, 1911, 1923), p. 512) gives some grammatical parallels for the MSS *humane commoda* (70): *impie gratus, mansuete obediens, comiter facilis;* but Brink, III,

pp. 304–5, prints Froelich's emendation (*haud sane commoda*) as making better sense.

35. Vv. 74–75 are a metrical tour de force: a "golden line" expresses the formality of the funeral procession, followed by a split line (diaeresis between feet 3 and 4) with a bold monosyllabic close (*ruit sus*) expressing the frantic actions of rabid dogs and muddy pigs racing this way and that. See G. Williams, *Tradition and Originality in Roman Poetry* (Oxford, 1968), p. 657; Brink, III, p. 307.

36. *Contracta*, though supported by a minority of the MSS, must be correct. The proper path for poets (from Callimachus on) is narrow: precise, learned, demanding, and original in its choice of material.

37. See Wilkins, *ad loc.* (and now Brink) for a summary. Wilkins considers it odd that some critics have supposed Horace himself to be the *ingenium* caricatured here and takes *hic ego* (84) to be too strongly adversative to admit of that. His case is undermined by Horace's own usage (cf. *Ode* 1.16.25 [*nunc ego*], *Sat.* 1.5.82 [*hic ego*]) of *ego* as a mild resumption of the first person subject. *Annos septem* need not be taken literally, although it could be so taken. (Horace was going on 23 at the time of Philippi; so he would have had to go to Athens at age 15 or 16, which does seem rather young.) McGann, p. 350, does not support an autobiographical reference here.

38. The MSS (83) vary between *insenuitque/libris et curis statua taciturnius exit* and /*libris et Curii statua taciturnius exit.* (Porphyrio read *Curii* too). See O. Keller, *Epilegomena zu Horaz* (Leipzig, 1879), *ad loc.* who argues strongly against *Curii* as only a "tasteless variant." (Why would a statue of Curius be especially silent?) But the epistle is liberally sprinkled with famous *exempla* of antiquity (Cato, Cethegus, Gracchus, Mucius), and one more would not be out of place. Curius Manius Dentatus (consul 290, 280, 275, 274, censor 272: an outstanding military and civil career) was famed for his humble, frugal, and incorruptible character. He it was who sent the traitorous physician back to Pyrrhus, and preferred earthen vessels to Samnite gold (Flor. 1.10–1.13). Val. Max. cites him as an *exemplum* of *frugalitas* and *severitas* (cf. Porph.). Livy recounts (*Epist.* 14) how he began to auction off the property of young Romans who did not report for military duty. Perhaps a change of punctuation to *libris, et curis,* would help, taking *curis* with *exit,* "because of his concerns" (cf. Cic. *Tusc.* 5.24.69; Hor. *Ode.* 3.21.15 [*sapientium curas*]; and v. 66 below [*inter tot curas*]). Either reading (*Curii* or *curis*) yields four relative clauses in 81–84a modifying *ingenium*, in apposition to *me* (79). Brink, III, p. 313, reads *curis*, taking *Curii* as a "mechanical slip."

39. See note 37 above.

40. McGann, p. 352, n. 26, defends the reading (87) *ut alter.* But see Brink, III, p. 87n., who obelizes. Transposing *frater* and *rhetor* might solve Brink's objections. (See my translation and the textual note on p. 84.)

41. Particularly known in oratory and law—very Roman, and of interest therefore to Florus especially.

42. Already young poets such as Celsus (1.3.15–20) find it hard to resist the potential for plagiarism in such a collection! The most famous description is that of Propertius (3.29). See A.J. Marshall, "Library resources and creative writing at Rome," *Phoenix* XXX (1976): 261, n. 56, for a survey of modern scholarship on this library. The wonder in Horace's description parallels that of Propertius. (See J.P. Postgate, *Select Elegies of Propertius* (London, 1884), p. xxxiii.) The idea that the library needs filling echoes *Epist.* 2.1.217, where the same point is pressed home to Augustus.

43. For this melancholic disposition of poets, cf. v. 53 (above); *Epist.* 1.8 (*POF*, pp. 38–39); Sen. *Dial.* 9.17.10 (*nullum magnum ingenium sine mixtura dementiae fuit*). Cf. *Tusc.* 3.5.11; Arist. *Probl.* 11.38.

44. *Optivo* (101) is another legal term (Gaius, *Inst.* 1.154), usually applying to a wife's right (if granted to her by her husband in his will) to choose a *tutor*. The opposite term is *dativus*. See Brink, III, p. 326.

45. Brink, III, p. 325, prefers "not to press the assumed biographical points" regarding Propertius. M.C.J. Putnam, *Artifices of Eternity* (Ithaca and London, 1986), rejects any notion that "the Roman 'Callimachus,' in *Epistles* 2.1 [sic], who is surely Propertius, is treated with any greater irony than that which Horace expends on himself, a latter day Alcaeus." See his review of recent opinion on this question (p. 28, n.8).

46. Contrast his independence of public acclaim in *Epist.* 1.19 (*POF*, pp. 18–24). Horace claims to have avoided public recitations in his early career (*Sat.* 1.4.23, 73), but Ovid heard him (*Trist.* 4.10.49) recite, perhaps in a private salon.

47. Cf. *Sat.* 1.9.20. Disagreement persists as to whether *impune* (another legal term) qualifies *obturem* (e.g., Wilkins, G.T.A. Krüger, *Des Q. Horatius Flaccus Satiren und Episteln. Zweites Bändchen. Episteln* (Leipzig, 1900); KHB, *Briefe*; Villeneuve; E.P. Morris, *Horace. The Epistles* (New York, 1909)) or *legentibus* (e.g., Orelli, Wickham). The former would imply that having given up poetry Horace no longer needs support from other poets and can afford to ignore them; the latter, that if he ceases to be *auditor et ultor* (1.19.40) there will be no one to reply to them. There is nothing wrong with accepting some ambiguity: both ideas are present and important! (*Impune legentibus* always did apply, since these poets do not acknowledge criticism—only praise: 107–8). The opening of Juvenal's First Satire owes much to this passage. Brink, III, pp. 327–28, supports Wilkins, i.e. "*obturem... impune.*"

48. We are reminded of the play on the expression *mala carmina* in *Sat.* 2.1.

49. The precise details of this allusion are not clear, but just as the Vestals were required to keep the sacred flame burning and to preserve the ancient Pal-

ladium from Troy, hoary ritual terms could be alluded to. The phrase *penetralia Vestae* is a Vergilian line-end (5.744, 9.259: see KHB, *Briefe*). Brink translates (III, p. 335): "within the recesses of Vesta."

50. Horace returns to the principle of *usus* ("utility," "need") at *Ars P.* 71. (Cf. Lucr. 5.1029.) For a full discussion of the history of this fairly recent controversy over whether Horace there means "usage" or "utility," see C.O. Brink, *Horace on Poetry*, Vol. II, *The Ars Poetica* (Cambridge, 1971), on *Ars P.* 71: pp. 158–60. Brink's own conclusion that Horace means "usage" is not conclusive. *Usus* (2.2.119) applies only to words new to poetry but which are nonetheless *ex consuetudine*. The basis for the "selection" (not "coinage") of a word from that reservoir is *usus* in the sense Horace always uses it: "need," "occasion," "advantage." "Need" must be determined on the basis of the poet's "experience" and "skill" (and may also be translated by *usus*). It would seem odd for general *consuetudo* to apply to poetry (cf. Varr. *L.L.* 5.1) even at *Ars P.* 71, without requiring the artistic selection of the poet. *Usus* in Horace implies the judgement of the poets, not the masses, and in that sense is the *arbitrium . . . et ius et norma loquendi* for poetry. One may compare Cicero's attempted synthesis of *ratio* with *consuetudo* (Cic. *Brut.* 259–61; Varr. *L.L.* 9.18). On Cicero's distinctions between good and bad *consuetudo* see the article by E. Fantham, "Cicero, Varro, and Marcellus," *Phoenix* XXXI (1977): 208–13. The rhetorical controversy between those who espoused selection (*analogia, ratio, lectus, elegantia*) as the criterion for diction and those who relied upon *consuetudo* is there lucidly explained and well documented. Varro's account of *natura, analogia, consuetudo, auctoritas* is cited (Diomedes 1.439 K) in n. 22. (As Brink points out, almost all other modern opinion favours *usus* = "need.") See also Becker, p. 60.

51. For the Callimachean image of the clear stream, cf. Cic. *Brut.* 79.274 (Wilkins). Wili, p. 312, compares *Ode* 4.2, *Sat.* 1.4.10. See also McGann, p. 353, n. 31, and J.K. Newman, *Augustus and the New Poetry* (Bruxelles, 1967), p. 347. McGann, p. 354 n. 32, cites studies by Nillson, Marouzeau, and Herescu showing how words such as *luxuriantia* demonstrate the fault referred to. See also Brink, III, pp. 339–43: "The desired qualities of the poetic user of words: intensity and lucidity, 120–21."

52. With this metaphor Wilkins compares Cic. *de Or.* 2.23.96 and Quint. 10.4.1. See Brink, III, pp. 343–44.

53. With Krüger, Keller, Munro (cited by Wickham), and E. Pasoli, "Per una lettura dell' epistola di Orazio a Giulio Floro (*Epist.* 2.2)," *Il Verri* XIX (1965): 129–41.

54. Wilkins suggests "be worried" for *ringi*, citing Ter. *Phorm.* 2.2.27 as an analogy. (The word is *hapax* in Horace.) Persius uses the same image (1.108–10) but in more abstruse language: "vide sis, ne maiorum tibi forte/limina frigescant: sonat hic de nare canina/littera." The growl is in-

tended to keep away the unwelcome person from the door (there, the outspoken literary critic). Brink's interpretation, I, p. 190, "rather be a dilettante with a craze than know—and growl" is rather different. See also
Brink, III, p. 350: "snarl, chafe, pull a wry face, be disconcerted."

55. *Beatus* is the word used by Horace of such self-infatuation (*Satt.* 1.1.19,
1.4.2.) or the bliss of ignorance.

56. *Epist.* 1.1.97-end. Cf. such other quoted sermons as *Satt.* 2.2, 2.3, 2.4, 2.6
(the mouse fable).

57. For this *atra bilis* (melancholy) of artistic temperaments, see note 43 above.

58. Becker, p. 55.

59. Cf. *Epp.* 1.1, 1.4, 1.10–12, 1.16. See Wickham, *ad loc.*

60. Cf. the analogy of specifics in medicine and moral philosophy in *Epist.* 1.6.

61. For the logic of v. 155–57, see R. P. Winnington-Ingram, "Two Latin
idioms," *CR* V (1955): 139–41.

62. See the Lucretius commentaries of Merrill and Bailey. *Epist.* 1.12 also exploits the legal concept of *usus*. Brink's note, III, pp. 367–69, is now fundamental on this concept.

63. I.e., the principle of *usucapio*. (See Wilkins's note.) The allusion to *libra et
aere* is a technical one, continuing the age-old means of purchase with
bronze by weight. See Brink, III, pp. 367–69.

64. *Odes* 2.3.20, 2.14.25, 3.24.62, 4.7.19; *Satt.* 2.2.132, 2.3.122 (145, 151),
2.5.86.

65. Wickham knows of no other author who describes the idea of the *genius* as
closely as does Horace (2.2.187). See Wilkins' notes (*ad loc.*) as well on
genius, *astrum* and *albus-ater* (in the sense of "character"), and now Brink,
III, pp. 385–86.

66. See Wickham, *ad loc.*, for this abrupt certainty in the indicative *curat*.

67. *Utar* (190) picks up the theme of *usus* developed earlier (158) and carried
through right to v. 189. For the *topos* of laying up a modest pile to draw
from as need or pleasure arise, cf. Tib. 1.1.77–78, Hor. *Epp.* 1.1.12,
1.7.39.

68. Some MSS omit both *domus* and *absit* (199); Bentley and other subsequent
editors have suspected these two words even where they occur. (See
Wilkins; KHB, *Briefe*; and Brink, *ad loc.*). The complete line sums adequate
in sense and meter. *Inmunda* means *sordida* (cf. *Sat.* 2.2.65); the dirty
house is familiar in Horace as a symbol for miserable poverty (*Ode* 2.10.7).
Paupertas and *pauper* by themselves can convey the idea of a laudable
tenuis victus, and require an adjective such as *sordida, immunda, angusta,
dura, importuna, contracta*, or some other sign in the context to give the
sense of "misery." Brink argues that there is a contradiction between the

rejection of "squalid poverty of house," and the acceptance of *either* a large or small ship. However, "pauperies *immunda* domus" represents an extreme lying beyond mere "pauperies." (The latter would be the equivalent to "*parva navis.*")

69. Horace is clearly thinking of *Ode* 2.10 here with the combination of house and voyage images illustrating the "golden mean."

70. Cf. *Epist.* 1.2.70–71.

71. Some editors take *mortis* with both *formidine* and *ira* (207), citing Liv. 1.5 and Lucr. 3.1045. (Wickham, *ad loc.*). This is not necessary and limits *ira* drastically. *Epist.* 1.2 is a sermon to Lollius on *ira*. (See *POF*, pp. 26–32.)

72. The *lemures* were roaming spirits of those who were wicked in life. (Contrast the *lares.*) There was an annual festival, the *Lemuria*, each May (Ov. *Fast.* 5.419–92).

73. Cf. *Sat.* 1.3.35; *Epist.* 1.14.4–5; Cic. *Tusc.* 2.5.13. On v. 213, see McGann, p. 358, and Klingner, pp. 467–68.

74. See KHB, *Briefe, ad loc.* "*Vivere si recte*" reminds us strikingly again of *Ode* 2.10 (*Rectius vives*).

75. E.g., *Satt.* 1.2, 1.3, 1.4, 1.7, 1.8, 1.9, 2.3, 2.6, 2.7; *Epp.* 1.1, 1.13, 1.19, 2.1.

76. Cf. *Odes* 1.25, 3.15, 4.13, and *Epodes.* 8, 12 for the mocking of presumptuous old age. In *Ode* 4.13 Lyce has lost her *decens motus* (17–18): *Ludisque et bibis impudens* (4) *et cantu tremulo pota Cupidinem lentum sollicitas* (5–6). Young men will see her as *multo non sine risu dilapsam in cineres facem* (27–28).

77. Cf. *Ode* 2.2.13, *Epist.* 1.1.34.

78. Cf. Mart. 10.23.1–4.

79. I.e., 23 of 70 lines (Becker, pp. 54–55).

80. Cf. *Sat.* 2.1.2; *Ars P.* 135, 274.

81. As Brink points out, I, p. 185, "The literary criticism of the letter is fitted into this pychological setting with great skill. . . . Although comparatively brief, it comes with much emphasis right in the centre of the poem and its bearing on poetry is clearly greater than the scope of the letter would lead one to expect."

82. Brink also observes, I, p. 189: "Horace's precepts deal with revision rather than drafting" in the three areas of ornamentation, ruggedness, and lack of *virtus*. Horace is careful to avoid excessive technicalities.

83. Becker, p. 62, sees *Epist.* 2.2 as a transition between *Epp.* I and the literary epistles.

3 *The Epistle to the Pisos*

1. Brink, I and II. The majority of Brink's reviewers continue to be very positive; but see G. Williams, "Review of C.O. Brink, *Horace on Poetry* [Vol. I], *JRS*, LIV (1964), 186–96, and Brink's response (II, pp. xv-xxi); also Williams's review of vol. II (*CR*, XXIV [1974]: 52–57).

2. Brink, I, p. 245. E. Norden in "Die Composition und Litteraturgattung der Horazischen Epistula ad Pisones," *H* XL (1905): 481–528 (cited from *Kleine Schriften zum klassischen Altertum* (Berlin, 1966), p. 356) regarded the *Ars Poetica* as the most Greek of all Horace's poetry.

3. Brink, I, p. 246; II, p. vii.

4. Brink, I, p. 247. Scaliger's famous dictum *"ars sine arte tradita"* is mistaken. Contrast W.K. Wimsatt, "'IAM NUNC DEBENTIA DICI': Answers to a Questionnaire," *Arion* IX (1970): 226: "There is no such thing as a successful poem, a classic, which turns out on study to be disorderly."

5. Brink, I, p. 248.

6. Norden, p. 316, Brink, I, p. 248. Wimsatt, p. 227 distinguishes 32 topics in the *Ars Poetica*. (See his schema, pp. 227–33.)

7. Brink, I, p. 251.

8. Brink, I, pp. 90–134.

9. Brink, I, p. 255.

10. Brink, I, p. 219; C.J. Cody, *Horace and Callimachean Aesthetics: Coll. Lat.* CXLVII (Brussels, 1976), p. 5.

11. Brink, I, p. 72; II, pp. 76–77; Villeneuve, p. 196.

12. Brink, I, p. 256.

13. Quint. *Inst.* 8.3.60. Brink classifies *Ars Poetica* as a "nickname" (I, p. 233).

14. C.M. Wieland, *Horazens Briefe aus dem lateinischen übersetzt und mit historischen Einleitungen und anderen nöthigen Erläuterungen versehen* (Leipzig, 1837), pp. 185–209. O. Weissenfels ("Aesthetisch-Kritische Analyse der *Ep. ad Pis.* von Horaz," *Neues Lausitzisches Magazin* LVI (1880): 118–200) vigorously attacked this view because it "distracted attention from Horace's wider message" (pp. 130–31); he quotes K. Lehrs, *Q. Horatius Flaccus* (Leipzig, 1869), p. CCX, with approval: "Nicht für die Pisonen schrieb Horaz die *Ars Poetica*." (See also L. Spengle, "Horatius de arte poetica," *Phil* XVIII (1862): 108.) But G. Boissier, "L'art Poétique d'Horace et la tragédie romaine," *RPh* XXII (1898): 5, concludes that Piso major has proposed to write, but offers him no encouragement. Cf. J. Vahlen, "Über Horatius' Brief an die Pisonen," *SBPA* (1906), cited from *Gesammelte*, p. 755. E. de Saint-Denis, "La fantaisie et le coq-à-l'âne dans l'*Art poétique* d'Horace," *Lat* XXII (1963): 668–70, reads the *Ars Poetica* as a letter, "essayant de me mettre dans la peau des destinateurs. . . . " Wil-

liams (*JRS* LIV (1964)) believes that Horace is creating the *impression* of a real person intimately and immediately addressing his correspondents. Becker, p. 128, sees only a superficial connection with the Pisos.

15. Brink finds no conclusive evidence, I, p. 216; *Appx. III*, for its date, but believes it to have been written after 14/13 B.C. Suggested dates range from 20 B.C. (e.g., Wilkins; H. Nettleship, "The De Arte Poetica," *JP* XII (1883): 43–61) to 10 B.C. (e.g., O.A.W. Dilke, "When was the *Ars Poetica* Written?" *Bull. Inst. Cl. St.* V (London, 1958): 49–57; J. Perret, *Horace* (Paris, 1959; trans. B. Humez, N.Y., 1964)).

16. Two contemporary Pisones have been suggested as the *pater* of the *Ars Poetica*: L. Piso Pontifex (b. 48 B.C., cons. 15 B.C.: Porphyrio, Wieland, Nettleship, Williams, Rostagni, Perret), whose age might suit a date of 13 B.C. or later. Velleius Paterculus gives a glowing account of his capacities and character (2.98; cf. Sen. *Epist.* 83); Antipater of Thessalonike (*A.G.* 9.93, 428) testifies to his warm interest in poetry and poets (cf. Porph.). We know of no sons of this L. Piso (but one daughter). If sons did exist, the year of their father's consulship (15 B.C.) would be about as early a date as could make their relationship with the poem plausible; Cn. Piso (*cons. suff.*, 23) did have two sons: Cn. Piso (*cons.* 7 B.C.) and L. Piso, the augur (*cons.* 1 B.C.). Unlike his suffectus colleague of 23 (L. Sestius Quirinalis), Cn. Piso was not named in the *Odes* (1.4.14). Both of them had been republicans. (This identification would facilitate an earlier date; possibly as early as Cn. Piso's consulship, when Quintilius Varus was already dead). R. Syme's conclusion, after a thorough examination of the evidence is: "Perplexity subsists" ("Piso Frugi et Cassius Frugi," *JRS* L (1960): 12–20). Dilke supports L. Piso Pontifex.

17. Brink, I, pp. 233–34.

18. Brink, I, p. 266. Brink's work has made the bewildering mass of scholarship on the *Ars Poetica* accessible and intelligible.

19. Brink, I, pp. 56–90.

20. See (e.g.) Saint-Denis, p. 670.

21. See Wieland; Boissier, p. 5; St. Denis, pp. 664–71.

22. On the relationship of Ciceronian rhetorical theory to the *Ars Poetica* see Norden, p. 355; Becker, p. 97; Brink, "Cicero's *Orator* and Horace's *Ars Poetica*," *Atti del II Colloqium Tullianum, Ciceroniana* n.s. II (Rome, 1975): 1–12.

23. See Wickham, II, p. 383; Vahlen, *Gesammelte*, pp. 752–74. Horace's use of *vos* and *tu* needs to be explored.

24. H.L. Tracy, "Horace's Ars Poetica: A Systematic Argument," *G&R* XVII (1948): 104–15.

25. Wickham, II, pp. 327–35, 383–86.

26. Wickham, II, pp. 383–84.

27. D.A. Russell, "Ars Poetica," in C.D.N. Costa, ed., *Horace* (London, 1973), pp. 113–34, Rostagni; pp. x, xl. See also Nettleship, p. 57: "more causerie than treatise"; G. Ramain, "Horace, Art Poétique," *RPh* I (1927), 249: "une causerie intime"; P. Cauer, "Zur Abgrenzung und Verbindung der Theile in Horazens Ars Poetica," *RhM* LXI (1906): 243: "tragt den Charakter einer zwanglosen Plauderei"; C.J. Classen, "Orazio Critico," *BStudLat* I (1971): 403: "non e un' opera didascalica."

28. Wili, p. 314.

29. Cic. *de Or.* 2.41.177; *Orat.* 28.99.

30. Norden, p. 356.

31. E.g., Juvenal VI.

32. E.g., L. Herrmann, "Les deux parties de l'Art Poétique d'Horace," *Lat* XXIII (1964): 507. (The rest of his article is an attack on Saint-Denis.)

33. See Cic. *Part* 7.28–17.60. Rhetorically, the *Ars Poetica* is a *suasoria*, perhaps divisible as follows: *exordium* (1–37), transition (38–41), *narratio* (42–284), *confirmatio* (285–365), *peroratio* (366–476). That it is an *hypothesis* (*causa: Part.* 18.61) addressed to him is not discovered by Piso Major until the *peroratio*, for vv. 1–365 seem to be a *thesis* (*propositum, consultatio*). Both *cognitio* and *actio* are stressed (*Part.* 18.62). Saint-Denis, p. 671, denies any similarity between the *exordium* here and that of a didactic poem or a letter.

34. See K. Gantar, "Die Anfangsverse und die Komposition der horazischen Epistel über die Dichtkunst," *SO* XXXIX (1964): 91, who compares this monstrous composition to Zeuxis' "Hippocentaur" (Luc. *Zeux.* 3).

35. Saint-Denis, p. 687, is struck by the absence of any invocation to deity, announcement of subject, or even *captatio benevolentiae*, devices common to didactic poetry.

36. For *diatribe* in 1–23, see F. Klingner, "Horazens Brief an die Pisonen," *BVSA* LXXVIII (Leipzig, 1937). (See *Studien*, pp. 357–400.)

37. This first major transition is one of the hardest to demarcate. Brink prints vv. 38–41 as a separate paragraph, but belonging to what precedes (1–37). Klingner sees them as the first precept.

38. See Brink *ad loc.* on *facundia* and *ordo*.

39. The interdependence between *ars* and *ingenium* is a major theme of the poem and is introduced again in greater detail at 295ff and 408ff. On this technique of interlacing, see Williams, *TORP*, p. 356.

40. An analysis of the vocabulary of the *Ars Poetica* reveals how pervasive *ars* and related concepts are. E.g., 6 times *ars* (31, 214, 262, 295, 320, 408) (cf. 1 time *iners*, 1 time *sollers*); 1 time *auctor* (45); 1 time *audere* (9); 5 times *dis-*

cere (88, 326, 370, 380, 418); 5 times *docere* (306, 308, 318, 336, 474); 3 times *ingenium* (41, 295, 323); 1 time *limae labor, mora* (291); 3 times *natura* (108, 353, 408); 5 times *nescire* (35, 88, 371, 379, 418); 15 times *poeta* (9, 87, 264, 285, 291, 296, 299, 307, 308, 333, 361, 372, 420, 455, 463); (1 time *poesis*, 361); 5 times *sapere* (212, 309, 367, 396, 455); 6 times *scire* (11, 20, 158, 336, 424, 462); 10 times *scribere* (38, 74, 120, 136, 235, 306, 309, 346, 354, 387); 2 times *vates* (24, 400); 1 time *vena* (409); 1 time *venia* (264).

41. Laughter words occur at least 8 times (5, 105, 113, 139, 356, 358, 433, 452). The last 23 vv. all emphasize the two ridiculous situations: Empedocles and the bear.

42. Cicero too recognized that poetry was entitled to a *verborum licentia liberior* (*de Or*. 1.16.70).

43. Williams, *TORP*, p. 333, sees v. 24 as an example of the abrupt making of a new point (cf. 38, 73, 99, 153, 251, 275 etc.). See also P. Händel, "Zur Ars Poetica des Horaz," *RhM* CVI (1963): 185.

44. Wieland's construct of the dramatic background to the *Ars Poetica* shares this view of the importance of ridicule (pp. 192–93). He goes too far in assuming that Piso's son's "lack of talent" may disgrace the family, however. It is more likely his lack of craftsmanship.

45. Vv. 38–41 are transitional, reaching backwards and forwards.

46. See J.H. Waszink, "Bemerkungen zu den Literaturbriefen des Horaz," *Mnem* XXI (1968): 394, for a convincing defence of the MSS order of vv. 45–46 (transposed by Bentley and Brink).

47. *Callidus* means "practised." Cf. its collocations in other authors: *docta et callida* (Plaut. *Poen*. 234); *c. et docta . . . desertum* (Ter. *Eun*. 1011); *c. et nulla in re tironem* (Cic. *de Or*. 1.50.218); *prudentes natura, callidi usu, doctrina eruditi* (Cic. *Scaur*. 24); *callidus excusso populum suspendere naso* (Pers. 1.118); *verba togae sequeris iunctura callidus acri* (Pers. 5.14).

48. Cicero describes the creative process of coining certain Latin words on the analogy of Greek (*de Or*., 1.34.155): "sed etiam exprimerem quaedam verba *imitando*, quae *nova* nostris essent, dummodo essent *idonea*." Horace's meaning of *usus* here (71) is important to determine. (See Brink *ad loc*., for the points under contention, and M. Ruch, "Horace et les fondements de la *iunctura* dans l'ordre de la création poétique (*A.P*. 46–72), "*REL* XLI (1963): 246–69.) Brink rejects the senses of "need" or "necessity" (Ruch). (Horace does so use it at *Epist*. 2.2.119). He argues cogently for "usage," "practice" (*consuetudo*), although Horace does not so use it elsewhere. I believe that here Brink is correct in rejecting "need," if somewhat off the mark in equating *usus* with *consuetudo*. First, a distinction must be drawn between the *usus* ("practice") of orators (Ruch, p. 248), and that of poets. When Cicero writes "dicendi autem omnis ratio in medio

posita, communi quodam in *usu* atque in hominum more et sermone ver-
satur" (*de Or.* 1.3.12), he is speaking only of oratory, in which the speaker
must select his diction from the words in common use at the time. Oratory
is by definition a *vulgare genus orationis* and draws upon *consuetudo com-
munis sensus* (*ibid*). Poetry, however, is not a *vulgare genus*, and while the
poet is *finitimus oratori*, he is granted *verborum licentia liberior* (1.16.70).
Other arts draw from *un*common sources: "ceterarum artium studia fere
reconditis atque abditis e fontibus hauriuntur" (1.3.12). Therefore, when
Horace defines *usus* as the *arbitrium et ius et norma loquendi*, he is referring only to the poetic usage of practised poets in determining which ob-
solete words are to be revived, and which words in current poetic use are to
be dropped; i.e., "if (poetic) practice consents." On the general topic of *consuetudo* see Fantham, pp. 208–13.

49. See Brink, *ad loc.* (and II, *Appx.* 1.1) for the controversy over the force of
   -que in *tuque* (128). He (with Mueller) translates "and therefore," against
   G. Williams (*JRS*, LIV (1964), p. 190). More recently P. White, "Horace
   A.P. 128–30: The intent of the wording," *CQ* XXVII (1977): 197, has
   argued for use of *-que* here to indicate a shift from the general to the
   specific. White compares *Odes* 1.7.17, 2.18.17, *Epist.* 1.18.87, *Ars P* 426.

50. Cf. the advice of Mozart's father, Leopold, to his son: "I recommend you to
   think when at work not only of the musical but also of the unmusical public.
   You know that for ten true connoisseurs there are a hundred ignoramuses!
   Do not neglect the so-called popular, which tickles long ears." (Letter of
   11th Dec., 1780, trans. M.M. Bozmann, *Wolfgang Amadeus Mozart, Letters*, selected and edited by M. Mersmann (London, 1928).)

51. For the moral implications of the use of the flute, cf. Plat. *Rep.* 399c1, 397a;
   Aristox. 2; Plut. *De Mus.* 30; and esp. Cic. *Leg.* 2.39. See E. Bolaffi,
   "Probabili influssi platonici su Orazio," *Athenaeum* n.s. XI (1933): 125.

52. For the scant evidence for Roman satyr-plays, see Brink, II, pp. 274–77.
   Boissier, p. 16, sees an even greater lack of evidence for choruses in such
   plays. In his view Horace is advocating strict adherence to classical Greek
   canons in tragic drama—including the satyr-chorus. (He need not imply the
   trilogy form, although such is not excluded.) Only one line of satyric drama
   in Latin survives (Mar. Vict. 4.143 K.)

53. Williams, *TORP*, p. 356, views this section only as a "leg-pull"—a
   "humane and humorous treatment of a subject whose practitioners pre-
   served the most pompous and boring solemnity." Brink, I, p. 265, is closer
   to the truth in viewing this elementary instruction on the iambus as aimed
   at "elementary ignorance."

54. Cf. *Epist.* 2.1.

55. Cicero's Crassus (*de Or.* 1.25.113) sees *ingenium* and *natura* as the sources
   of the orator's *vis maxima*; the *artes*, on the other hand, can give polish,

but *doctrina* cannot make better what is already good (G. Pierleoni, "L'Arte Poetica di Orazio e il De Or. di Cic.," *Atene e Roma* VIII [1905]: 254ff.) Brink, I, p.4, sees v. 295 as the true beginning of the final section (295–476) on general questions of poetic criticism.

56. *Sapere* is difficult to translate by a single word so as to suggest its range of meanings. The verb retained its original meaning of "have a taste," "smack" (then "to taste," "sense") while acquiring its general intellectual connotation "be discerning."

57. E.g., *de Or.* 1.3.9.

58. This clear critical distinction goes back at least to Aristophanes (*Ran.* 1334).

59. For the sentiment, cf. Dryden, *Mac Flecknoe* 19f.

60. See n. 32 above.

61. In Cic. *de Or.* 1.27.124, the view is put forward that actors are judged more leniently than orators.

62. Cic. *Fam.* 7.1.1; *Sat.* 1.10.38. (See Brink.)

63. See Brink on this crux. Perhaps *animi latentes* could be construed as "the secret vanity" and self-deception of the crow/poet, under the spell of the fox (*sub vulpe*). The word order could be the difficulty.

64. See Brink on 438.

65. Cic. *Amic.* 24.88: "multaeque causae suspicionum offensionumque dantur, quas tum evitare, tum elevare, tum ferre sapientis est."

66. See Cic. *De Or.* 2.18.75–76, 3.14.55; *Orat.* 28–29; *Off.* 1.97.94; and G.C. Fiske, M.A. Grant, "Cicero's *De Oratore* and Horace's *Ars Poetica*," *University of Wisconsin Studies* XXVII (1929): 45

Horace, *Epistles* II and *Ars Poetica*

For a full bibliography see:

Brink, C.O. *Horace on Poetry*. Vol. I, *Prolegomena to the Literary Epistles*. Cambridge, 1963, pp. 273–86.

———. Vol. II, *The Ars Poetica*. Cambridge, 1971, pp. 524–27.

———. Vol. III, *Epistles, Book II*. Cambridge, 1982, pp. 573–77.

Kissel, W. "Horaz 1936–1975: Eine Gesamtbibliographie." *ANRW* II.31.3 (1981): 1403–1558.

Sbardone, F. "La poetica oraziana alla luce degli studi più recenti." *ANRW* II.31.3 (1981): 1866–1920.

Viola, A. *L'Arte Poetica nella critica italiana e straniera*. 2 vols., Napoli, 1901, 1906.

The following works are cited at least once in the notes.

Alföldi, A. *Die zwei Lorbeerbaüme des Augustus*. Bonn, 1973.

Allen, W., Jr. "'O fortunatam natam. . . '." *TAPA* LXXXVII (1956): 130–46.

Becker, C. *Das Spätwerk des Horaz*. Göttingen, 1963.

Boissier, G. "L'art Poétique d'Horace et la tragédie romaine." *RPh* XXII (1898): 1–17.

Bolaffi, E. "Probabili influssi platonici su Orazio." *Athen* n.s. XI (1933): 122–27.

Bringmann, K. "Struktur und Absicht des horazischen Briefes an Kaiser Augustus." *Phil* CXVIII (1974): 236–56.

Brink, C.O. "Cicero's *Orator* and Horace's *Ars Poetica.*" *Atti del II Colloquium Tullianum, Ciceroniana* n.s. II Rome, 1975, pp. 1–12.

———. *Horace on Poetry.* Vol. I, *Prolegomena to the Literary Epistles.* Cambridge, 1963, pp. 273–86.

———. Vol. II, *The Ars Poetica.* Cambridge, 1971, pp. 524–27.

———. Vol. III, *Epistles, Book II.* Cambridge, 1982, pp. 573–77.

Cauer, P. "Zur Abgrenzung und Verbindung der Theile in Horazens Ars Poetica." *RhM* LXI (1906): 234–43.

Classen, C.J. "Orazio Critico." *BStudLat* 1 (1971): 402–18.

Cody, J.V. *Horace and Callimachean Aesthetics: Coll. Lat.* CXLVII, Brussels, 1976.

Dilke, O.A.W. "When was the *Ars Poetica* Written?" *Bulletin of the Institute of Classical Studies* V, London, 1958: 49–57.

Doblhofer, E. *Die Augustuspanegyrik des Horaz in formal historischer Sicht.* Heidelberg, 1966.

Fantham, E. "Cicero, Varro, and Marcellus." *Phoenix* XXXI (1977): 208–13.

Fishwick, D. "Genius and numen." *HThR* LXII (1969): 356–67.

Fiske, G.C., Grant, M.A. "Cicero's *De Oratore* and Horace's *Ars Poetica.* *Univiversity of Wisconsin Studies* XXVII (1929).

Fraenkel, E. "Zur Form der αἶνοι." *RhM* LXXIII (1920): 366–70.

———. *Horace.* Oxford, 1957.

Gantar, K. "Die Anfangsverse und die Komposition der horazischen Epistel über die Dichtkunst." *SO* XXXIX (1964): 89–98.

Giuffrida, P. "Horat. *Epist.* II. i.118–138: Elogia o parodia?" in *Studi in Onore di Gino Funaioli*, Roma, 1955, pp. 98–119.

Gros, P. "Horace et la tentation du desert. Note sur *Epist.* I. II v. 7–10." *Mélanges P. Boyancé*, Rome, 1974, pp. 367–74.

Händel, P. "Zur Ars Poetica des Horaz." *RhM* CVI (1963): 164–86.

———. "Zur Augustusepistel des Horaz." *WS* LXXIX (1966): 383–96.

Herrmann, L. "Les deux parties de l'Art Poétique d'Horace." *Lat* XXIII (1964): 506–10.

Hupperth, W. *Horaz über die scaenicae origines der Römer.* Diss. Kölm, 1961.

Keller, O. *Epilegomena zu Horaz.* Leipzig, 1879.

Kettner, G. *Die Episteln des Horaz.* Berlin, 1900.

Kiessling, A., Heinze, R., Burck, E. *Q. Horatius Flaccus, Briefe.* Erklärt von Adolf Kiessling, bearbeitet von Richard Heinze. 7th ed. Berlin, 1961.

Kilpatrick, R.S. "Juvenal's 'patchwork' satires: 4 and 7." *YCS* XXIII (1973): 229–41.

———. *The Poetry of Friendship: Horace, Epistles I.* Edmonton, 1986.

Klingner, F. "Horazens Brief an Augustus." *SBBA* V (München, 1950) [*Studien*, pp. 410–432].

———. "Horazens Brief an die Pisonen." *BVSA* LXXVIII (Leipzig, 1937) [*Studien*, pp. 352–405].

———. "Horaz-Erkärungen." *Phil* XC (1935): 277–93, 461–68 [*Studien*, pp. 305–24]. (For *Epistle* 2.2 see pp. 464–68 [*Studien*, pp. 321–24].)

———. *Studien zur griechischen und römischen Literatur.* Zürich und Stuttgart, 1964.

Knoche, U. "Betrachtungen über Horazens Kunst der satirischen Gesprachsführung." *Phil* XC (1935): 469–82.

Krüger, G.T.A. *Des Q. Horatius Flaccus Satiren und Episteln. Zweites Bändchen. Episteln.* Leipzig, 1900.

Lehrs, K. *Q. Horatius Flaccus.* Leipzig, 1869.

Lejay, P. *Quintus Horatius Flaccus. Satires.* Paris, 1911.

Marouzeau, J. "L'art du nom propre chez Horace." *AC* (1935): 366–74.

Marshall, A.J. "Library resources and creative writing at Rome." *Phoenix* XXX (1976): 252–64.

McGann, M.J. "Horace's Epistle to Florus." *RhM* XCVII (1954): 343–58.

Mommsen, Th. "Die Literaturbriefe des Horaz." *H* XV (1880): 103–15.

Morris, E.P. *Horace. The Epistles. With Introduction and Notes.* New York, 1909.

Nettleship, H. "The De Arte Poetica." *JP* XII (1883): 43–61.

Newman, J.K. *Augustus and the New Poetry.* Bruxelles, 1967: 345–49.

Norden, E. "Die Composition und Litteraturgattung der Horazischen Epistula ad Pisones." *H* XL (1905): 481–528 [*Kleine Schriften zum Klassischen Altertum*, pp. 314–57].

———. *Kleine Schriften zum Klassischen Altertum.* Berlin, 1966.

Orelli, I.G. *Q. Horatius Flaccus*, 2 vols. Turin, 1852.

Packer, M.N. Porter. "Cicero, Horace and the New Academy." *TAPA* LXXX (1949): 430–31.

Pasoli, E. "Per una lettura dell' epistola di Orazio a Giulio Floro (*Epist.* 2.2). *Il Verri* XIX (1965): 129–41.

Perret, J. *Horace.* Paris, 1959. [Trans. Humez, B. N.Y., 1964].

Pierleoni, G. "L'Arte Poetica di Orazio e il De Or. di Cic." *Atene e Roma* VIII (1905): 251–59.

Pietrusinski, D. "L'apothéose d'Auguste par rapport à Romulus-Quirinus dans la poésie de Virgile et d'Horace." *Eos* LXIII (1975): 273–96.

Postgate, J.P. *Select Elegies of Propertius*. London, 1884.

Putnam, M.C.J. *Artifices of Eternity. Horace's Fourth Book of Odes*. Ithaca and London, 1986.

Ramain, G. "Horace, *Art Poétique*." *RPh* I (1927): 234–49.

Rostagni, A. *Arte Poetica di Orazio*. Torino, 1930.

Ruch, M. "Horace et les fondements de la *iunctura* dans l'ordre de la création poétique (*A.P.* 46–72)." *REL* XLI (1963): 246–69.

Rudd, N., ed. *Epistles Book II and Epistle to the Pisones ('Ars Poetica')*. Cambridge, 1989.

———. "Horace's poverty." *Hermath* LXXXIV (1954): 16–25.

Russell, D.A. "Ars Poetica" in Costa, C.D.N., ed. *Horace*. London, 1973, pp. 113–34.

Rutherford, R.B. "Horace, *Epistles* 2.2: Introspection and Retrospective." *CQ* XXXI (1981): 375–80.

Saint-Denis, E. de "La fantaisie et le coq-a-l'âne dans l'*Art poétique* d'Horace." *Lat* XXII (1963): 664–84.

Scaliger, J.C. *Poetice*. Lyon, 1561: *Praefatio in libros poetices ad Sylvium filium*. a.iiii, v. [repr. Stuttgart-Bad Cannstatt, 1964, intro. Buck, A.].

Schanz, M., Hosius, C. *Geschichte der römischen Literatur bis zum Gesetzgebungswerk des Kaiser*. München, 1927.

Sellar, A.Y. *The Roman Poets of the Augustan Age: Horace and the Elegiac Poets*. Oxford, 1899.

Spengle, L. "Horatius de arte poetica." *Phil* XVIII (1862): 94–108.

Syme, R. *History in Ovid*. Oxford, 1978.

———. "Piso Frugi et Cassius Frugi." *JRS* L (1960): 12–20.

Tracy, H.L. "Horace's Ars Poetica: A Systematic Argument." *G&R* XVII (1948): 104–15.

Vahlen, J. *Gesammelte philologische Schriften*, 2 vols. Leipzig und Berlin, 1911, 1923.

———. "Über Zeit und Abfolge der Literaturbriefe des Horatius." *Monatsber. Berlin, Ak.* (1878) [*Ges. Phil. Schr.* II (1923), pp. 46–61].

———. "Zu Horatius' Brief an Florus (II2)." *Zeit. f. öster. Gym.* XXV (1874) [*Ges. Phil. Schr.* I (1911), pp. 511–15].

Villeneuve, F. *Horace. Epîtres. Texte établi et traduit*. Paris, 1934.

Waszink, J.H. "Bemerkungen zu den Literaturbriefen des Horaz." *Mnem* XXI (1968): 394–407.

Weissenfels, O. "Aesthetisch-kritische Analyse der *Ep. ad Pis.* von Horaz." *Neues Lausitzisches Magazin* LVI (1880): 118-200.

White, P. "Horace *A.P.* 128–130: The intent of the wording." *CQ* XXVII (1977): 191–201.

———. "Horace, *Epistles* 2.1.50–54." *TAPA* CXVII (1987): 227–34.

Wickham, E.C. *The Works of Horace with a Commentary*, 2 vols. Oxford, 1891.

Wieland, C.M. *Horazens Briefe aus dem lateinischen übersetzt und mit historischen Einleitungen und anderen nöthigen Erlaüterungen versehen.* Leipzig, 1837.

Wili, W. *Horaz und die augusteische Kultur.* Basel, 1948.

Wilkins, A.S. *The Epistles of Horace. Edited with notes.* London, 1892.

Williams, G. *Horace.* Oxford, 1972.

———. "Review of C.O. Brink, *Horace on Poetry.*" [Vol. I], *JRS* LIV (1964): 186–96.

———. *CR* XXIV (1974): 52–57.

———. *Tradition and Originality in Roman Poetry.* Oxford, 1968.

Wimmel, W. "Apollo-Paupertas. Zur Symbolik von Berufungsvorgängen bei Properz, Horaz und Calpurnius." *Festschrift Büchner.* Wiesbaden, 1970, pp. 291–97.

Wimsatt, W.K. "'IAM NUNC DEBENTIA DICI': Answers to a Questionnaire." *Arion* IX (1970): 224–33.

Witte, K. "Der Literaturbrief des Horaz an Augustus." *Raccolta . . . in onore di F. Ramorino.* Milano, 1927, pp. 404–20.

Winnington-Ingram, R.P. "Two Latin idioms." *CR* V (1955): 139–41.

Special Bibliography to note on emendation of *Ars P.* 65 (pp. 84-85).

Delz, J. "Glossen in Horaztext," *MH* XXX (1973): 51–54.

———. "Textkritische Versuche an der *Ars Poetica* des Horaz," *MH* XXXVI (1979): 142–52.

Fabri, G. *Ravenna Ricercata.* Bologna, 1578.

Hutton, E. *The Story of Ravenna.* London and New York, 1926.

Jacini, C. *Il Viaggio del Po*, 4 vols. Milano, 1937–1945.

Jordanes, *De origine actibusque Getarum (Getica).* Ed. Mommsen, MGH (English trans. and comm. C.C. Mierow). Princeton, 1915.

Kiepert, H. *Lehrbuch der Alten Geographie.* Berlin, 1978.

Myers, A.L. *The Use of the Adjective as a Substantive in Horace.* Diss. U. of Penn., 1919.

Nicol, J. *The Historical and Geographical Sources Used by Silius Italicus.* Oxford, 1936.

Olschki, L. *The Genius of Italy.* New York, 1949.

Philippson, A. *Das Mittelmeergebiet.* Leipzig, 1904.

Radke, G. "Die Strasse des Konsuls P. Popillius in Oberitalien." *Lat* XXIV (1965): 815–23.

Salmon, E.T. *Roman Colonization under the Republic.* London, 1969.

Schwartz, J. "Horace, Art Poétique, v. 63–69." *RPh* XXI (1947): 49–54.

Tozzi, P. *Saggi di Topografia Grafica.* Firenze, 1974.

———. *Storia Padana Antica.* Milano, 1972.

Uggeri, G. *La Romanizzazione dell' Antico Delta Padano.* Ferrara, 1975.

Ward-Perkins, J.B. *Cities of Ancient Greece and Italy: Planning in Classical Antiquity.* New York, 1974

Ancient Authors

General Index

● CONTENTS

List of contributors (alphabetical)

Jon Atkins	Emma Kirk	Sally Rendall
Rob Barkworth	Stephan Lucks	Ceri Roderick
Sean Boyle	Joe MacAree	Paul Rose
Clíona Diggins	Ken McKenzie	Maraliese Spies
Polly Howard-De La Mare	James Meachin	Clair Thurgood
Holly Jones	Padraig Neary	Emma Trenier
Simi Jutla	Neil O'Brien	Maggie Van Den Heuval
Laura Haycock	Paula Philips	Louise Weston

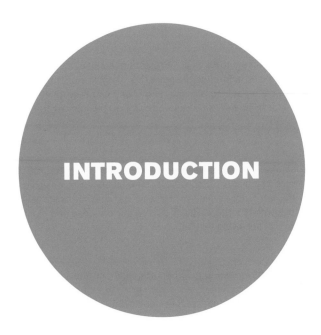

INTRODUCTION

This book is one of three in a series of leadership books based on the coaching experiences of Pearn Kandola Business Psychologists. Any manager aspiring to lead others will have a compelling interest in their own personal development. As coaches and experts in leadership skills, we have created iLEAD™, a series of three unique books based on the most important elements of business psychology.

Over the past thirty years we have coached leaders from hundreds of different organisations across all sectors. Using a combination of our own models and the best emerging research, we have helped those leaders to engage in change and further their development.

Now, for the first time, we have captured these models in three distinct books, one focused on people leadership, one on task leadership and one on thought leadership. Each book offers a chance for any manager to use some basic but essential psychology to help to improve and develop your approach.

A Model of Leadership

Each iLEAD™ tool provides immediate insights and new ways of thinking about management and leadership challenges. There are also a range of interactive exercises to develop new understanding and practise new skills.

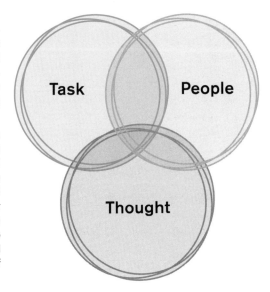

The iLEAD™ tools are based on our own strategic model of leadership, known as the Leadership Radar™. The model recognises that there are three core areas of leadership: People, Task and Thought. We use the analogy of a radar because leaders need to have an awareness of these three core areas to fulfil their role and be aware of where and how they use their time across each of the three areas.

People Leadership

The people leader inspires others towards achievement of ambitious goals through a combination of communication, influencing and engagement skills. They are openly passionate about what they aim to achieve, yet caring and considerate in the way that they approach others. They know that people are their most valuable resource and will do their utmost to secure and retain the commitment of their teams.

Task Leadership

The task leader drives others towards achievement of ambitious goals through a combination of determination, resilience and clarity of focus. They take ultimate responsibility for the quality and delivery of results, and are highly skilled in the way that they delegate tasks and ensure that others are aware of the priority targets. They optimise performance and realise the full talents of the people around them in achieving results.

Thought Leadership

The thought leader constantly looks to new opportunities and the future. They quickly evaluate complex and ambiguous situations and are ready to analyse and challenge tough decisions. The thought leader initiates changes and improvements, and is imaginative and open to taking entrepreneurial risk.

Leadership Styles

There is clearly more than one way to lead. Leadership draws on a diversity of talent and resources, and the most effective leaders understand how to make the most of the situations and people around them. The keys to successful leadership therefore are self-awareness and the capacity to change. While we may at times understand the attributes of leadership, we can often struggle to demonstrate these at the times when they are most needed.

Our aim, therefore, is always to equip leaders with the skills they need, and more importantly to provide them with the motivation and desire to lead. The iLEAD™ tools address both of these challenges.

We hope you not only enjoy reading the tools, but also find ways to make immediate and practical use of them in your own approach to leadership.

OWNING

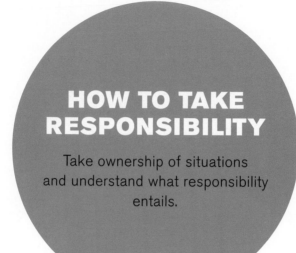

HOW TO TAKE RESPONSIBILITY

Take ownership of situations and understand what responsibility entails.

● ISN'T IT INTERESTING?

What would you do in an emergency?

Calm in an emergency?

Everybody likes to think that they would keep a calm head in a crisis, help another in a time of need or at least call the police in an emergency. However, research into a phenomenon known as the 'bystander effect' may suggest otherwise.[1] When others are present, observers can assume that someone else will intervene, and so they each individually refrain from doing so; in effect we feel less responsible. People may also assume that other bystanders are more qualified to help, such as doctors or police officers, and their intervention would thus be unnecessary or even unwanted. This can be due to a fear of losing 'face' in front of others or being superseded by a better helper.

'Using your loaf'

Before the discovery of the 'bystander effect' there was an investigation into a similar effect which occurred in the structure of work. What was discovered is a phenomenon commonly referred to as 'social loafing'.[2] This is where a group of individuals working on a task together will personally contribute less effort than if they were working on their own. This is a subtle effect and was first shown in a simple rope-pulling exercise, where individuals exerted less energy pulling the rope as part of a group than as an individual.[3]

There are ways to prevent yourself and others from being a 'loafer', such as recording individual work, assigning specific roles, and increasing communication and collaboration within the team. Often, the most common reason for loafing is feeling that any effort will not be utilised or recognised, so a sense of personal responsibility can be critical to our overall effectiveness in work.

This tool can help

Standing by or taking responsibility in an emergency is not a situation that most of us have to face very often. However, there are everyday instances at work when there is the chance to take responsibility. This tool is all about **how to take responsibility** and will help you to take ownership of situations and understand what responsibility entails.

● TAKING RESPONSIBILITY

Imagine you're in the office, about to print off those reports but the copier's out of toner. Why didn't whoever used it last replace it? The stationery cupboard is chaotic and you need to step over things and look behind other things to find what you need. Why do people leave such a mess? Why isn't someone responsible for keeping it tidy – and checking the copiers, too, come to think of it? And, why don't you?

It's the kind of mildly irritating situation we all recognise, and undoubtedly contribute to. What about, however, a situation similarly caused, but cranked up to a critical level – resulting in major catastrophe or even loss of life? What about the whole concept of 'collective responsibility' and what history reveals about that?

It's complex. However, for your purposes, we offer some general principles to help you to be more responsible and thereby more productive, efficient and motivated. This diagram's a good start:

The 'Taking Responsibility' model presents us with five potential blockages to taking responsibility. Here we will look at the evidence for how they can affect you and others, and show you how to tackle the challenges they present.

Fear of failure

Psychologists would argue that we're conditioned from childhood to seek approval from others. This can result in many of us avoiding opportunities to try something new in case we might get it 'wrong'. In the workplace we sidestep relatively trivial actions we wouldn't think twice about at home or elsewhere, rather than risk criticism or failure. However, there are ways of overcoming fears which stop us from applying ourselves when we can't guarantee success. We'll also demonstrate the benefits we can gain from our efforts, whatever the outcome. We'll explain these in the following sections.

Lack of interest

If we don't want to do something we'll avoid it if we can, or get someone else to do it. In the following pages, you'll discover ways to motivate people by linking their personal goals to those of the team, or the organisation.

Lack of time

You'd be surprised, but if you look closely you'll notice how unproductive 'busy' people can be! We'll talk about this later, too.

Lack of expertise

Expertise, knowledge – they're words that frighten a lot of us. Usually, you'll discover you only need to focus on what is specific to the task in hand, and it's often easily available. We'll describe how to find it.

Not knowing how to take responsibility

You may be willing to take responsibility, but not sure how to or how to persuade others that you are. We'll guide you.

● FEAR OF FAILURE

Step 1 – Identify

Take some time to think about what it is, exactly, that you're frightened of. Write it down, all of it. Once it's defined, it's easier to tackle.

Step 2 – Evaluate

Is your fear irrational? Again, write down exactly what might happen if you did fail. Will you have to leave the country? Will it be the main item on the ten o'clock news? Or, are you just telling yourself it'll confirm all the negative self-talk that's been going on since you let in that penalty, when you were eleven? We're often our own harshest critics. Consider whether you would be as critical of a friend who failed at this task – then, treat yourself in the same way.

Here are some ways to get fears in proportion:

Challenging Your Worries	
Keep a journal	Jot down what's worrying you. In a few days or weeks, write the outcome. Things usually work out better than we imagined.
Focus on now	The next time a thought threatens to escalate into anxiety, bring yourself back into 'now'. Snap your fingers, focus on your breathing or do something else to distract yourself.
So, prove you're a failure	Visualise important events during the last 10 years. In most cases we can't remember how we worried about them beforehand. Even if you do remember a little, it'll help to prove that things generally turn out well. Tell yourself that what's worrying you now will fade away, too.

Step 3 – Re-interpret

If you think a thought often enough, it becomes a belief. Try to work through the layers of your fear and find what the root of it really is. Is it, in fact, just that you really, really want to succeed and are uncertain how to ensure you do? Or, is it something someone else has said, or experienced, which you have 'taken on board'?

Step 4 – Take action!

Doing nothing is often counterproductive, because the longer you do nothing the more your fears take root and grow! Think, instead, of the positives that will result from each small decision or step you take, and what you will gain or learn from them. If you're still convinced some of your fears are justified, remember that there is more than one way to achieve anything – get creative. Having alternative strategies will give you confidence.

> If you can, it's often useful to involve others, if only to sound out your ideas or put your fears into perspective.

● LACK OF INTEREST

Step 1 – What motivates you?

Each of us is motivated by different things. You may be surprised by research which reveals that the opportunity to learn frequently motivates people more than money. So, what motivates you or your colleagues, which could relate to the current situation? Suggesting what people may achieve personally will often spur them into action.

Step 2 – Appreciate the bigger picture

The task you or others have been avoiding might seem mundane or unrewarding, but have far-reaching overall impact. Recognising how a single issue or task dovetails into a 'bigger picture' can re-ignite flagging interest.

Step 3 – The 'Psychological contract'

This is the implicit understanding and trust between people engaged in fulfilling objectives or tasks together, or between those who give instructions and others who carry them out. Unlike a legal contract, it's unwritten and usually unspoken, yet understood and expected by those involved. It accounts for the kind of things we all do (or don't do!) in the workplace and elsewhere, which aren't detailed in job descriptions, but to which we 'psychologically contract', as members of a larger group or organisation. (For example, checking the office building's secure when you're last to leave is something you might do, even though you're not the caretaker, it's a pain to do and you're already late, anyway.)

Step 4 – Be the benchmark for others

They don't, so why should I? An organisation's ethos or 'culture' is determined less by its policies and procedures than by the behaviour of its employees. It only takes the example of a single individual to influence many others.

Remember, the tool 'How to motivate others' might help you to identify what motivates you.

● LACK OF TIME

Step 1 – What is there to do?

Write it down, all of it. Simple, but best. This way, your mind stops buzzing and you can finally hear yourself think. Not only does it look less than you were imagining or trying to remember, but you'll find you'll start coming up with the 'how to's' as you list and define things.

Step 2 – The need to prioritise: 'The 80:20 rule'

Why is it that some 'busy' people never seem to finish what they're busying about? The Pareto Principle (also called the '80:20 rule') reveals that, generally, 80% of what we achieve results from only 20% of the effort we put into it! There'll always be 'too much to do' if we don't focus on the most immediate tasks, first. In other words, to be more effective, prioritise…

Step 3 – How to prioritise

High urgency and low importance	High urgency and high importance
Low urgency and low importance	Low urgency and high importance

- Put each task on your 'to do' list in one of the boxes on the table.
- Break them down into smaller, manageable bits with a deadline for each bit.
- Assess (seriously, now!) whether the less urgent tasks are, in fact, just distractions.
- If not, add them to the lower boxes on the table.
- Get going with your priorities!

Step 4 – Ask for help

If you really do have too much to do, then get some help. You may be able to delegate some items, or, if you've been given things to do by someone else, ask them to help you prioritise your workload in the time you have available. Much overload results from our saying 'yes' out of habit or because we want to appear helpful. If demand on your time is going to make you ineffective, however, you're not doing yourself or anyone else any favours.

Step 5 – Avoid distractions

Here are the worst offenders:

Distractions and Solutions	
Emails	Just because you can, you really don't have to reply to that message RIGHT NOW! The best thing about speedy communications and other techno wizardry is that you can make it work around you. For now, you could turn your screen alert off.
Colleagues	Just let them know you need to concentrate for a while and that you look forward to catching up with them later. It's not a big deal, we all need a bit of time and space from time to time to get on with important tasks. You'll understand when they ask the same of you.
Ourselves	It's surprising, the things we suddenly notice that need our attention, before getting down to whatever it is we haven't had time to do yet! You may tell yourself you'll concentrate better once you've tidied the cupboard/desk/room, or nipped out to get that thing before stocks run out, but we know it's all nonsense. Just think, once you really have done it, won't that feel good?

By applying the tips and skills in this section you can optimise your effort to ensure that you concentrate as much of your time and energy as possible on the most important and relevant tasks. This ensures that you achieve the greatest benefit possible with the limited amount of time available to you.

KNOWING HOW TO TAKE RESPONSIBILITY

Step 1 – What is your objective?

Make sure you know where your responsibility starts and ends and exactly what you've been asked to achieve.

Step 2 – What needs to be done?

And by when? Once you're clear about this you can 'map' separate stages against a timescale, so you can monitor progress or delays. Reaching each stage will also give you a sense of achievement along the way.

Step 3 – Who needs to be involved?

Even if a team has already been chosen for the task or project, check that each member is assigned a role in which they feel confident.

Step 4 – Ensure others know you are leading

Make yourself a part of the team and easily available to give and receive feedback. It's a mistake to think you can lead effectively by marching ahead and shouting over your shoulder.

Step 5 – Get stuck in!

Look for some 'quick wins' to develop confidence and gain momentum – it'll help confirm your leadership to yourself as well as others!

NEXT STEPS

Having read the tool the next step is to act in order to take responsibility. All the research suggests that planning how you will achieve your goal makes it much more likely that you will do so in reality:

- Consider what you've read here, and what is most relevant to you
- Identify how you can apply it to a specific situation
- Think, not only about what you could do but what may deter you
- Think of solutions for these potential problems in advance, so you can deal with them or produce alternatives, if necessary.

FINALLY...

Finally, enlist the support of others. Knowing you have access to advice will increase your personal and professional effectiveness.

● FURTHER INFORMATION

If you found this tool useful then you are likely to find the following tools both insightful and relevant:

- How to take control
- How to develop strategic long-term goals
- How to focus on the bigger picture
- How to balance risk with potential benefits
- How to be confident in making judgement calls
- How to make timely decisions
- How to delegate.

● REFERENCES

1   Darley, J. & Latané, B. (1968). Bystander intervention in emergencies: Diffusion of responsibility. Journal of Personality and Social Psychology, 8, 377-383.

2   Liden, R. C., Wayne, S. J., Jaworski, R. A., & Bennett, N. (2004). Social loafing: A field investigation. Journal of Management, 30(2), 285-304.

3   Latané, B., Williams, K. & Harkins, S. (1979). Many hands make light the work: The causes and consequences of social loafing. Key Readings in Social Psychology, 1, 297.

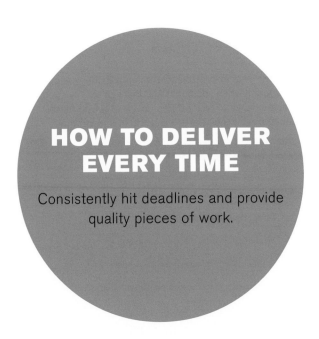

HOW TO DELIVER EVERY TIME

Consistently hit deadlines and provide quality pieces of work.

● ISN'T IT INTERESTING?

Aeroplanes are remarkable machines that can, depending on your view of the world, do wonderful things. But each aeroplane needs people to make it work.

Deliver every time

In 1974, researchers Tversky and Kahneman[1] described how an Israeli flight school decided to employ an interesting approach to try enhance trainee pilots' performance, to ensure perfect delivery of manoeuvres every time.

To praise or not to praise?

The instructors' initial approach was to praise students when they made excellent landings and criticise when the landings were less smooth. However, they soon noticed that the performance of those students who had warranted praise would nearly always decline on their next attempt, whereas those who had received criticism for particularly bad landings almost always subsequently improved. The solution seemed clear; criticism must be more effective than praise in managing performance and ensuring perfect delivery of manoeuvres. Instructors, they suggested, should refrain from giving praise and use criticism instead.

What the flight instructors didn't realise, however, is that they were witnessing a statistical principle called 'regression to the mean'; regardless of the type of feedback a pilot received, an outstanding performance can be expected to deteriorate at the next attempt and a terrible performance can be expected to improve. This is because it's difficult, perhaps impossible, to maintain an extreme performance at either end of the spectrum. At some point the performance will move towards the average.

This tool can help

It seems that giving or receiving criticism is only one part of the puzzle to enhancing performance, and should be combined with other methods to help ensure delivery. This tool is all about **how to deliver every time** and will help you to consistently hit deadlines and provide quality pieces of work.

● THE DELIVERY PROCESS

We'll bet you sometimes feel your efforts to achieve things in the time given are taken for granted, because you only hear about it when you don't! And that's exactly our point. While those you work with are undoubtedly appreciative of your efforts, failure to deliver reliably (however infrequently), inevitably raises issues of trust, especially if it impacts their own work.

However, as is so often the case, once you have a method, it's easy. Our model outlines the processes necessary to ensure effective, timely delivery:

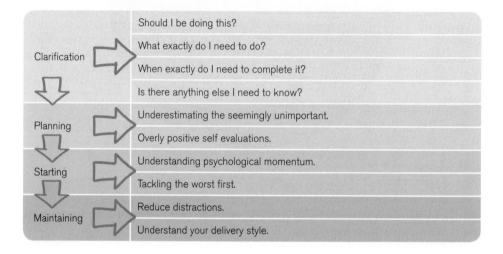

Clarification	Should I be doing this?
	What exactly do I need to do?
	When exactly do I need to complete it?
	Is there anything else I need to know?
Planning	Underestimating the seemingly unimportant.
	Overly positive self evaluations.
Starting	Understanding psychological momentum.
	Tackling the worst first.
Maintaining	Reduce distractions.
	Understand your delivery style.

● CLARIFYING WHAT NEEDS TO BE DELIVERED

The way to make sure you always deliver is to ask yourself (and whoever else may be involved) the following questions – don't be tempted to steam ahead before doing this...

- **Should I be doing this?**
  Never begin a task without checking the appropriateness of your involvement – and do it in a way that makes it clear you're not trying to avoid responsibility! Explain that effective delivery is dependent upon giving the task to whoever is most able or likely to fulfil it successfully.

- **What exactly do I need to do?**
  Effective delivery is about more than 'getting things done', it's about producing what is needed. Clarify your understanding of the task in as much detail as you can. Contact the key stakeholder (by email ideally, so you have a written record) and ask for confirmation that you correctly understand requirements and expectations.

- **When exactly do I need to complete it?**
  You might complete the task successfully, but if it's a day after the deadline it'll still be less effective, less useful or even redundant. Make sure you clarify when the work is needed.

- **Is there anything else I need to know?**
  Sometimes, you may only discover something which would have been useful to know while you were working on the task, after its completion. This could be unknown requirements or end uses which you need to factor into your planning.

Now, you should have a much clearer idea of the 'what' 'why' and 'when', which makes it easier to work out 'how.'

● PLANNING A TASK EFFECTIVELY

Although you can learn how to plan, you may not realise that there are predictable, psychological processes which will affect the process. Understanding these processes will greatly assist you to deliver consistently. Two of them are described below:

Never underestimate what you think is unimportant

When planning a project we have a natural tendency to pay attention to obvious requirements. These are things that will be time consuming and/or important. As a result, they are uppermost in our minds. However, the opposite is also true. We will naturally underestimate the impact of small or seemingly unimportant demands on our time. Examples include unexpected requests from clients or colleagues, dealing with administrative tasks and responding to emails and phone messages. These seem unimportant because they're never very prominent in our thinking. However, they all add up and can take up a significant amount of our available time. Think, for example, about the kind of project you estimate would take about five days to complete. Now, try to remember the last time you had five totally free days in which you could concentrate on one task, without having to deal with other demands or people. Probably never!

Don't overestimate positive self evaluations

We have a natural tendency to overestimate our own abilities. As Myers[2] noted: 'On nearly any dimension that is both subjective and socially desirable, most people see themselves as better than average.' Because planning and completing a task is as much art as science, our estimates are inherently subjective. In other words, we often discover we can't do something as quickly or as well as we thought we could!

● STARTING A TASK

Even those of us who are good at planning tasks effectively often find it hard to get started. Most people know how to prioritise tasks, but still put off important things. Here are another two psychological principles that are key to helping you get going.

Understanding psychological momentum

We are likely to put off a task if we feel we don't have the 'momentum' to get started (and we all know how easy that is). However, by better understanding how we (wrongly) think about 'psychological momentum', you can avoid this common pitfall.

The way we think about psychological momentum is similar to the way we think about the physical momentum of objects.[3] For example, there's the story of the basketball players who were told that the team they were about to play had previously beaten their arch rivals in a tough local derby. They predicted that their chances of winning were much less than other teams, who were told only that the team had won their last match. This is because the idea of a 'tough local derby' gave the team's psychological momentum greater 'mass'!

Similarly, imagine pushing a heavy weight along the ground, then losing your momentum. How hard do you think it would be to get started again? We tend to think progress will be harder after we've had psychological momentum, but then lost it. For example, students were told that a woman called Jane was working on a research paper before being interrupted by a phone call.

Students who were told Jane had been focused and 'on a roll' before the call, rated her chances of completing the paper after the phone call as much less than other students, who'd been told Jane was simply working at a steady pace prior to the interruption.

Tackling the worst first

Avoidance-based coping (that is, putting off tasks that you've been dreading) is an ineffective strategy. It makes you more likely to miss deadlines and the cumulative anxiety it causes will distract you from other responsibilities, also.

● MAINTAINING EFFORT

Once you have started working, delivering every time means maintaining effort and concentration. When our concentration is interrupted (for example, to make a phone call, or check an email), it is difficult to re-engage in what we were doing beforehand. Regular interruptions have the same effect as temporarily reducing our IQ. In particular, it has been found that the average worker's functioning IQ temporarily drops 10 points when multitasking. This highlights the importance of reducing distractions.[4]

Decide which method of delivery you use and how you maintain momentum – or change your approach in different situations:

Delivery Style	Definition
Initiator	Starts but gets bored quickly. Has a strong push to initiate tasks and projects but after initial effort loses momentum to complete the work.
Completer	Always finishes work they start. Maintains momentum throughout the task until completed. May not initiate tasks.
Interested	Only completes the work if interested in the content. Otherwise, will move on to or be distracted by something more interesting.
Plodder	Takes a methodical approach when undertaking the task or project and proceeds slowly but steadily through the work. They may seem to lack energy to work quickly and effectively.
Delegator	Gives various elements of the work to other people to complete. May not have enough time for the work or would rather use others to complete the tasks.
Gladiator	Someone who always points out risks and challenges if the work is not being completed to their standards. They may come across as obstructive or combative.
Daydreamer	Not focused on the practical delivery, rather enjoys the more abstract, strategic element of the work. Prefers to do the thinking and leave others to carry out the practical elements of the task.
Procrastinator	Will not complete the work until the last minute. Leaves difficult things to the end and often does the planning rather than the activity required.
Enthusiast	Two steps ahead of everyone else. Highly involved and keen for the work to be completed but often works at own pace and leaves others behind. Can get frustrated easily.

Now, consider the different situations outlined in the table on the next page and write down how you (honestly) think you would go about achieving an objective to deadline and what you would do in each situation to maintain momentum. If this reveals that you would use different methods in the various situations, think how, in future, you could amalgamate these methods to achieve consistent, effective delivery.

Situation	My Delivery Style	What to do to Maintain Effort	My Ideal Delivery Style
Typical style			
Under general pressure			
Feeling great			
Time pressured			
Delivering through others			
Deadline approaching			

Where different situations have caused you to alter your method of delivery think about the following:

- What you can do to begin incorporating your 'ideal style' in that situation. It may be that your ideal style is simply your typical style, but that in certain situations it's less effective. If this is so, think about how you can try to use your typical delivery style in as many situations as possible, while being flexible when necessary.

- If your ideal style is different from your current approach, think of people around you who demonstrate both methods, and then work out what you need to do differently to begin adopting the behaviour/results you would like to emulate.

● ENSURE THAT YOU DELIVER EVERY TIME

When trying to deliver work on time you may have problems to overcome. Some of the most common are listed below – with solutions!

Issue	Solution
Underestimating the seemingly unimportant	The solution is to recognise our tendency to underestimate the impact of seemingly unimportant events and to build in a 20% contingency to our initial plan. For example, instead of allowing 5 days for the project, we would allocate 6 days.
Overly positive self evaluations	The solution, as before, is to allow a 20% contingency and to ensure that all of the potential risks and threats have been considered. Covering all angles will ensure that you don't have an unrealistic perception of success.
Maintaining momentum	It is important to understand what people will respond to in order to maintain momentum. Some people may need positive reinforcement to keep going; others will need strict deadlines and guidance. Think about what it is that will help you to maintain momentum. For more information see the tool 'How to maintain momentum until the completion of every task'.
Putting off difficult tasks	If the worst task on your schedule can be completed first thing in the morning, then think how much more enjoyable and productive the rest of your day will be!
Maintaining effort	Identify regular sources of disruptions (e.g. instant messaging or internet surfing) and minimise them. For example, turn off your email message alert and switch your phone over to voice mail.

In the tables on the following pages, write the names of three managers you have worked with or for, under the titles at the top of the table.

From the five solutions listed, identify two demonstrated by each of your managers. Then, for each manager, choose one solution which has influenced your own way of trying to achieve effective delivery. As you write your answers in the table (or in a notepad, if it's easier) think about the following:

- How did this solution impact on the delivery of the work or project?
- Was it a key driver for success?
- Think of a time when you have used that solution; how effective was it?
- What did you learn about your ability to deliver?

● DELIVERY SOLUTIONS EXERCISE

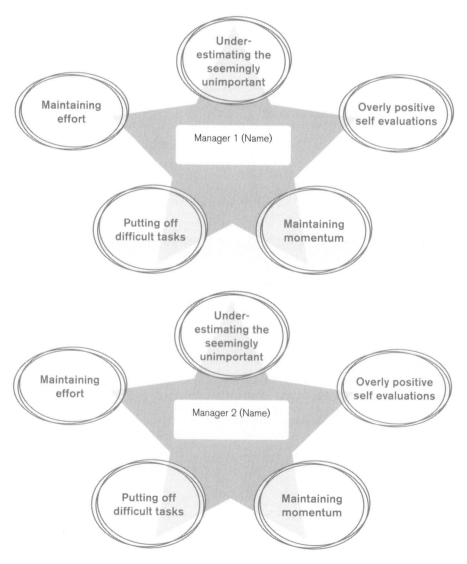

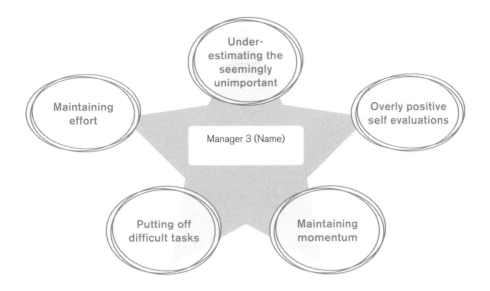

● NEXT STEPS

Now you know what effective and consistent delivery of tasks and projects involves, here are suggestions about what to do next (although this list is by no means exhaustive).

Gather feedback on existing performance

You may find it useful to ask for formal or informal feedback, to understand how other people perceive you and get advice about where you can make modifications or improvements. You can also use this information to manage people's future expectations about your approach and ability to deliver.

Consider your role model

Try and identify someone you know who you admire for their delivery. Think about what it is you admire about their approach. This is the starting point for you to develop a plan to improve – see below.

Discuss delivery style with someone

Talk about your delivery style with someone you trust, such as your line manager, mentor, coach or colleague. Think about what you want from this person – do you want a sounding board? Do you want advice and guidance or do you want someone to help review and check your progress?

Write a development plan

Use this tool to write out a personal, focused development plan.

Look for opportunities to practise

Watch out for opportunities in your current work or elsewhere, where you can study the kind of methods you admire.

● FURTHER INFORMATION

If you found this tool useful then you are likely to find the following tools both insightful and relevant:

- How to maintain momentum
- How to prioritise tasks ready for action
- How to direct people
- How to take control
- How to cope with setbacks
- How to win and manage resources
- How to delegate
- How to engage others to deliver.

● REFERENCES

1   Tversky, A. & Kahneman, D. (1974). Judgement under uncertainty: Heuristics and biases. **Science**, 185, 1124-1131

2   Myers, D. (1996). **Social Psychology.** McGraw-Hill, New York.

3   Markman, K. & Guenther, C. (2007). Psychological momentum: Intuitive physics and naïve beliefs. **Personality and Social Psychology Bulletin**, 33, 800-812.

4   Hewlett Packard. (2005, April). **Abuse of technology can reduce UK workers' intelligence: HP calls for more appropriate use of "always-on" technology to improve productivity.**

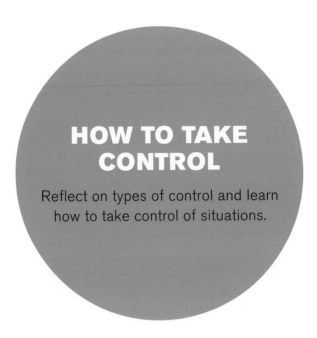

HOW TO TAKE CONTROL

Reflect on types of control and learn how to take control of situations.

● ISN'T IT INTERESTING?

An orchestra is a collection of highly talented, dedicated individuals, but only one person, the conductor, can assume responsibility and take control of proceedings. If this doesn't happen, chaos results.

The right blend

The study below shows the types of qualities that might make up a great conductor. Just like an orchestra conductor, understanding how and when to take control is one of the critical attributes of being a leader. Vroom & Jago[1] outlined some common decision making styles of leaders ranging from making decisions alone, consulting with others before making decisions, to having a fully collaborative approach. They noted that each approach has its own merits but all have far reaching consequences.

Virtuoso performance?

In 2007, two psychologists, Boerner & von Streit,[2] examined orchestral performance. They found two key elements; suggesting that the orchestra's individual players must be emotionally 'in tune' with each other and also that leadership style of the conductor affects group success.

They studied 22 German orchestras, looking at leadership style (as well as cohesiveness of the orchestra), and rated the orchestras on their overall level of artistic quality.

The results showed that the most highly rated orchestras had conductors who were charismatic (the orchestra was proud to work with them), inspirational (motivate the orchestra by making it clear what is required) and intellectually stimulating (often suggest new interpretations).

This tool can help

Taking control is a demanding process – the manager or team leader has to understand if their approach and abilities are matched to the task and the people at hand. Awareness of our strengths and limitations is necessary if sound decision making is to result. This tool is all about how to take control and will help you to reflect on types of control and provide you with guidance on taking control of situations.

● A CONTROL MODEL

Collins English Dictionary defines control as 'the power to direct something'. Controlling situations at work is an important aspect of a manager's job. You need to demonstrate an ability to control or direct a situation to achieve the best possible outcome for the business.

'A person's ability to control his or her work activities'[3] as the theory tells us, requires knowledge of which skills are needed to achieve a particular result, an ability to make decisions – and the authority to do so. Simple, except when (and we've all been here) your team is unmotivated or you don't have the authority to make a particular decision. Or perhaps you're faced with an unusually tricky or ambiguous situation and your confidence in your own abilities suddenly evaporates! iLEAD™ is the very thing to help you in any of these circumstances…

Lack of autonomy at work is a key 'stressor', especially when yours is a demanding job. Here's a model of how control – or the lack of it – affects stress levels.[4]

Control	Demands	
	Low	High
High	Low strain	Active
Low	Passive	High strain

So, the optimum combination would be to have a demanding job plus a high degree of control over how you do it, which promotes 'active learning' (learning through doing). The most stressful combination is a demanding job with little control over how you do it.

We want to help you gain greater control so that, depending on how demanding your job is, you are either less stressed or have more opportunity to 'actively learn'.

Here are two ways of taking control of a situation:

1. Through direct, personal control, using skills and resources to get the desired outcomes.

2. Through 'socially mediated, proxy control', which means influencing others to get the result you want – you'll need to be charming and/or persuasive for that one!

● LOCUS OF CONTROL

Your 'locus of control' is one factor that will influence your direct personal control. Some people think what they do and the mistakes they make affect what happens to them, so they feel in control of outcomes. Others believe that fate plays a large part in what happens and that 'what will be, will be' no matter what they do. These feelings relate to their 'locus of control' which is best thought of in terms of a continuum:

External   Internal

Believe in fate, things happen independent of their actions.

Outcomes are determined by your hard work and decisions.

Whilst there is no 'right' or 'wrong' with either belief, research reveals that having an internal locus of control makes a person feel more in control of outcomes. Without this you are likely to be less motivated to take control at work.

Identify your locus of control

Here are two situations to help you think about your potential reaction to certain situations and whether they are typical of someone with an internal or external locus of control (LOC). For each, consider which reaction you think is most like your own and look at the positive and negative factors associated with it.

Scenario 1

Scenario: Imagine you have applied for a job that you really want. You are very excited about the type of work and think the company will be great to work for. You're asked to attend an interview, but it doesn't go very well and you're not successful in getting the job.

Possible reaction (internal LOC): You're really disappointed that you did not get the job and decide that, next time an opportunity arises, you must work really hard to be the best candidate.

Positives: You are going to take control and give yourself a better chance of getting the job you want next time.

Negatives: You may feel very disappointed and negative about your abilities. You may need to control your emotional response.

Possible reaction (external LOC): You quickly get over the disappointment as you decide that it obviously wasn't meant to be.

Positives: You can quickly overcome the setback.

Negatives: You may not be giving yourself a good chance of getting the job you want in future because you fail to recognise your weaknesses.

Scenario 2

Scenario: You have moved to a new organisation, and due to being a new arrival, your internal network is not excellent, and you feel you are missing out on support and exciting projects.

Possible reaction (internal LOC): You have decided to organise an informal meeting with influential people in your area in order to become acquainted.

Positives: You will now be on approachable terms with individuals who can provide you with resources and allow you to influence decisions through them.

Negatives: Some people may feel that you are trying to increase your influence without it having occurred naturally over time, which may give the wrong impression.

Possible reaction (external LOC): You don't take specific action and wait to bump into people by chance. You think that meeting the right people is down to fate.

Positives: You can allow yourself to influence people based on your merits, and allow yourself to be noticed due to your positive traits.

Negatives: You may continue to miss out on key events while you wait to become a more integral part of a work network.

● TIPS FOR TAKING CONTROL

External locus of control

If you have an external locus of control you may avoid taking action because you feel the outcome is beyond your control. However, feeling you lack control can negatively affect your performance and ability to meet demands. Try to focus more on the things that could positively influence your situation.

Here are some tips to help you:

> **Set yourself clear and challenging goals** (See 'Goal Setting' on page 25). This will help you to define what you want to achieve and see a clear link between your actions and the desired outcomes.

Build your self-confidence in your ability to influence outcomes

Setting yourself challenging and achievable goals will help. Once you have achieved them, your confidence will grow. Evaluate your performance – think constructively about something you did that led to a positive outcome and something else that didn't. Consider what you could do differently next time.

Motivate yourself to take control and influence the situation

See section on Gaining Control on pages 25 and 26 of this tool.

Develop your problem-solving skills

Try to break down a problem or situation into manageable tasks/goals. Start by defining the desired outcome (the objective) and think about how you might go about achieving it (goals). Think about the influence you can have rather than the influence you don't have.

Internal Locus of Control

If you have an internal rather than external locus of control you are likely to be more prepared to take control of a situation. This is because you already believe that what you do will influence a situation and are likely to work hard towards achieving your desired outcome. You may, therefore, feel you don't need advice. However, there are potential negatives. People with a strong internal locus of control tend to be very achievement-orientated, which can mean those around you feel overlooked. Because you focus on making things happen, you may try to control everything! Again, this may damage your relationships with others and cause you to overload yourself.

> Think about others, especially if you're managing a team. Involve all team members in setting (and achieving) goals. Don't steam ahead with the task in hand leaving others behind.

When taking control try to remember

Consider others' feelings. You tend to be very achievement-orientated and may give little consideration to your team's feelings. However, you need your team's commitment to perform at their best, so make sure you have regular meetings or catch-ups and listen to what others tell you.

Don't overload yourself, delegate some responsibility to others

You can do this while maintaining overall control, and this will enable you to focus on the 'bigger picture' while letting others feel involved.

Don't be too hard on yourself

We can control much of what happens in our lives – but not everything!

● GAINING CONTROL

The following section is about how to use motivation as a positive force at work. Motivation will help you to take control of a situation. This includes motivating yourself (direct personal control) and others (socially mediated proxy control).

Goal setting[5]

Increase both your, and your team's, motivation by setting specific or challenging goals. Encouraging your team's input in the goal-setting process will increase their sense of involvement and shared control, because achieving goals grows self-esteem and the incentive to take on more. Give them feedback about their performance, or if you are goal setting for yourself, evaluate your own performance. So, when setting goals:

- Make them clear and specific
- Make them challenging and achievable
- If you are setting goals for others, involve them in the process
- Provide feedback on performance or self-evaluate your own performance.

What's in it for me?[6]

Most people are motivated to do something if there's something in it for them! For your team or yourself consider:

- Do you and your team possess the necessary skills to complete the task?
- What is the reward for completing the task?
- Is the reward of value to you and your team?

It's important you and your team feel you can complete the task, so set challenging but achievable goals and make the rewards clear. This could simply be the satisfaction of completing a project to a high standard and on time, improved morale in the team or something more tangible. Whatever the rewards are, they need to be recognised by those involved as something worth having, or they'll fail to motivate.

Motivating your team through 'proxy control' means getting them 'on side' or to act on your behalf. Be sure to:

- Think about who you're talking to and pitch what you're saying at the right level (don't overcomplicate things or confuse people by talking about things of which they have no knowledge)
- Clearly state your objectives and why they're important
- Explain the benefits of the intended outcomes – especially if they're of value to your audience
- Act with integrity – they need to know you're trustworthy
- You need to come across as someone with expertise – show you know what you're talking about.

Gaining control: Exercise

Many of us will have been in a situation where we have 'derailed'; that is, where we had control of a situation and then, for whatever reason, we lost it again. In this exercise, we will look at how to prevent yourself from being 'derailed' in the future.

Step 1: Think of a time when you lost control of a situation. You may have thought you had everything covered, but things can go off track. Think of the impact it had on your team, and the task you were all doing. Remember, we learn more from our mistakes than our successes. Don't beat yourself up about it, but think instead of the insight it gave you and that it made you aware of skills you can now develop, as a result.

Step 2: Discuss the situation with a mentor or line manager. Using what you've read so far, identify the locus of control you applied. Was it external, internal, or half-way between the two? Identify when it all began to derail. Did you overlook something in the planning stage? Or did you assume a level of competence in a team member that they didn't have (and which you could now help them to develop)?

Step 3: With your line manager, make a plan of action for your future development. It might be helpful to recreate the situation that went off the rails at a team training event, so that you and your team can learn from the experience. It can be challenging to face up to mistakes in front of others. However, doing so openly and sharing the insights gained can do much to build trust and enable you to manage future projects better – and your team will be clearer about what is expected of them.

> Do not overload yourself. Delegate some responsibility to others. You can do this whilst maintaining overall control and it will enable you to focus on the bigger picture while letting others feel involved.

● NEXT STEPS

Now you've read this far, here's a selection of things you can do to reinforce what you've learned:

Look for opportunities to practise

Think about opportunities at work, or elsewhere, where you can practise taking control. Are there projects you can lead? Meetings you can attend? Presentations to give?

Discuss the gaining control exercise

Arrange a meeting with someone appropriate to discuss your reflections, using the Gaining Control exercise. This could be your mentor, line manager, coach or a colleague. Ask more than one person to get different perspectives.

Set up an evaluation meeting

Set up a further 'evaluation meeting' for a later date to ask whether your skill in taking control has noticeably improved or whether there are aspects that still need development.

Write a development plan

Make 'taking control' a specific objective and factor this into your own, personal development plan. Make sure you give yourself clear tasks and objectives to ensure measurable improvements.

● FURTHER INFORMATION

If you found this tool useful then you are likely to find the following tools both insightful and relevant:

- How to be assertive
- How to create team identity
- How to take responsibility
- How to delegate
- How to build resilience
- How to get the most out of yourself.

● REFERENCES

1   Vroom, V. & Jago, A. (1988). The new leadership. Upper Saddle River, NJ: Prentice-Hall.

2   Boerner, S., & von Streit, C. (2007). Promoting orchestral performance: the interplay between musicians' mood and a conductor's leadership style. Psychology of Music, 35(1), 132.

3   Karasek, R. (1979). Job demands, job decision latitude and mental strain: implications for job redesign. Administrative Science Quarterly, 24, 285-308.

4   Häusser, J. A., Mojzisch, A., Niesel, M., & Schulz-Hardt, S. (2010). Ten years on: A review of recent research on the Job Demand–Control (-Support) model and psychological well-being. Work & Stress, 24(1), 1-35.

5   Locke, E. A., Shaw, K. N., Saari, L. M., & Latham, G. P. (1981). Goal setting and task performance: 1969–1980. Psychological Bulletin, 90(1), 125.

6   Van Eerde, W., & Thierry, H. (1996). Vroom's expectancy models and work-related criteria: A meta-analysis. Journal of Applied Psychology, 81(5), 575.

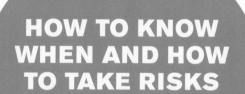

HOW TO KNOW WHEN AND HOW TO TAKE RISKS

Determine your own level of risk-taking behaviour and how this might impact on your decisions.

● ISN'T IT INTERESTING?

How much would you bet on the toss of a coin? £5? £10? £50? £1000?

Risk versus reward

The answer to this question depends on a logical interpretation of the odds and the associated risks and rewards. However, as much as we like to think of ourselves as logical beings, under certain circumstances this is far from the case. The study below clearly shows the logical errors we can make when making decisions.

Risky decision making

In 1979, two psychologists published influential research that would ultimately lead them to receive the Nobel Prize. Daniel Kahneman and Amos Tversky[1] investigated the apparent strange and illogical behaviour demonstrated when people take risks.

Participants were asked whether they would be willing to bet £10 on the toss of a coin if they stood a chance of winning £20. So a 50% chance of winning £20 and a 50% chance of losing £10. It's clear that you have more to potentially gain than to potentially lose, so it's interesting that people tended to avoid this bet. It seems that when there are potential gains, we tend to become more risk averse.

Conversely, consider this example. You have two options available to you. The first is that you have an 85% chance of losing £1000 and a 15% chance of losing nothing. The second option is that you have a 100% chance of losing £800 – not much of a choice I hear you cry. Still, sometimes it is best to cut your losses and the maths states that the second option is the most sensible. However, most people will prefer the 85% chance of losing £1000 over the absolute certainty of losing £800. It seems that when there are potential losses, we tend to become more risk seeking.

It seems then that when faced with taking risks, our decision making processes can turn themselves on their head.

This tool can help

Life poses endless 'gambles'. Each and every day, we weigh up the pros and cons of multiple options before arriving at our decisions. This tool is about **how to know when and how to take risks** and provides advice on determining your own level of risk-taking behaviour and how this might impact on your decisions.

● WHAT IS RISK TAKING?

We're not talking about the 2.30 at Kempton Park, but without taking risks we'd be nowhere. Every day presents us with a variety of risks to assess — we've been doing it since we were born. Our experiences and personality shape our adult approach but here we'll help you consider whether yours helps or hinders you in the workplace and how you can maximise your chances of successful risk taking.

The adrenalin junkies amongst us are exhilarated by unpredictability, others unsettled by it or 'risk averse'. Whichever extreme you think you tend towards seems to depend on the amount of information you need before making a decision and how quickly you make it.[2] Psychologists assess the likelihood of us taking risks according to personality — if we're conventional and abide by rules and norms we're less likely to be risk takers than those who are impulsive, spontaneous or entrepreneurial. However, a taste for risk taking doesn't indicate an instinct for successful decision making! Being successful as an individual or an organisation isn't a matter of 'nothing ventured nothing gained' — it's about knowing when and how to take risks to maximise their chances of success.

Approaches to risk taking

People have three broad approaches to risk taking or 'risk orientation':[3]

- Risk avoiders: those who won't take any if they can help it
- Risk reducers: those who do things in spite of the risk involved
- Risk optimisers: those who do things specifically because of the risk involved.

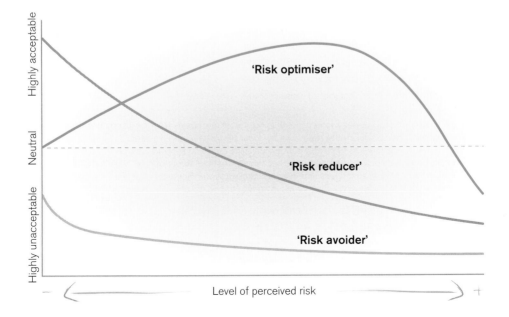

● HOW RISKY ARE YOU?

Develop an understanding of your personality style...

One way to understand how 'risky' you really are, or are likely to be, is to complete a personality questionnaire and get some feedback on the outcome. The most useful questionnaires are based on the Five Factor Model of Personality and all include assessment of risk-taking tendencies.

In the situations[4] described below, imagine you're helping someone make a decision. Indicate the minimum odds you'd need to recommend one of the available options.

> **Increase your self-awareness: are you a risk taker?**
>
> 1. Mr. B, a 45-year-old accountant, has recently been told by his doctor that he has a heart condition. It's serious enough to force him to make several fundamental changes to his lifestyle including reducing his work load, drastically changing his diet and giving up favourite leisure pursuits. The doctor suggests a delicate operation which, if successful, would cure the condition. However, its success can't be guaranteed, and it may prove fatal. Listed below are probabilities or odds of the operation being successful. Indicate the lowest probability you'd consider acceptable for recommending it.
>
> ☐ Tick here if you think that Mr. B should not have the operation, no matter what the probabilities are (10 in 10).
> ☐ The chances are 9 in 10 that the operation will be a success.
> ☐ The chances are 7 in 10 that the operation will be a success.
> ☐ The chances are 5 in 10 that the operation will be a success.
> ☐ The chances are 3 in 10 that the operation will be a success.
> ☐ The chances are 1 in 10 that the operation will be a success.
>
> 2. Mr. D is captain of University X's sports team. University X is playing its traditional rival, University Y, in the final game of the season. The game is in its final seconds, and University X is losing. University X has time for one more play. Mr. D, the captain, must decide whether it would be best to settle for a score to tie the match that would almost certainly work or, on the other hand, try a more complicated and risky play that would bring victory if successful but defeat if not. Tick the lowest probability you'd consider acceptable for the risky play to be attempted.
>
> ☐ Tick here if you think that Mr. D should not attempt the risky play, no matter what the probabilities.
> ☐ The chances are 9 in 10 that the risky play will work.
> ☐ The chances are 7 in 10 that the risky play will work.
> ☐ The chances are 5 in 10 that the risky play will work.
> ☐ The chances are 3 in 10 that the risky play will work.
> ☐ The chances are 1 in 10 that the risky play will work.
>
> 3. Ms. K is a successful businesswoman who has done a lot of valuable work for the community. She has been approached by the leaders of her local school as a possible councillor in the next election. Ms. K would like to become a school councillor but to do so would involve a serious investment because of the time she needs to campaign to the parents who will vote in the elections. She would also have to spend less time with her family and with her other charities. Tick the lowest probability you'd consider worthwhile for Ms. K to run for political office.
>
> ☐ Tick here if you think that Ms. K should not run for office, no matter what the probability.
> ☐ The chances are 9 in 10 that Ms. K will win the election.
> ☐ The chances are 7 in 10 that Ms. K will win the election.
> ☐ The chances are 5 in 10 that Ms. K will win the election.
> ☐ The chances are 3 in 10 that Ms. K will win the election.
> ☐ The chances are 1 in 10 that Ms. K will win the election.

4. Ms. L, a 30-year-old research physicist, has been given a five-year appointment by a major university laboratory. As she contemplates the next five years, she realises that she might be given the opportunity to work on a difficult, long-term scientific problem, a solution for which would win accolades for her. If no solution were found, however, Ms. L would have little to show for her five years in the laboratory and would find it difficult to get a good job afterwards. On the other hand, she could, as most of her professional associates are doing, work on a series of short-term problems for which solutions are easier to find but of less scientific importance. Tick the lowest probability you'd consider acceptable to make it worthwhile for Ms. L to work on the more difficult, long-term problem.

☐ The chances are 1 in 10 that Ms. L will solve the long-term problem.

☐ The chances are 3 in 10 that Ms. L will solve the long-term problem.

☐ The chances are 5 in 10 that Ms. L will solve the long-term problem.

☐ The chances are 7 in 10 that Ms. L will solve the long-term problem.

☐ The chances are 9 in 10 that Ms. L will solve the long-term problem.

☐ Tick here if you think Ms. L should not choose the long-term, difficult problem, no matter what the probabilities.

Scoring key: These situations are taken from a longer questionnaire. Your results are an indication of your general orientation toward risk but not a precise measure. To calculate your risk-taking score, add up the chances you were willing to take and divide by 4.

Use the chance rating that you gave, so for example a 7 in 10 chance should be calculated as 7.

For any of the situations in which you would not take a risk regardless of the probabilities, give yourself a 10.

The lower your number, the more of a risk taker you are.

Implications and considerations

Score: 1–4: If you take risks easily, you're likely to be extremely confident or optimistic. You need to be careful of being either – consider the risk to your reputation as well as for company resources if, for example, you were to commit funds to an unproven product or service. Try to analyse the risk and decide if the benefits outweigh them regardless of your own inclination. Consider how you're perceived by others – they may consider you reckless or a bit of maverick!

Score: 5–7: If you take calculated risks, you'll probably weigh up the pros and cons and your decision is likely to depend on your own confidence in a particular situation. Consider gathering additional information or other opinions for when you feel less confident, rather than relying on your inclinations alone.

Score: 8–10: If you hesitate to take risks or avoid them you're probably wary of change or leaving things to chance. This may be exacerbated after a setback of some kind. At work you can probably be relied upon to highlight potential risk or threats or be cautious and pessimistic. Try focusing on the potential benefits and opportunities in a situation as well as the obstacles. Consider how you may be perceived by your colleagues or manager – as well as your attitude to change and innovation, generally.

● STOP AND THINK BEFORE YOU TAKE THE RISK...

Steps for knowing when and how to take risks

The following grid is designed to help you analyse your 'risk' in context and therefore take a more informed approach to how and when to take risks.

	Describe the Activity/Situation			
Which element in the context makes it 'risky' (please circle)	The People	The Environment	The Resources	The importance of the Outcome
	Yes/No	Yes/No	Yes/No	Yes/No
If yes, can you manage the risks?				
	Yes/No	Yes/No	Yes/No	Yes/No
	If yes		If no, should you really take the risk?	
If yes, think about how you can utilise the following:				
	Your signature strengths (what are they?)	Your networks (who, how?)	The resources (what are they, how?)	External influences (what are they, how?)

If you feel unable to control the riskier elements of the situation, you may be relying too heavily on chance. Consider the following hints and tips to manage your risk.

● HINTS AND TIPS

- Write down the key questions that are worrying you about the situation, e.g. what resources are needed to complete the work? Take some time to gather more information about these issues to give you more clarity and reduce ambiguity. This will help to increase your confidence levels.

- Consider how you could reward yourself in order to provide a greater incentive to take the risk.

- Think about the benefits and opportunities that taking the risk will bring you. Looking at the situation from a different angle can help you highlight the positive aspects and potential openings.

- Take some time away from the activity in order to consider whether the risk is really as bad as it seems.

- Talk to people who you know take more risks than you. Get their take on this situation in order to gain a different perspective.

- Consider past projects and experiences you have gone through and learn from these successes or failures to help make your decision.
- Categorise potential problems into high and low risk areas. When doing that, consider how likely it is that the problem will occur and how damaging it would actually be. Carry out a risk analysis using a grid like the one below:

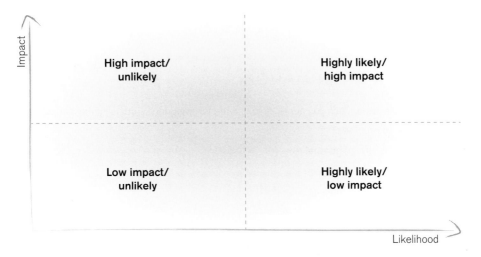

Your objective is to think of strategies that will result in any risk that falls in the top right corner moving ideally to the bottom left or at least to one of the other corners. This process will also help you to identify which issue you should tackle first and which issues you can afford to leave to last or even not deal with at all.

● NEXT STEPS

Now that you know more about what's involved in managing risk and have some practical tools, think about what to do next. Here are a few suggestions, but be willing to take other opportunities to develop your risk taking.

Gather feedback on existing performance

You may find it useful to benchmark your current performance by asking for formal or informal feedback. You could help others, too, by making yourself available to share your views and experiences with them.

Use the exercises in this tool

Use the techniques outlined in this tool to help you manage your risk taking. This should increase your confidence that you're taking more calculated risks.

Seek out role models

Consider how you would like to manage risk and find someone who you think does it well. Consider what you particularly admire about them or their approach and make comparisons with yourself. By being aware of the differences in your approaches, you may be able to provide potential steps to flex your style.

Write a development plan

Use the tool in this document to highlight your approach to managing risk. Once you have established the way you'd assess risk in different situations write a plan for addressing any shortcomings.

Look for opportunities to practise

Find opportunities in your current work or elsewhere to practise assessing situations and making decisions involving various degrees of risk.

● FURTHER INFORMATION

If you found this tool useful then you are likely to find the following tools both insightful and relevant:

- How to reframe problems
- How to focus on the bigger picture
- How to make reasoned judgements
- How to be confident in making judgement calls
- How to balance risk with potential benefits
- How to use optimism to achieve.

● REFERENCES

1   Kahneman, D. & Tversky, A. (1979). Prospect Theory: An Analysis of Decision Making Under Risk. **Econometrica**, 263-291.

2   Robbins, S. (1998). **Organisational Behaviour: Concepts, Controversies and Applications.** Prentice Hall.

3   Llewellyn, D. (2003). The psychology of risk taking: The case for a multidimensional model of risk taking behaviour. Paper presented at the 2003 O2 Risk Conference.

4   Kogan, N. and Wallach, M. (1964). **Risk Taking: A Study in Cognition and Personality.** New York: Holt, Rinehart & Winston, 256-61.

DRIVING

HOW TO MAINTAIN MOMENTUM

Take ownership of situations and understand how you can keep going to the finish.

● ISN'T IT INTERESTING?

You may or may not have experienced the phenomenon known as hitting the wall, synonymous with the last few miles of a marathon...

Hitting the wall

When people hit the wall they describe feelings of fatigue, shifting focus or unintentional changes in pace. This phenomenon can partly be explained through physiological perspectives.[1] Depleted glycogen supplies means the body converts fat into energy, which is slower and less efficient than normal. But there is a far more psychological element to overcoming this barrier, as by using our mind, we can dictate how long we are able to keep going.

Anticipate the finish

Ulmer and colleagues devised a theory that we tend to anticipate where the finish point is and work backwards to regulate the effort required – known as 'teleoanticipation'.[2]

In this way we moderate intensity and effort to complete the task. Researchers carried out a study to investigate this and found that runners who were told that they had 30 minutes to run but actually ran for 20 were less exhausted than those who were told that they had 20 minutes to run. The implications are that we are subjective about how fatigued we get and can therefore control this by setting realistic expectations.

Further research into psychological momentum[3] has shown that success breeds success. Students were told that a basketball team had just beaten another in a local derby. The students rated that team as more likely to win the next game based on this information. This is commonly known as 'being on a roll'.

There is however a caveat; in another study, participants were told that an author had been working on a research paper but was then interrupted. Some were told that she was 'on a roll', others that she was working steadily. The participants rated her chances of completing the work as higher if she had been working at a steady pace. This implies that once on a roll, momentum is easier to lose than if working steadily.

This tool can help

The research shows that we can influence our own momentum to complete a task, reducing fatigue and focusing on success. This helps to stave off 'the wall' which we will all feel at some time and stay focused on the task to hand. This tool is all about how to maintain momentum until the completion of every task and will help you to take ownership of situations and understand how you can keep going to the finish.

● PHYSICS AND TASK LEADERSHIP

'How to maintain momentum until the completion of every task'.

Let's consider this statement by applying some basic physics:

Momentum refers to the 'quantity of motion that an object possesses'; in other words, momentum refers to the 'amount of "stuff" that is moving and how fast the "stuff" is moving'. Any mass that is in motion has momentum and the implication of this idea is that people also have momentum. Is this really the case though?

People can have momentum too. For example, it is a well known phenomenon in sport that the 'momentum' can be with a particular team or individual, and this is generally assumed to be a good predictor of improved performance. This is attributed to the fact that the agent in question has developed a temporary 'winning habit' and this is giving them extra motivation and confidence, that the opponent no longer has.

Especially important to the definition of momentum is 'energy'. Here the laws of physics also apply. In brief, the law of conservation of energy states that 'energy cannot be created or destroyed, it can only be changed from one form to another', as when electrical energy is changed into heat energy – or for our purposes, when an idle employee changes into an active employee!

So, for the purposes of our discussion, let's imagine ourselves as existing in a type of energy field where our movement towards task completion is influenced by driving and restraining forces, respectively. In terms of momentum, driving forces include those factors that push employees towards task completion, whereas restraining forces inhibit the employee's progress towards task completion. The exact nature of these forces will become clearer as you continue reading.

The following section delves a little deeper into the concept of an energy field. You might find it useful to refer to the Energy field model that visually depicts what we mean by this on page 39.

● YOUR ENERGY FIELD DECIPHERED

The idea of driving and restraining forces originated from the work of Kurt Lewin on Force Field Analysis.[4] He stated that when the sum of driving forces equals the sum of restraining forces, a so-called state of equilibrium is achieved. Equally, when one force is stronger than the other, this unbalances the equilibrium:

> **Driving > Restraining = Positive effect**

Vs.

> **Restraining > Driving = Negative effect**

If we translate Lewin's ideas for use in the working environment, the state of equilibrium could represent an employee's present level of productivity, in terms of working towards task completion. If we want to maintain this level of productivity we have to maintain equilibrium; that is, ensure that the individual experiences a balanced state of being.

In thinking about maintaining momentum, it's also worthwhile considering the concept of 'flow'.[5] Flow is a mental state in which a person is fully immersed in what he or she is doing. It is characterised by a feeling of energised focus, complete involvement in the task at hand and success in the process of the activity. In other words, flow appears to be a state of being where a person is optimally engaged in an activity and constantly moving towards a successful outcome. Considering flow from this angle indicates its potential value for maintaining energy and, therefore, momentum, over a period of time.

Interestingly, people who have described their 'flow experiences' in research studies used the metaphor of a 'current carrying them along' to describe it. Once again the idea of movement and momentum is reinforced.

You might say: 'so what?'

From the above, we can deduce that in order to maintain momentum for the purpose of task completion, one should aim to achieve a state of flow.

...and then ask: 'how does one obtain a state of flow?'

In order to arrive at an answer, it's important to note that flow is an ideal state and that its attainment is not guaranteed for every task. The good news, however, is that there are certain factors or conditions that contribute to the experience of flow – and better still, not all of these factors are needed for flow to be experienced!

The implications are that:

- We can manipulate situations and tasks so that the probability of experiencing flow is enhanced.
- Individuals can discover which factors make them work more effectively (i.e. move them towards the flow experience) and introduce these factors to their working lives.

We can roughly link some of the factors that contribute to the flow experience to the driving and/ or restraining forces (also see the Energy field model on the next page) albeit not perfectly.

FLOW FACTORS	Matched to: DRIVING FORCES	Matched to: RESTRAINING FORCES
Clear goals	Goal-setting (according to SMART formula)	
Concentration and focus		(Opposite of) boredom
Loss of the feeling of self-consciousness	Positive emotional state	
Direct and immediate feedback	Constructive feedback	
Balance between ability level and challenge	Motivation	
Sense of personal control	Coping skill	Workplace/personal stressors
Activity is intrinsically rewarding	Motivation	
Absorption in and complete focus on the activity, with distorted sense of time	Positive cognition/ positive emotional state	

● ENERGY FIELD MODEL

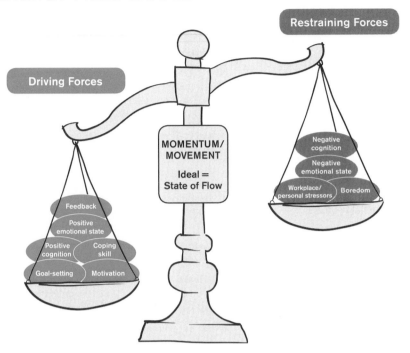

Key to the Energy field model

The Ideal situation is when moving from the start of a task to completion you achieve a state of 'Flow', whereby you're balancing the momentum/movement. You achieve this by countering the negative restraining forces with the positive driving forces.

Driving Forces*

- **Motivation** (Intrinsically + Extrinsically motivating factors).
- **Goal-setting** (SMART objectives) – see 'How to formulate action plans' tool.
- **Positive cognition** (Positive thinking; Constructive thoughts; Building positive mental schema).
- **Positive emotional state** (for example, positive emotions, happiness, humour, optimism, etc.).
- **Coping skill** (for example, access to, and/or creation of, resources; Emotional/Instrumental/Informational Support).
- **Feedback** (continuous feedback from others leading to corrective actions).

Restraining Forces*

- **Negative cognition** (Negative thinking; Destructive thoughts; Breaking negative mental schema).
- **Workplace/personal stressors** (for example, workload, role conflict/role ambiguity, lack of support, interpersonal conflict, work-life imbalance, etc.).
- **Negative emotional state** (for example, negative emotions, pessimism, etc.).
- **Boredom** (in a sense, the opposite of 'flow').

*Note: This is not an exhaustive list of possible 'forces!'

● TIPS FOR MAINTAINING MOMENTUM

The information here focuses on the concept of an energy field influenced by driving and restraining forces respectively. Your task is to 'construct' your energy field (working environment) in such a manner that you move towards the flow experience to maintain momentum towards task completion. The importance of flow in the equation is that:

- It entails an energised focus on an activity – it is not a passive state of being. On the contrary, the individual is actively absorbed in what they are busy with.

- In addition to being an energising experience, flow also sustains activity. In other words, the emphasis is on the maintenance of movement (momentum) towards the successful completion of a task.

Once you have created the conditions for experiencing flow, following these **practical actions** and 'tips' can help you maintain momentum to complete a task. They can also be integrated into the energy field.

1. **Consider your job and list five motivating and five de-motivating factors.** Identify what steps you can take to reduce the impact of any blocks or hindrances to your enthusiasm.

2. **List your current work and personal goals/tasks.** For each one, make a realistic assessment of how far along you are to achieving this goal/task, the steps that need to be taken from now on and any potential blocks you anticipate to your progress.

3. **Identify ways to minimise these hindrances, set your milestones** against a realistic timeframe, and determine a **process to monitor and review** your achievements over time.

4. **Seek feedback from a colleague about your level of 'negativity'** and, if necessary, modify your behaviour and dispel any lack of interest or enthusiasm.

5. **Create a running list of completed goals/tasks** and break complex or extended projects into chunks with set milestones. Recognise and celebrate your achievements as they occur.

6. **Meet with your team, and identify all the achievements** made over the past 3-6 months. Ensure all your direct reports are aware of the collective accomplishments of the entire group or department.

7. **Treat failure as a learning opportunity.** Analyse why problems arose and what could have been done differently or better. Similarly, review instances of success and identify the key factors that contributed to the overall result in order to incorporate them in future operations.

8. **Recognise perseverance and tenacity in your direct reports** and acknowledge effort and progress, as well as the final achievement.

9. When faced with difficulties, **apply the technique of Force Field Analysis** to identify the factors serving to help (driving forces) or hinder (restraining forces) you in achieving your goal/task.

10. **Consider how you react to disappointment, and your capacity to bounce back.** Note that your emotional resilience will be generally weakened under conditions of ongoing stress and pressure. Take action to increase your resilience by addressing any chronic stressors in your work or personal life. For more information on resilience or coping with setbacks see the tools 'How to build and maintain resilience' and 'How to cope with setbacks'.

11. **Assess the amount of personal energy that you bring to work.** Consider your current levels of physical fitness, health and relaxation. Implement strategies to improve your diet, increase your exercise and develop your coping resources.

12. **Become 'realistically optimistic' when considering setbacks or disappointments.** Just as you should not give up too soon, neither should you obstinately persist when a situation is deemed 'hopeless'. Apply a sound cost/benefit analysis when deciding if and what action you will take to overcome the presenting obstacles.

● ENERGY FIELD EXERCISE

In order to complete the following exercise you should:

- Have read through this tool and understood the key messages about driving/restraining forces, equilibrium and flow.
- Have looked at the example model of an energy field.
- Think laterally and be creative!

Your task:

1. Refer back to the Energy field model to consider your 'flow factors'. Use the table on the following page to note down your flow factors.

2. Think about the following questions in order to identify the driving and restraining forces in your own working environment:

Identify your Driving and Restraining Forces

1. Which conditions or factors need to be present for you to function optimally?

2. When (at which times) do you operate at your best?

3. Alternatively, when don't you operate at your best?

FLOW FACTORS	DRIVING FORCES	RESTRAINING FORCES

3. Once you've completed Step 2, think of ways you can increase the probability of experiencing 'flow'. Consider the following questions:

Enhance Probability of Flow

1. How will you deal with, and/or manage, the restraining forces, so that they don't upset your flow experience?

2. What action do you need to take to maintain equilibrium?

4. Once you've completed this exercise for yourself, you can then share it with the rest of your team and/or facilitate a session whereby each team member draws their own energy field.

● BOREDOM PRONENESS EXERCISE

Boredom is the aversive state that occurs when we (a) are not able to successfully engage attention with internal (e.g. thoughts or feelings) or external (e.g. environmental stimuli) information required for participating in satisfying activity.[6]

As a tool for identifying predisposition to boredom, Farmer & Sundberg[7] devised the Boredom Proneness Scale, which has been included below. To find out your own relationship with boredom, look at the following statements and rank your affinity with them from 1 (not representative of yourself) to 7 (completely representative of yourself).

Statement	Rank
In situations where I have to wait, I get very restless.	
Many people would say that I am a creative or imaginative person.	
It takes a lot of change and variety to keep me really happy.	
Among my friends, I am the one who keeps doing something the longest.	
I would like more challenging things to do in life.	
I often find myself at loose ends, not knowing what to do.	
Having to look at someone's home movies or travel slides bores me tremendously.	
When I was young, I was often in monotonous and tiresome situations.	
I have so many interests I don't have time to do everything.	
Many things I have to do are repetitive and monotonous.	
I have projects in mind all the time, things to do.	
I feel that I am working below my abilities most of the time.	
I often find myself with nothing to do – time on my hands.	
I often wake up with a new idea.	
It takes more stimulation to get me going than most people.	
I am often trapped in situations where I have to do meaningless things.	
Frequently when I am working I find myself worrying about other things.	
Much of the time I just sit around doing nothing.	
Unless I am doing something exciting, even dangerous, I feel half-dead and dull.	
In any situation I can usually find something to do or see to keep me interested.	
I am seldom excited about my work.	
Time always seems to be passing slowly.	
It seems that the same things are on television or the movies all the time, I'm getting old!	
It would be very hard for me to find a job that is exciting enough.	

When you have worked through the questionnaire, simply add up the values of all your answers; this is your overall score. You can then use this to compare to the table we have designed overleaf based on the average values of others who use this test.

This table will help explain your rating in more detail.

Score	Category	Implication
>115	Distractable	You'll get bored easily. Try to identify three or four of the answers on the previous page that really stand out for you. Think about what really excites you and what keeps you doing that activity. Maybe you need to have variety in your life in order to keep you stimulated or be working on several things at the same time. Think about how you sustain your momentum at work and focus on completing your work.
100-115	The Plate Spinner	You're likely to get bored with certain things and will want to keep busy. Look back over your responses and note down where you agreed with the statements. Look for common themes. You're probably someone who likes to have more than one activity happening at the same time and will stick to several things rather than concentrate your efforts on one. Think about your work environment and how you work to meet deadlines.
85-100	Racing Drivers	You're not likely to get bored easily. Like a Formula One racer, you'll be able to sustain momentum with only a few pit stops. Think about how you can use your ability to stick with a task to help you in the areas where you may get bored more easily. Try to bear in mind how flexible you need to be in your current work environment and how you prefer to work.
<85	The Power Station	You're not likely to get bored at all. Lucky you! You're probably able to stick with a task or activity when others around you may give up or get diverted. Consider how you work when you have a number of activities to complete with limited time and resources. Can you adapt your style to multitask, or prioritise and focus on doing one thing at a time?

Maintain momentum in others

Consider how 'results-orientated' you are with your team, and list the methods you use to motivate and enthuse your direct reports. Identify the business outcomes you're focused on to sustain and increase their drive, enthusiasm and effort.

● NEXT STEPS

Now you know how to maintain your momentum, here are a few suggestions about what to do next.

Gather feedback on existing performance

You may find it useful to ask for formal or informal feedback, to understand how other people perceive you and get advice about where you can make modifications or improvements. You can also use this information to manage people's future expectations about your approach and ability to deliver.

Consider your role model

Try and identify someone you know who you admire for their ability to see things through. Think about what it is you like about their approach and what works well for them. Then consider how you can adapt your style. This is the starting point for you to develop a plan to improve – see below.

Look for opportunities to practise

Watch out for opportunities in your current work or elsewhere to practise some of the tips and exercises that you have picked up from this tool.

Write a development plan

Use this tool to write out a personal, focused development plan.

● FURTHER INFORMATION

If you found this tool useful then you are likely to find the following tools both insightful and relevant:

- How to raise energy levels
- How to prioritise tasks ready for action
- How to direct people
- How to deliver every time
- How to cope with setbacks
- How to engage others to deliver
- How to use optimism to achieve
- How to get the most out of yourself.

● REFERENCES

1   Buman, M., et al (2008). Hitting the wall in the marathon: Phenomenological characteristics and associations with expectancy, gender, and running history. **Psychology of Sport and Exercise**, 9, 177-190.

2   Ulmer, H. (1996). Concept of an Extracellular Regulation of Muscular Metabolic Rate During Heavy Exercise in Humans by Psychophysiological Feedback. **Experientia**, 52, 416-420.

3   Markman, K. & Guenther, C. (2007). Psychological momentum: Intuitive physics and naïve beliefs. **Personality and Social Psychology Bulletin**, 33, 800-812.

4   Lewin, K. (1961). Quasi-stationary social equilibria and the problem of permanent change. 238-244.

5   Mihaly Csikszentmihalyi (1991). **Flow**. SOS Free Stock.

6   Eastwood, J. D., Frischen, A., Fenske, M. J., & Smilek, D. (2012). The Unengaged Mind; Defining Boredom in Terms of Attention. **Perspectives on Psychological Science**, 7(5), 482-495.

7   Farmer, R. & Sundberg, N. (1986). Boredom proneness: The development and correlates of a new scale. **Journal of Personality Assessment**, 50, 4-17.

HOW TO COPE WITH SETBACKS

Understand what causes setbacks
and develop the skills you need
to overcome these obstacles.

● ISN'T IT INTERESTING?

At one time or another, we all come across the proverbial 'brick wall'. Do you tend to bang your head fruitlessly, or do you navigate yourself around it successfully?

How hardy are you?

Darwin's theory of 'natural selection' explains that only the most hardy and adaptive of plant and animal life survives. The same logic (if less dramatic) can be applied to working life too. The study below describes the culmination of 30 years of research into the skills and attitudes needed to overcome setbacks and work past the wall.

How hardy are you?

In the late 1970s, psychologists Suzanne Kobasa[1] and colleagues undertook a long-term research study into the impact of stress on a large organisation's senior executives during its break-up. The executives were either being moved to other roles or departments or were losing their jobs entirely.

Over this period, the team found two broad ways in which the executives reacted to the news. On one side, employees became increasingly distressed, developing psychological and physiological ailments. Conversely, the other group demonstrated few or no medical symptoms. In fact, they seemed to rise to the challenge, becoming more healthy and robust in the process.

So what factors led some employees to crumble and some to thrive? The researchers put this down to the concept of hardiness – a particular pattern of attitudes and skills that helps you to be resilient, thrive under stress and cope with setbacks.

Perhaps most importantly, though, whereas under Darwin's theory we either have the genes to survive or not, Kobasa's research suggests that we can actually develop the skills and attitudes needed to enhance our ability to deal with what life throws at us.

This tool can help

Research has shown that resilience to overcome setbacks is not an inborn personality trait, it is something that can be learned.[2] This tool is all about **how to cope with setbacks** and helps you to understand what causes setbacks and develop the skills you need to overcome these obstacles.

● THE SPORT MODEL

We hope we've caught you at a good time. If you're reading this thinking about some prolonged disappointment, or how you might nurse a colleague through one, you'll agree with us that everyone experiences them and, of course, we can all think of successful people who've had their fair share of them. If, on the other hand, you're still occupied by a more recent experience, you may feel you'd prefer to sit there a bit longer, staring at the wall.

So, we'll say this quietly: It's a fact that we learn more when things don't go according to plan than when it's a breeze. The trick is how you deal with it – and that's what marks out those infuriatingly successful people from the rest. Don't assume you're a failure, and don't allow negativity or anxiety to spiral until it engulfs you. Take the time to work out what went wrong and why – and what insights this gives you for next time. This may sound impossible right now, but how you react is a choice, and like anything else, training yourself to think in ways that benefit you gets easier with practice.

And, we have a strategy of our own for you to follow whenever you experience a setback at work, in your relationships or anything else that affects your general wellbeing. First, whether you want to analyse what went wrong with a previous plan or are about to create a new one, separate the planning process into 5 essential stages, best remembered as the acronym **SPORT**:[2]

(S) pecific – so that everyone involved knows what is expected.

(P) ositive – in outlining what success looks like and how this will be achieved.

(O) bservable – with clear measurable stages to show how the final goal was achieved.

(R) ealistic – to ensure that there is a practical focus to the plan.

(T) imed – so that deadlines and timeframes are clearly established and followed.

Making sure a plan incorporates SPORT will give it a better chance of success, because even if a setback occurs you'll be able to identify the problem more easily, work out how to put it right and continue working towards your goal, rather than abandoning it as a failure.

There's a model of a SPORT plan, on the next page.

In the model, the line of arrows at the top shows the 5 stages of the plan (it's backwards, but the acronym's easier to remember!). We've indicated that a setback occurs, just as everything looks as if it's all working out nicely!

The backward-pointing arrows below the SPORT indicate what needs to be done to overcome the setback and realign with the original goal – or an amended goal if necessary. What's needed will depend on the stage at which the setback occurs, but as a general rule, it's a good idea to start with review and identify and then move through SPORT to work out where the setback has occurred.

This is a method which allows review of an objective and the process used to achieve it. More importantly, it demonstrates that setbacks don't automatically signify failure, but our attitude to them can! For more detail on how to review and identify and approach the other steps, there is help overleaf.

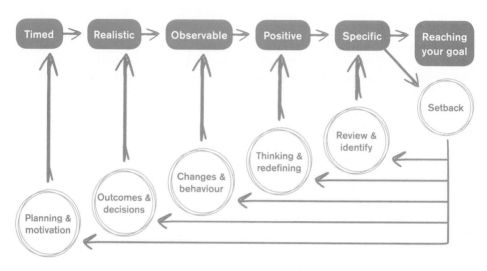

Review and identify

In what context are you working at the moment? It could be that you're in a new job, or have a new team or a difficult team member to manage. Even if the situation is subject to influences beyond your control, it's important to maintain communication with those you work with and for – and don't be afraid to ask for help. You need to be aware of possible political or cultural influences which may determine the success or otherwise of your plan as well as the kind of setbacks which may occur.

Identify any other external or personal 'stressors' that could affect your ability to achieve your goal. Going through a divorce, bereavement, illness or even moving house can themselves be setbacks. Reviewing circumstances as well as specifics will produce an overall perspective and banish needless self reproach. It will clarify your objectives and what needs to be altered to achieve them.

Thinking and redefining success

What does success look like to you? Is this setback such a critical issue? If your strategy didn't work first time, think of how you could make it more flexible rather than giving up altogether. Or, what would the consequences of getting that new job have been for your family? A coveted promotion may have meant less time with them.

Flexibility offers more options than rigid attachment to a particular outcome – there is usually more than one way to achieve anything. Achieving goals is not always a linear process and flexibility often overcomes the bleakest outlook, as this account of the building of Brooklyn Bridge proves:

> The Brooklyn Bridge spans the East River between Manhattan and Brooklyn. Several setbacks occurred during its construction, but the worst involved its suspension cables. Over six months or so, a crooked contractor delivered more than 200 tons of defective steel cables which had already been installed by the time the fraud was discovered. They couldn't be removed because, as the bridge engineer calculated, this would have weakened the cables from the required margin of 'six times maximum required strength' to only 'five times maximum strength'. He finally solved the problem by adding an additional 150 wires to each cable, and they remain in place to this day! The contractor involved had succeeded in his deception by replacing cables of an acceptable standard with substandard ones between inspection and delivery. At the time, the public was unaware of what had happened, and the contractor's only penalty was to pay for all the additional wires used.

The engineer running the Brooklyn Bridge project had to review his plans after that setback, but he didn't let it prevent the bridge being built. He found a way of reinforcing the cables to meet safety requirements which kept the budget down and disrupted the project as little as possible.

Changes and behaviour

What kind of person am I; how will I respond to this setback?

Throughout our lives we all experience setbacks to what we most want to achieve. It could be finishing an important project to deadline at work or trying to get your children somewhere important on time. Your personality will affect how you react. When something unexpected looms in front of you, do you spin out of control or do you grab the steering wheel and steer out of the spin? How you deal with a problem determines its outcome. Try to remember that a setback is temporary and you can steer yourself back on track, with determination. If you don't, you're just setting yourself up for more setbacks ahead. Try to determine how much of the situation you can control and what you really cannot. For more information about how to make this decision effectively, see the tool 'How to take control'.

Step back and assess the situation. Make sure you take responsibility when appropriate and don't blame others for your slip-ups. Is the setback really that significant or is it just a matter of applying yourself a little more to get things back on track? Never be shy about asking for help if you need it, including emotional support. You don't have to be perfect — no one else is!

Outcomes and decisions

Being 'self aware' means allowing yourself to be objective about significant events and their impact on you. We tend to label any events as either 'good' or 'bad', depending on how you felt at the time. In fact, most experiences are neither wholly good nor bad — and our view of them can change in retrospect. We all have memories we can smile at, but which felt anything but amusing at the time.

Planning and motivation

Give yourself credit for small successes while working towards your main goal. Remember, however, that they may not come as regularly as you'd like — you may hit a plateau during which nothing seems to change. If so, give yourself time and be flexible rather than abandoning your goal altogether.

Stick to your goal, not to your strategy. Perhaps, for example, a trainer at your gym suggests a different programme to what you thought you needed, but you find it works. Or, you may have been working towards a promotion but illness has prevented you from learning some of the necessary skills. Negotiate a new timetable for training and move your target date for the promotion. Having a time-bound goal is one of the best cures for procrastination!

● SIGNIFICANT LIFE EVENTS EXERCISE

Think of some significant events. Start by considering one with happy associations where you achieved something that pleased you, without setbacks. Passing an exam, perhaps, or being promoted, accepting a new job offer or taking a trip abroad. Now ask yourself the following (and write your answers in the top box):

- Were there any results from this action that were less than satisfactory?
- What other options did I rule out for myself by the action that I took?

Now repeat the exercise (using the bottom box) with an event that didn't turn out so well; one where you did encounter a setback. Maybe a poor performance at a meeting or interview, failing your driving test, the ending of a relationship?

Answer

- What came out of this experience that turned out to be good?
- What did you learn from the experience that has stood you in good stead for the future?

Answer

Thinking about the choices you have made objectively, and whether you would choose differently now, helps you identify factors you hadn't considered before. It will help you relax about possible future setbacks, knowing that there is usually more than one way to achieve things – and that the first time you encounter a difficulty, it doesn't mean you've failed.

● THE ZIG ZAG EXERCISE

We are our own harshest critics. The Zig Zag technique[3] is designed to bolster your belief in yourself, by being your own devil's advocate. The more you argue the case for believing in yourself and challenge your own negative self-talk, the more you defend and believe in your 'cause.'

How the zig zag technique works

1. First box – write down in the top left hand box a belief that you want to strengthen; maybe, after a setback you want to re-establish your confidence. Rate your confidence in percentage on a scale of 1-100%.

2. In the next box down on the right, write your doubts, reservations or challenges to that belief in box 1.

3. In the next box dispute your attack and re-defend your belief.

You can repeat steps 2 and 3 until you exhaust all your self criticisms. Be sure to address all the doubts that surfaced after your setback, and give a good argument for proving to yourself that there is a new, healthy and alternative way of thinking. Use as many forms as you need and be sure to stop while defending rather than attacking. If you can't help finishing with a criticism, ask a friend to provide an alternative, final defence. It may be helpful to do this exercise with a mentor or line manager to demonstrate the reasons for your self-doubt and discuss training or other means to help you overcome it.

Zig Zag Example: Presentations

Healthy belief 40% sure

When I do my presentation I want people to be honest about my ability; if they don't like it, I will not take it personally and it doesn't mean that I'm an unlikeable person.

Defence

Lots of people criticising my presentation would be unfortunate, but not the worst thing in the world. It doesn't follow that some of them don't like me just because their feedback was negative.

Attack

Yes, but lots of people not liking me must mean there's something wrong with me; it proves that I'm disliked and just not cut out for this post.

Defence 70% sure

I'm more likely to assume people don't like me but I don't know if that's really true. I simply cannot be liked by everybody, and not liking my presentation is totally different from not liking me. After all, I like some people better than others, but that doesn't mean that if they are not good at giving presentations I will like them any less. I will continue to learn from this experience, it's not failure – just a setback.

● NEXT STEPS

This tool is designed to focus your thoughts on how you cope with setbacks. Consider the following suggestions for practical next steps (although these are by no means exhaustive):

Use the exercises in this tool

Use the zig zag model to help you to cope with setbacks. Try and find opportunities to practise it. Use the 'significant life events' exercise to help you to think about how you have dealt with different situations.

Discuss how you cope with setbacks

Consider discussing these findings with someone you trust, such as a line manager, coach, mentor, colleague or even friends and family to gain different perspectives and to consider your way forward.

Seek out role models

Do you know someone who seems to cope well with setbacks? Think about what it is that you admire about them or their approach – and then compare yourself with them. The differences may at first seem too great, but it's a start and could reveal aspects of your own approach of which you were previously unaware.

Write a development plan

If you don't already have a personal development plan it's worth the time spent creating one. Make sure to set yourself clear objectives and practical things to do to help make a real improvement. For a start, this will indicate how much your attitude and ability to deal with setbacks has improved.

'A final thought'

Fear of failure is common to many of us but people can just as easily be hampered by fear of achievement. Often, people don't do things they're capable of because they want to 'fit in', rather than be set apart by success. Being good or 'the best' at something can be lonely and the pressure of people's expectations can itself prove to be a setback.

● FURTHER INFORMATION

If you found this tool useful then you are likely to find the following tools both insightful and relevant:

- How to raise energy levels
- How to reframe problems
- How to take control
- How to maintain momentum
- How to formulate action plans
- How to build resilience
- How to use optimism to achieve.

● REFERENCES

1 Kobasa, S. (1979). Stressful life events, personality, and health: An inquiry into hardiness. **Journal of Personality and Social Psychology**, 37, 1-11.

2 Caza, B. B., & Milton, L. P. (2012). Resilience at work: Building capability in the face of adversity. **The Oxford handbook of positive organizational scholarship**, 895-908.

3 Lindenfield, G. (1999). **Success from Setbacks.** Harper Collins.

4 Adapted from "CBT Training Course for Relate counselling training", East London University (1997).

HOW TO FORMULATE ACTION PLANS

Break down overall plans into more manageable chunks in order to more easily achieve your goals.

● ISN'T IT INTERESTING?

Everyone loves mazes. But what is the best plan of action in finding your way out of a maze? Try out this one below:

So what strategy did you use, if you used one at all?

Most people tend to either work through from the entrance to the exit using a process of trial and error or work back from the exit. You are likely to be engaging the logical part of your brain to work out a route to follow. When you take a wrong turn you will make a mental note not to repeat the error. When you are physically in a maze you will form a mental picture of your position and use this as a guide. This requires you to form a mental map which can be hard to maintain and update when you keep adding new information. So what would make life easier?

The right-hand rule

The right-hand rule, sometimes referred to as the wall-follower, is thought to be the best-known rule for traversing mazes; this rule works on the fact that all the walls of the maze are connected together or to the maze's outer boundary. By keeping one hand in contact with one wall of the maze 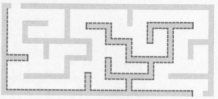 the player is guaranteed not to get lost and will reach a different exit if there is one; otherwise, they will return to the entrance. This strategy works best when implemented immediately upon entering the maze.

This tool can help

There is not always such a straightforward rule or plan of action to follow, but by planning ahead you are increasing your chances of reaching your destination quickly and effectively. This tool is all about **how to formulate action plans** and provides you with details of how and when plans should be evaluated or adjusted. This will help you to break down overall plans into more manageable chunks in order to more easily achieve your goals.

● SEVEN-STAGE ACTION PLAN MODEL

Action planning can be applied to any task or project, big or small, and is critical to the timely achievement of your goals. Effective action planning will help you to understand the breakdown of your task, what you need to do to achieve each stage and, where appropriate, how one task may be dependent on another.

It is fair to say that the action planning process can be seen as a cycle. The way in which you plan your actions will have an impact on the outcomes. In turn, the outcomes will impact the way you plan your next action. This model depicts the stages of an action plan and outlines some of the points that need to be considered at each stage of your plan.

This type of approach also works if there are several goals combined into an 'I need to clear my desk' requirement.

The seven stages

● THINGS TO CONSIDER AT EACH STAGE OF THE PROCESS

1. Pre goal-setting planning
   - Think about what you want – what is your desired outcome?
   - Why do you want it?
   - Think about whether you should want it – is it worthwhile?
   - Weigh up benefits and costs of your outcome.
   - Consider past experience.

2. Goal-setting
   - Set a target that is SMART.
   - Specific | Measured | Agreed | Realistic | Timed.

3. Plan how to get there
   - Think about what needs to be done to meet your target.
   - Break down your target into manageable chunks if it makes it easier.
   - Prioritise; what is most important?
   - Think about what resources you will need to help you achieve your goal.
   - Consider the barriers to your goal – what is likely to stop you from attaining it?

4. Take action

5. Review actions and adjust strategies
   - Take some time to review whether things are going to plan.
   - If things are not going to plan, consider why this is the case.
   - Take stock of new information or changes to the situation.
   - Be flexible and ready to rethink your strategy, if need be.
   - Be resilient – don't be disheartened if you don't get it right first time.

6. Achieve target

7. Evaluate outcomes
   - Congratulate yourself if you have achieved the desired outcome.
   - Consider what you could have done differently.
   - Think about your key learning for:
     > Your outcomes
     > Your action planning process
   - How can you incorporate your learning into your next action plan?

● WHAT IS A SMART TARGET?

SMART targets[1] are a very simple concept and in recent years have become one of the most popular ways of breaking down goals into measurable chunks. There are a number of differing opinions as to what SMART actually stands for. Here, we have outlined them all and explained the most popular. These steps are relevant whether you are setting your own target, or a target for an employee.

Specific or Significant or Stretching

 Measurable or Meaningful or Motivational

 Agreed or Attainable or Acceptable

 Realistic or Relevant or Rewarding

Timed or Timely or Tangible

Specific or Significant or Stretching – It is important that the goal is well defined and clearly articulated to ensure that you know exactly what you want to achieve. It will be easy to know when you have achieved your goal if you know exactly what it is in the first place!

For example, working towards a target such as '£10,000 a day' is more specific than a goal of having to 'do well at selling today'. This will help you and those around you to have a clear view of the plan and its progress.

It is also important for the goal to be specifically tailored to the individual and the situation. If, for example, it is the week before Christmas and you are putting in extra shifts, it is likely that the target would need to be adjusted to suit this specific situation.

Measurable or Meaningful or Motivational – Once you have your specific target and know exactly what is expected, it is important to consider how your performance will be measured against this target; it is not always as straightforward as just assigning monetary values!

For example, if your target is to become proficient at giving presentations, this may not be as easy to measure as whether you take £10,000 or not. Consider ways in which your outcomes can be measured – maybe feedback from those you are presenting to or a more quantitative measure, such as how many questions you garner at the end of the presentation. In order to make the measure valid, make sure to have planned it in advance to avoid the pitfall of choosing a favourable measure after you've taken the action.

Agreed or Attainable or Acceptable – This refers to agreement of what the target will be, between manager and managee. This is an important element of the process, because if you have not agreed what the target will be you may be working towards different aims!

For example, if a manager gets buy-in from the other party at the time of setting the target, it is more likely that the managee will feel that they have some ownership over it as they have had a say in what is to be achieved. They are then more likely to be motivated to achieve the goal. Where goals are decided by one party and rejected by the other it may be less likely that they are achieved.

Realistic or Relevant or Rewarding – This seems obvious, as there is no point in setting an unattainable goal. People generally find that the hardest part is to strike the right balance. A difficult, yet attainable, goal will lead to higher performance than will an easily attainable goal or, indeed, an impossible one. If a goal is too easy, an individual may lower their effort levels and so the motivation to complete the task will decrease. On the other hand, if the goal is seen as impossible there may be little motivation to work towards it as there is no point.

For example, it is important to work with an employer/employee to agree what is realistic for you and your situation. If there is a 200-page report to be written by the end of the week and the individual is out with clients for three days and in meetings for one day, it is unrealistic to expect that they will have time to complete it to a high standard in the timeframe required.

Timed or Timely or Tangible – It is most productive when setting targets to work to specific timescales. It is often useful to provide a deadline to work to in order to be clear about when the target needs to be achieved. This also provides you with a point in time to work towards, which is particularly useful if the outcome of a project is otherwise ambiguous.

For example, if the project comprised finding general information about a particular topic on the internet, you could be searching forever as there may be limitless information out there on that subject. If you have set your target in terms of how long you will spend on the task, you can work towards delivering your output at a certain time. As well as this, of course, it would be useless to set a sales person a target of £10,000 if they don't know whether this needs to be achieved in a day, a week, or a month!

● TIPS FOR ACHIEVING YOUR SMART TARGETS

The SMART system has been reviewed several times over the last 30 years, and modern studies[2] have shown that SMART is still an effective means of attaining long-term goals. Here are some recommendations for maximising the impact of SMART plans.

As far as possible, align your goals with your values

If your goal does not reflect your character or your beliefs, then it is less likely that you will be motivated to achieve it. Recent reviews[2] have shown that one of the key means of success with SMART is to tailor it to your own feelings and thoughts.

Let 3 to 5 key people know about the goals you have set for yourself

Finding supportive people who can encourage you is the key to successful goal-setting. Similarly, if someone other than you knows your plan it may help you to feel more motivated to carry it through!

Get things that you might need ready before you need them

If you prepare well, it will save a lot of time wasting and frustration later on.

Minimise potential challenges

Follow these three easy steps:

1. Create an action plan that is as thorough as possible including all the steps you need to go through to achieve your goal. These steps should be measurable and have due dates for each stage of the plan.

2. Incorporate all your actions into your schedule. Add them into your calendar and make sure you include some flexible time in case of extenuating circumstances that may cause delays.

3. Evaluate your progress regularly. There is nothing wrong with adapting plans as circumstances or priorities change. Anticipate any changes that need to be made so that you are not caught off guard.

Aim to complete one task associated with your target every day

Consistent actions will propel you towards your goal. Even if the task is a small one, remember that each action adds up and ticking something off your to-do list may even motivate you to do more!

Ensure that you have a support system in place

Consider the people around you who can provide encouragement, advice or feedback.

Reward yourself

Make sure you take time to congratulate yourself at each milestone; you don't have to wait until you achieve the overall goal, especially if the goal is a long-term one. Something as simple as taking some time out for yourself or indulging in a special treat can motivate you to keep going to achieve the end goal.

● NEXT STEPS

Now that you have considered the factors involved in formulating action plans and have some practical tips to guide you it is worth thinking about what to do next. Here are a number of suggestions to maintain momentum (although these are by no means exhaustive):

Reflect on your approach

Ask yourself what part of action planning you find most challenging or need most support with. Be honest with yourself to identify the positive and negative consequences of your current approach and think about what you would like to modify to improve.

Gather feedback on existing performance

You may find it useful to benchmark your current performance by asking for formal or informal feedback. This can help you understand how well others perceive your action planning. You can also help others around you by managing their expectations or by modifying your approach.

Look for opportunities to practise

Think about the opportunities that you have in your current work, or elsewhere, to practise action planning. This could involve your team or colleagues, so think about how this might play out.

Write a development plan

Use the tool in this document to highlight your action planning approach. Once you have established your preferences you could put together a focused development plan to improve your effectiveness.

● FURTHER INFORMATION

If you found this tool useful then you are likely to find the following tools both insightful and relevant:

- How to develop strategic long-term goals
- How to think about problems laterally
- How to prioritise tasks ready for action
- How to take responsibility
- How to delegate.

● REFERENCES

1 Doran, G. (1981). There's a SMART Way to Write Management Goals and Objectives, **Management Review** (AMA Forum).

2 Day, T., & Tosey, P. (2011). Beyond SMART? A new framework for goal setting. **Curriculum Journal**, 22(4), 515-534.

HOW TO WIN AND MANAGE RESOURCES

Understand what it takes to coordinate people in order for work to be carried out in the most effective way possible.

● ISN'T IT INTERESTING?

Many resources are won at the negotiating table. But who normally wins?

A matter of economics

The true fundamental of economics is the designation of finite resources to a population. This happens in many amazing and mundane ways in different scenarios every day. But one scenario you might be more familiar with is the battle for resources within your workplace. Whether it is the latest piece of technology, the new intern, or face-time with stakeholders, there's often not enough to go around. Some of the most successful people in business are experts at not only garnering these key resources, but justifying their ownership of them by managing them effectively. The most common way of (fairly) acquiring these sorts of resources is at the negotiating table, and the study below will help give you an insight into some of the nuances of negotiating.

We all have to start somewhere...

In a 2011 study by Michelle Marks & Crystal Howard,[1] 149 new recruits into a large field of industries were studied for their use of negotiation in starting salaries. It was found that those who used negotiating tactics got a starting salary $5000 higher, on average, than those who used no negotiating techniques.

The most successful were those who negotiated using competing and collaborative strategies. These are chacterised by an open and expansive attitude and were more likely to increase their salary by over $5000. Those who used compromising strategies took less on average, but still more than those who did not negotiate. Interestingly, men were far more likely to negotiate, and negotiate effectively, than women, although the reason for this was not clear.

To put it into perspective, if someone negotiated a $55,000 starting salary rather than a $50,000 salary, with an average 5% per year increase, they would earn over half a million more in a 40-year career than their colleague. So, it pays to negotiate.

This tool can help

Negotiating is certainly going to be a key factor in being able to win resources in your current job. But this tool aims to address all of the issues that you will face when trying to win and then manage resources.

● RESOURCE MANAGEMENT CYCLE

Effective management can be as much about acquiring appropriate or sufficient resources as deploying them – whether people, equipment or funds. Preparing a business case and persuading decision makers to provide what you need takes as much careful planning as the day-to-day running of a project or business.

Managing resources is an ongoing, cyclical process which we'll separate into stages to help you ensure daily and long-term smooth running – here's a simple model of what we mean:

Winning
resources

User
acceptance
testing

Building the
project team

Managing
Resources

Project
meetings

Planning

Recording
problems

Risk
management

● WINNING RESOURCES

You'll need to show that you've given careful, objective thought to why the success of your project requires the resources you're asking for. Give timescales for each stage as well as its overall completion and, importantly, describe the benefits it will deliver. You'll need negotiating and influencing skills:

Interpersonal awareness

What concerns might other people have about you winning the resources you're requesting? If it's money, is it wanted elsewhere? Try to find out information like this so that you can argue your case with some insight into what resistance you might encounter. If there's a general, financial concern, highlight how your project could improve productivity or bring other opportunities.

Bargaining

Negotiate a mutually beneficial outcome. If you know that someone else wants the same resources, try to agree a compromise. You may want someone with expertise from another team, which would leave it short staffed, so offer a replacement from your own team. Compromise on the less important issues to gain bargaining power for other issues!

Relationships

Building rapport with others can help win their support when you need it. Show interest in their work and concerns and offer solutions where appropriate.

Buy-in

To gain commitment from key decision makers, build their interest and involvement by demonstrating the practicality and benefit of your ideas. (There's more information about this in the tool: 'How to gain buy-in and commitment'.)

Organisational values

Show how your project aligns with the organisation's goals and objectives. The most persuasive argument for any organisation is one which positively impacts the bottom line!

Facts

Use facts and other information to support your business case. If you can, calculate the likely return on investment in your project – and the current, negative impact of any weaknesses your project might address.

Negotiation

Hopefully, your arguments will be sufficiently compelling to achieve the resources you want; if not there are three approaches that you could take:[2]

1. Request fewer resources or agree to a counter-request that someone else wants.

2. Refuse to give someone else what they want unless they give you something that you need in return. However, it is better to push ahead with strong arguments for the resources you need.

3. Team up and work with others to find a mutually beneficial outcome.

To reach a mutually beneficial outcome, identify shared interests and goals to create a cooperative atmosphere.

Where interests and goals differ you may agree 'trade offs' to accommodate each other. Also, remember to consider the other side's position – put yourself in their shoes. What kind of solutions are they looking for? Is there any way you can alter your requests to accommodate the other party?

● MANAGING RESOURCES

Now you've got the resources you need, the model we introduced back on page 60 will help you with the cyclical process of managing them effectively. The key aspects are:

Building the project team

Who's in your project team and what are their skills, methods of working and relationships? To work effectively, a team has to be more than a group of people with the collective skills required to, theoretically, achieve an objective. They need to identify with and cooperate amongst themselves for a common purpose. Consider not only their skills and experience but teamwork skills, existing relationships with other members of the group and any other factors which may also affect the outcome of the team's work.

Research into diversity[3] in the workplace suggests it's beneficial to have team members from different working backgrounds and with varied strengths and approaches to problem solving to resolve complex tasks. It might include those who'll focus on knowledge, strategy and ideas with others who will be action- or people-oriented. There's not much point in having a team of creative thinkers without one or two practically minded individuals who can work out how to make new ideas work.

Identifying team members' preferred methods of working helps everyone involved understand the group's dynamic – who's best placed to take on particular tasks and what to expect from each other, as well as how to counter possible weaknesses and forestall problems. Factoring knowledge like this into your style of management helps you support and motivate people to maximise the chances of your project's success.

Planning

Develop a formal plan so that everyone involved understands the requirements for each stage of the project, the deadlines and who's responsible for what. It could look like this:

No.	Task/Action	Start Date	End Date	Complete?	Owner

The following stages will help you to break down the project and plan the tasks:[4]

- Identify key 'milestones'.
- Identify the tasks needed to reach each milestone.
- Organise the tasks into a logical sequence.
- Work out any 'dependencies' between tasks. For example, if one task can't start before another's completed, plan this into your timeframes and deadlines.

- Provide a timescale for each task.
- Identify how each task will be done and by whom.
- Translate your timeframe into calendar dates.
- Allow for contingencies. If you schedule tasks too closely you'll have no leeway if things slip a little.
- Be flexible – your plan may need to alter during the project's course.
- Update your project plan. Record when each deliverable is completed.

Once you've got your plan sorted, a Gantt chart[5] is a great, quick visual reference. It'll help you stick to your timeframes and identify the knock-on effects of any missed deadlines, immediately.

	Week 1	Week 2	Week 3	Week 4
Task 1	██			
Task 2				
Task 3		██		
Task 4		██		
Task 5			██	
Task 6				██
Task 7				
Task 8				██
Task 9				██
Task 10				██

Meetings

Hold regular meetings with key stakeholders to update and discuss any changes in objectives, priorities and timeframes. Hold weekly meetings with the project team to check the progress and timeliness of each task. Check everyone's managing his or her workload and re-distribute tasks to maintain momentum, if appropriate.

Risk management

Take time to identify potential risks before the project starts. For each task involved, consider:

- What are the risks?
- How likely are they?
- If they did happen, what are the implications?
- What can you do to minimise them?

Recording problems

Record any problems during the project. The cause, when it happened, its impact on the progress and whether and how it was resolved. When evaluating the project after its close, a record of any problems will help you learn and refine future projects.

User acceptance testing (UAT)

As each key milestone is reached, check that any deliverables so far meet acceptable standards. For example, if you're developing a website for a client, ask them for an appraisal (UAT) at each milestone so that amendments can be easily incorporated. If this is left until later on, alterations may be much more difficult and have more impact on other aspects of the project.

● SELLING YOUR STRENGTHS

The following exercise will make you more aware of the best way for you to win and manage resources, according to your preferred methods of working – or to ensure you 'play to your strengths' and operate as effectively as possible. There are more, but we'll focus on the eleven working styles and strengths which relate to most of us.

Exercise: Using your strengths to win resources

Using the table below, identify what strengths[6] you think you have and how you could use them to win resources for a particular project.

Strength	Characterised by...	How to use it...
Analyser	You need evidence and proof for assertions and to understand broad implications.	Analyse any information you have to prove the relevance of your project; for example, how it can improve sales figures. Your analytical nature will enable you to build a strong business case using facts and figures. The organisation will be keen to see what impact you can have on the bottom line. However, be careful not to forget the 'people' side of things.
Values driven	Strong beliefs in values and ethics. Easy to trust.	Show how your project benefits the company while complying with or reinforcing its values. However, don't forget to make your argument practical and commercial.
Communicator	You like to enliven your ideas by using stories and images to capture the imagination of others.	Use your excellent communication skills to persuade others. Using a story is a good way of bringing your pitch to life and making it memorable. Use these skills to make your requests easy to understand and relate to. However, be careful not to appear to be relying on theory alone. Use some facts and figures, too.
Risk avoider	You are careful, vigilant and risk averse. You like to identify the risks in life, assess them and think about how they can be minimised. You like to plan ahead.	Your preference for planning and minimising risks could be a real strength when winning resources. Before pitching for your resources carefully plan out your project, identify your risks and how you will manage them. Presenting your information in a structured way will show you as well organised. However, be careful not to appear to lack imagination or be unreceptive to new suggestions and innovations.

Strength	Characterised by...	How to use it...
Planner	You have a natural affinity for project planning. You like planning, organisation and structure and working to timeframes and deadlines. You like breaking projects down into smaller, achievable tasks.	You'll be great at managing your resources but first you need to get them! Plan your project in detail to show how it would work and why you need the resources you've described but be careful of seeming inflexible. Don't come across as a bit of a 'control freak!'
Empathiser	You're able to see things from others' perspectives whether you agree or not and are able to anticipate their needs. You choose your words and tone to suit circumstances and people.	Use your empathetic skills to anticipate objections with prepared answers. However, don't be so concerned with what others want that you become distracted from your original purpose.
Innovator	You can energise people with your imagination and enthusiasm for finding ways to improve or invent ideas, processes and methods.	Use your creativity to inspire and engage people but be careful to include practical detail – remember some people can't visualise things as easily as you and are wary of change.
Optimist	You are quick to give praise, optimistic and enthusiastic. Others like to be around you and your enthusiasm's contagious! You make every project exciting and celebrate all achievements.	Use your ability to get people to like you and feel your enthusiasm to get them 'on side'. Tell them about past achievements to build their confidence in what you are proposing now. Play on the excitement that you are able to create in them to gain the resources you need. However, be careful not to let your positivity blind you to potential risks.
Problem solver	You love the challenge of identifying underlying problems and finding solutions.	Use your love of problem solving to structure your approach in two ways. First, explain the problems you've identified and their implications, then describe your solution, how it will work and its benefits. Secondly, treat winning resources as a problem solving exercise in itself. If you don't get agreement, ask if you can have more time – you might offer previously overlooked solutions and impress with your tenacity and ingenuity!
Self-assured	You're sure of your abilities and judgement, so exude and invite confidence.	Your air of confidence and track record will help persuade that you're able to deliver, but don't appear arrogant.
People person	You're great at winning people over. You like meeting new people and find it easy to build rapport.	Being able to build rapport is a great strength as people will like you and are more likely to be receptive. Use your skills to gain commitment but be careful not to become complacent. It's not enough that people like you; you still need to put forward a good business case!

● TEAM BUILDING

Exercise: Identifying team roles

People in teams have different methods of working and preferred roles. Research has identified nine clusters of behaviour typical in team working, known as Belbin's team roles.[7] It's useful to identify and understand the interplay of strengths and 'allowable weaknesses':

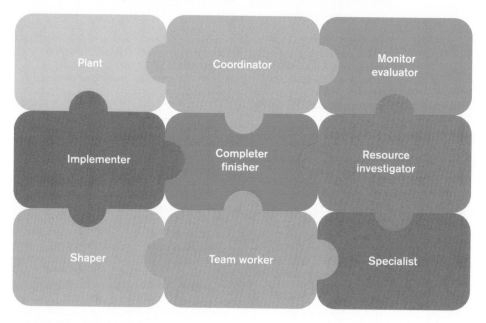

The following exercise is designed to help you understand your team's working styles and their potential strengths and weaknesses and, therefore, how best to assign roles or tasks.

Follow these steps:

1. Give each team member a set of the nine team roles with descriptions.

2. Ask each team member to describe which team roles best describe other members, using the card descriptions in the visual above.

3. Describe the roles to the team and agree as a group what each member's role preference is (remember to listen to each team member, too!)

4. Once everyone's team role has been decided, the team discusses who's most suited to undertake each task in the project.

5. Assign responsibility for tasks according to people's strengths.

6. Record who's responsible for each task and what their deadline is, in line with the overall project plan.

7. Ask team members to give one single promise and make one request connected with the project, for example: 'I promise to keep my mobile on so I can be contacted during the day. It really frustrates me if tasks are not completed on time so, please meet deadlines or promise to let me know if you can't!'

● NEXT STEPS

Once you have completed the exercise above, having identified team roles and assigned responsibility for tasks:

- Consider whether the absence of certain roles will be a problem; for example, if there's no 'implementer', how will ideas be made to work? In this situation think who else in the team may have the skills and be willing to accommodate another role. If there's no one, do you need to source an extra team member with appropriate skills?

- Think about whether there are too many people in the team with the same role; for example, if there are four 'plants', will there be conflict? Perhaps tasks should be assigned to individuals rather than 'roles' to avoid problems.

- Think about any gaps in the team's skills. For example, are there any necessary roles not represented?

Plant
This person is creative, imaginative and unorthodox. They solve difficult problems. However, they may ignore incidentals and be too preoccupied to communicate effectively.

Coordinator
This person is mature, confident and a good chairperson. They clarify goals, promote decision making and delegate well. However, they can be seen as manipulative and may offload personal work.

Monitor evaluator
This person is sober, strategic and discerning. They see all options and tend to judge accurately. However, they may lack drive and ability to inspire others.

Resource investigator
This person is extroverted, enthusiastic and communicative. They explore opportunities and develop contacts. However, they can be over-optimistic and lose interest after initial enthusiasm.

Completer finisher
This person is painstaking, conscientious and anxious. They search out errors and omissions. They deliver on time. However, they are inclined to worry unduly and are reluctant to delegate.

Shaper
This person is challenging, dynamic and thrives on pressure. They have drive and courage to overcome obstacles. However, they are prone to provocation and tend to offend people's feelings.

Team worker
This person is cooperative, mild, perceptive and diplomatic. They listen, build and avert friction. However they tend to be indecisive in crunch situations.

Specialist
This person is single-minded, self-starting and dedicated. They provide knowledge and skills in rare supply. However, they only contribute on a narrow front and tend to dwell on technicalities.

Implementer
This person is disciplined, reliable, conservative and efficient. They turn ideas into practical actions. However, they can be somewhat inflexible and slow to respond to new possibilities.

● FURTHER INFORMATION

If you found this tool useful then you are likely to find the following tools both insightful and relevant:

- How to influence others
- How to manage your impact
- How to create team identity
- How to build and maintain trust
- How to gain buy-in and commitment
- How to direct people
- How to delegate
- How to engage others to deliver.

● REFERENCES

1 Marks, M., & Harold, C. (2011). Who asks and who receives in salary negotiation. **Journal of Organizational Behavior,** 32(3), 371-394.

2 Pruit (1981) in Arnold, J., Cooper, C & Roberston, I. (1998). **Work Psychology.** Prentice Hall.

3 Jehn, K., Northcraft, G. & Neale, M. (1999). Why Differences Make a Difference: A Field Study of Diversity, Conflict and Performance in Workgroups, **Administrative Science Quarterly,** 44, 741–763.

4 http://www.jiscinfonet.ac.uk/InfoKits/project-management/pm-planning-1.1

5 Invented in 1917 by Henry Gantt as a project management tool.

6 Adapted from Rutigliano, T. & Smith, B. (2003). **Discover your Sales Strengths.** Random House Business Books.

7 http://www.belbin.co.uk/belbin-team-roles.htm

ENGAGING

HOW TO COMMUNICATE YOUR VISION

Think about ways of framing and communicating your vision clearly to enable others to carry out practical actions and tasks.

● ISN'T IT INTERESTING?

Communicating a vision to others involves translating an abstract concept into practical activities. Consider one of the most important translations in existence – the Rosetta stone.

Bringing people together

The Rosetta stone is an ancient Egyptian artefact, created in 196 BC. Currently in the British Museum, it features translations of a single passage in two hieroglyphic texts and Ancient Greek. In essence, the stone communicates a vision to the temple priests of a better tax system and in practice outlined restoration of tax privileges.

Translating a successful leadership vision into clear practical actions can bring people together, give them a sense of shared purpose and make the impossible possible. Evidence from a range of studies shows that successful communication of visions depends heavily on the leader being seen as identifying with group members and having a history of standing up for the group and its members in order for the group to be prepared to do the work necessary to realise the vision.

Together we stand

Social psychologists Julie Duck and Kelly Fielding[1] found in their research into leadership that group members show high levels of identification with their group when their leader is representative of that group – whatever course of action the leader chooses to pursue.

In 2001, Haslam and Platow[2] conducted a study to investigate how social identity affects translating visions into actions. They asked students to rate how much they would follow leaders based on videos of leaders outlining different visions for their campus. They found that students only generated arguments and ideas that backed up a leader's plans for improving their campus, if that leader had a record of making decisions that supported positions that the group related to (e.g. opposing government cuts).

This tool can help

Developing a vision into practical activities can bring a strategy to life and help to gain buy-in from those people responsible for making the idea a success. This tool is all about how to communicate visions into actions for others and will help you to think about ways of framing and communicating visions clearly to enable others to carry out practical actions and tasks.

● 3-STEP MODEL: TRANSLATING VISIONS INTO ACTIONS

You know the feeling? Maybe you had a great idea during the weekend, which you knew could really boost sales or solve some long running problem in the office. You could see it clearly, couldn't stop thinking about why no one else had come up with or understood it. So, on Monday, you approached the commercial director on her way out to lunch and ran it past her. She hasn't got back to you yet. When you put the idea to your team, it didn't come out the way it sounds in your head, somehow, but you're waiting to see what they come up with, after they've thought about it. You're feeling a bit crestfallen, even doubtful, maybe.

And so your vision lists, capsizes and sinks. This tool will help to make sure that next time, it'll be different. There are three separate stages to translating ideas into realities: Describing and communicating them effectively, winning other people's commitment and demonstrating what definitive action needs to be taken, and by whom. We can boil this down to Prepare, Explain and Ask or PEA for short.

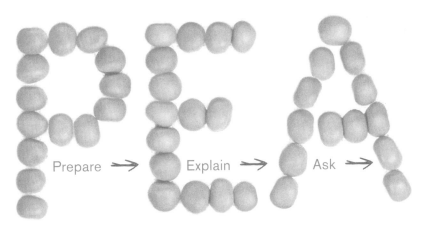

Prepare ➔ Explain ➔ Ask ➔

Step 1 – Prepare

Two key aspects of preparing to communicate your vision relate to personality and the context and task.

Personality – change oriented (big picture) or traditional (practical)?

You've got the idea, now comes the first, practical stage – thinking about the kind of people you're going to 'sell' it to, the situation or context it would apply to, and what it would involve, practically. This way, you can anticipate the kind of questions different people might ask and what will interest them the most.

People are very different; some are fired by the 'big picture', or overall concept, others by the detail and practical implications. You need to be aware also that some are more adventurous, or open to innovation and change, than others. These factors all make up a key element of your personality – how open to experience you are. So, think carefully about how to 'pitch' your idea in ways that will excite some and soothe or reassure others! (If you want to work out which 'type' you are, get in touch with us to complete a personality questionnaire such as the Myers Briggs Type Indicator (MBTI).

- Context and Task (CAT) – building meaning into actions.

Another acronym. As part of your initial, preparatory stage, you need to describe the CAT (Context and Task). This means the Context within which the people will be working, as well as the Tasks needed to achieve the outcome. If people understand only the situation (or Context), they may not fully understand what's expected of them. Or, if they understand only what's expected of them but without knowing why or what the final objectives are, they're likely to think their roles are unimportant or meaningless, which can affect performance.

The way you 'give actions meaning' impacts accuracy and performance. This is demonstrated in an example Richard Dawkins[3] uses, of an apprentice carpenter learning from a master craftsman. When the master builds a cabinet, he knows the purpose and result of everything he does, like measuring, matching grain, planing, oiling, etc.

Imagine the apprentice trying to learn without understanding what the master craftsman was making. The apprentice would try to copy him and do things without understanding why, making more mistakes as a result – or even producing something quite unlike what was intended!

If the apprentice knew what he was trying to make, he would make fewer mistakes, perhaps work out how to correct some of them himself, or at least understand that they were mistakes at all.

As for performance, research in the field of positive psychology[4] reveals that people are happier when they feel their work is 'meaningful'. That is, they know why they're doing it and what contribution it makes. In turn, the way people feel about their work impacts motivation, productivity and creativity.

So, hopefully you're convinced about the importance of preparation, in launching your idea. The next stage is how to 'Explain' it.

Step 2 – Explain

Once you've fully prepared, it's time to communicate your vision to others. Here's a diagram of what you need to do (we'll explain each bit afterwards):

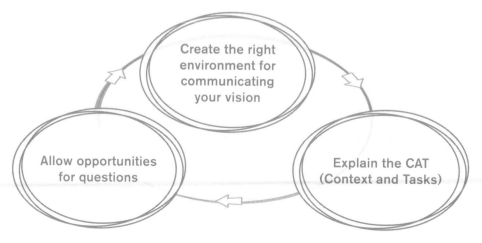

Creating the right environment for communicating your vision

The two most important elements of the 'environment' you create are making sure you allocate enough time, and how you communicate. By 'enough' time, we mean more than you first think is necessary, because if you're gabbling and checking your watch you'll seem disengaged from your audience, which won't win you any favours. Also, you need to give people time to assimilate what you're saying as you say it. Besides, if you seem rushed you'll be less engaging than you might otherwise be, or send an implicit message that 'this is not a priority'.

As to how you communicate, it's important to seem confident both in what you're saying and in your audience's ability to enable your vision. There's a psychological phenomenon known as the Pygmalion effect,[5] whereby high expectation elicits high performance – or, low expectation, low performance. There are plenty of examples where the expectations of influential people affect the performance of those around them.

Explain the CAT (Context and Tasks)

This is where your preparation will pay off. If you can clearly and confidently explain both the context and specific tasks required, you're half-way to translating your vision effectively. Please remember that explaining one (context or tasks) without the other will greatly reduce your chance of success.

Allow opportunities for questions

Try to anticipate potential questions and work out your responses or solutions. You might be asked:

- Who has responsibility for each part of the plan?
- What are the resources available for carrying out the activities?
- What support is there to help ensure that the project succeeds?

The final stage, 'Ask', is described below.

● STEP 3 – ASK

The last stage is to ask your audience to generate actions based on the CAT (Context and Tasks) that you have described. Involving your audience has several important benefits:

- It helps to promote buy-in and ownership, as people are more likely to feel responsible for the outcomes
- It allows you to check people's understanding of the CAT, as well as the suitability of their ideas
- It encourages them to generate their own mental models (i.e. understanding of the situation), which will be more elaborate and durable as a result.

More information about the importance of mental models and how effective models are generated is given below:

Developing effective mental models

People learn by developing 'mental models' (an understanding of how something works). The more accurate the mental model, the more effective the person will be at executing a given task. For example, a car mechanic will have a mental model describing how an engine works. Mechanics with the most elaborate and accurate mental models will be better able to diagnose and repair problems. Psychological research on learning[6] shows that effective mental models are those which are:

- Detailed – all of the important issues are understood
- Robust – long lasting
- Flexible – able to develop new insights.

To generate a detailed mental model, ask your audience to be as specific as possible when generating actions – not only will the detail be more tangible, but it will also be more readily applied.

To generate a robust mental model, encourage comments and feedback from others so that learning is shared amongst the group. Feedback is important so that people can refine their mental models.

Finally, to generate a flexible mental model, people must apply their own thinking rather than learning 'by rote'. This is why it is so important to involve your audience in the 'problem solving' of translating the CAT into more tangible and specific tasks.

● CONSOLIDATION: A GUIDANCE CHECKLIST

Here's a checklist to consolidate what you've read, based on the PEA acronym we talked about at the beginning of the tool:

Make a copy of it and tick off the sections as you complete them.

Activity	Checklist	Tick
Prepare		
Personality	Does my message cater for 'big picture' and 'practical, detail' people?	
Context and Task (CAT)	Am I being clear about the overall Context?	
	Am I clear about the Tasks that will contribute to achieving the Context – and making sure they're meaningful for those assigned to them?	
Explain		
Creating the right environment	Have I planned enough time for the meeting?	
	Have I thought about how to demonstrate confidence in the ability of my audience?	
Explaining the CAT	Have I clearly linked the Tasks to the Context?	
Allowing opportunities for questions	Have I allowed time for people to ask questions?	
	Have I thought about answers to likely questions from different people?	
Ask		
Involving	What specific tasks do the audience think will help them achieve the Context and enable my vision?	

● NEXT STEPS

You should now have an approach to translate your vision into action and a checklist to help ensure that you are successful in working through all stages of the process. Here are a number of suggestions for your next steps having read through this tool:

Look for opportunities to practise

Think of opportunities in your current work or outside, where you can translate a plan into action, using the PEA model and approach.

Gather feedback on existing performance

You may find it useful to think about which aspects you find easy or more difficult, then measure how you improve with practice, by asking for formal or informal comments and suggestions. This will help you to think about support that you may need moving forward.

Gauge other people's approaches

Ask colleagues or peers how they would describe an idea to a group. Do you know someone who's done a lot of this kind of thing? Ask them about their experiences; for example, what do they do that works well and what do they find particularly challenging? How have they improved their approach? What advice or support would they be able to provide?

● FURTHER INFORMATION

If you found this tool useful then you are likely to find the following tools both insightful and relevant:

- How to motivate others
- How to be assertive
- How to communicate effectively
- How to manage your impact
- How to create team identity
- How to gain buy-in and commitment
- How to develop strategic long-term goals
- How to make complex ideas simple, clear and concise.

● REFERENCES

1 Duck, J. & Fielding, K. (2003). Leaders and their treatment of subgroups: Implications for evaluations of the leader and the superordinate group. **European Journal of Social Psychology,** 33, 387-401.

2 Haslam, S. & Platow, M. (2001). The link between leadership and followership: How affirming social identity translates vision into action. **Personality and Social Psychology Bulletin,** 27, 1469-1479.

3 Dawkins, R. (2006). **The God Delusion.** Black Swan.

4 Linley, P. & Joseph, S. (2004). **Positive Psychology in Practice.** Wiley.

5 Rosenthal, R. and Jacobson, L. (1968). **Pygmalion in the Classroom.** New York: Holt, Rhinehart, and Winston.

6 Nadkarni, S. (2003). Instructional methods and mental models of students. **Academy of Management Learning & Education,** 2(4), 335-351.

HOW TO DELEGATE

Decide what kind of tasks may be delegated to your team, how to structure tasks to meet organisational goals, and ensure that professional development occurs in tandem.

● ISN'T IT INTERESTING?

You've got a report to write. You could give it to one of your team members, but it's easier to do it yourself. What would you do?

Understanding how and when to delegate

We've all been there, and in practice many managers find it hard to delegate. Reasons include the importance of the task or a lack of trust in others to get the job done. This line of thinking is self-defeating, as ultimately all tasks are kept on the manager's to-do list, adding to their stress and lessening the likelihood of task completion. In addition, staff are not stretched by taking on new tasks, and so their professional development suffers. Fred Fiedler[1] devised the 'contingency theory' to explain how behaviours should be matched to suit the team's characteristics. An effective leader will be able to predict how well the team members will respond to varying degrees of task clarity and understand individual strengths and team dynamics.

Time and time again

One of the most common reasons for not delegating is not enough time. An interesting recent study into time perceptions was carried out by Ola Svenson.[2] The research looked into how long we perceive things to take. Svenson set participants a number of mathematical tasks, like the two pairs (of a and b) below. Use your intuition to decide which option for each pair, a or b, will save the most time:

a) Travelling at 50km/h instead of 40km/h. a) Travelling at 50km/h instead of 30km/h.

b) Travelling at 130km/h instead of 80km/h. b) Travelling at 130km/h instead of 60km/h.

If you have assumed that option (b) saves the most time then you're like the majority of Svenson's participants. In fact, for the first pair, the time saved is roughly equal, and for the second pair, option (a) saves more time. If you don't believe us, do the maths on a piece of paper; whatever the distance it always works out the same!

This research provides evidence for a common error many of us make, which is underestimating how long things will take – known as the 'planning fallacy'.

This tool can help

Giving people time and space to carry out activities which may be a stretch (and that you think you can do in half the time) can often work out for the best in the longer term through individual development. This tool is all about **how to delegate** and will help you to decide what kind of tasks may be delegated to your team, how to structure tasks to meet organisational goals, and ensure that professional development occurs in tandem.

● DELEGATION AND THE PSYCHOLOGICAL CONTRACT

So many of us complain that we've got too much to do, both at work and elsewhere, but carry on chasing our tails, day after day. It's either because we don't trust anyone else to do things properly, or we think we might be suspected of not coping or 'passing the buck'. Often, too, people make a virtue of hectic busyness – as if it demonstrates indispensability, success – or just that their life is full of excitement!

Effective delegation, however, not only saves time but also speeds and increases the chance of successful outcomes. Indeed, it will also teach and motivate others. Most of the difficulties some of us experience are to do with the manner in which we delegate, or because what we say is incomplete or unclear. Stop, and consider for a moment or two, the fact that people are usually willing to help each other when asked – so why do we avoid delegating, and what goes wrong when we try to?

The role of 'psychological contracts'[3] in delegation

A formal contract is a written exchange of promises, but verbal agreements can be just as legally binding.

> The psychological contract refers to these same mutual beliefs, perceptions, and informal obligations between an employer and employee.

What we mean by 'psychological contract' is the implicit (not written or spoken) understanding between ourselves and the person with whom we make an agreement – or to whom we delegate a task. The relevance of it is that the parties involved may have different ideas about what that is and, therefore, about the way in which the agreement should be upheld or carried out.

You can see why people often unfairly accuse each other of not sticking to an agreement – and how often, too, you might complain that someone to whom you delegated something hasn't done it properly. Imagine, for example, agreeing with your line manager to spend a reasonable amount of time training and developing a new recruit. Now, imagine the kind of problems that would occur if you both interpreted 'reasonable amount of time' and 'training and developing' differently?

> When we are explaining or delegating something that's familiar or readily understood by ourselves, it's easy to assume we've made things clear – only to discover we didn't. Effective delegating is largely about the clarity of your instruction, and the more responsibilities you have, the more important it is to make sure people understand what you expect of them.

● WHAT TO DELEGATE?

It may sound obvious, but make sure you're not delegating things unnecessarily – things which are redundant, for example, and could be eliminated from your task list altogether. Or, are you delegating tasks for which you are not personally responsible?

On the other hand, even if there are routine things which you undertake as a matter of course and have not considered delegating, this may free up more of your time for other projects and provide someone else with an opportunity to learn, including:

- Things that aren't integral to your core specialism. For example, if you work in a small organisation you may have taken on extraneous responsibilities such as legal issues, HR functions, website design or IT support.
- Administrative tasks, including photocopying, printing, collating or data entry.
- Research assignments, or collecting of data for reports.
- Preparation of draft reports and problem analysis.

Delegating does not mean relinquishing all responsibility, either during or on completion of the task. Check that the person to whom you delegate has appropriate skills – or train them beforehand to ensure this is the case.

We've devised a model of the different levels of delegation which you may find useful.

● LEVELS OF DELEGATION

Level One: Following instructions only

At this stage all you're asking is that your instructions are followed, to complete the task. Be as clear as possible and, if you have time, describe the result you're expecting.

Level Two: Gathering data

Stage two is asking someone to gather information. Make it clear what you want. If you can, provide sources, but allow them to find some, too.

Level Three: Analysing data and providing recommendations

Now, you're allowing or 'empowering' the other person to complete the task. You require specific information but have enabled the other person to contribute input, also. Again, be as clear as possible.

Level Four: Deciding on course of action and seeing it through

When you are delegating a task at this stage you're entrusting the other person to decide the best course of action to achieve the result. Give guidance rather than instructions.

Level Five: Complete responsibility

This, highest, level of delegation requires you to describe your vision of what you want and give responsibility for its realisation to someone else. You will need to give strategic direction only and be available to review progress.

● DELEGATION – USING SMART GOALS

Use this framework to ensure the way you delegate is clear.

'SMART goals' is a framework which sets out stages to achieving goals generally.[4] Use the same stages to ensure effective delegating:

S pecific

- Clearly set out who and what is involved, and any requirements and restrictions.

M easurable

- It's important to set goals that are 'measurable' – that means break them down into stages to make them more manageable and so that you can gauge progress.
- Ensure that the person you are delegating to understands the result that is wanted.

A greed upon

- Make sure that you have 'buy-in', or commitment, from the person to whom you delegate.

R ealistic

- Are the necessary resources to complete the task available – including time, money and knowledge?

T imely

- Always give a time limit. Misunderstandings occur when people are asked simply, to 'complete it as soon as possible' or 'within a reasonable timeframe'.

● DELEGATION HINTS AND TIPS

You should ensure that the required standards are clear, alongside the expected outcomes. This means gaining agreement on what needs to be done, when by and to what standard. This will help ensure that the person you are delegating to has a clear understanding of what is required and has the opportunity to ask questions to clarify their understanding.

Here are some quick reminders of important things to remember when delegating:

- **Delegate the objective, not the procedure** – everyone has different working methods, so concentrate on the results rather than someone's methods of achieving them.
- **Get regular updates** – these keep everyone aware of progress and provide opportunities to deal with problems before it's too late! Set deadlines for various stages so that you have a timescale.
- **Delegate carefully** – be sure not to repeatedly give the tasks to the most experienced or first available person. These are not necessarily the most appropriate people for the task.
- **Delegate broadly** – to give people new experiences and training.
- **Gain clear feedback** – it will help you hone your delegating skills!

- **Delegate authority with responsibility** – giving people some 'ownership' of the task reduces their need to continually seek approval.
- **Trust people** – they don't want to fail! Take care not to continually check up on them, unless they request this.
- **Be prepared for the learning curve** – short-term errors can be traded for long-term benefits and results.
- **Check they have what is needed to complete the task** – always ask, 'What else do you need to get started?' or 'Is there anything else I can help you with?'
- **Praise and feedback** – this is important for you and the person to whom you've delegated the task, because it's a learning curve for both of you. Next time, the process will be easier for you, and he or she will better understand how you like to work and the kind of results you want.

● FURTHER INFORMATION

If you found this tool useful then you are likely to find the following tools both insightful and relevant:

- How to motivate others
- How to be assertive
- How to support and challenge in tandem
- How to develop others
- How to win and manage resources
- How to engage others to deliver.

● REFERENCES

1 Fiedler, F. (1967). **A Theory of Leadership Effectiveness.** New York: McGraw-Hill.

2 Svenson, O. (2008). Decisions among time saving options: When intuition is strong and wrong. **Acta Psychologica,** 127, 501-509.

3 Rousseau, D. (1996). **Psychological Contracts in Organisations: Understanding Written and Unwritten Agreements.** Newbury Park, CA: Sage.

4 DuFour, R., Eaker, R., & Many, T. (2010). **Learning by doing: A handbook for professional learning communities at work.** Bloomington, IN: Solution Tree Press.

HOW TO ENGAGE OTHERS TO DELIVER

Recognise the qualities of individual team members, delegate tasks appropriately and engage people to take ownership of their roles and deliver to the best of their abilities.

● ISN'T IT INTERESTING?

Have you ever been in a tug of war to get people to do their work?

Knowing how to engage others to deliver

How do people become engaged in their jobs? Is it something about them, the job itself or can you as a manager motivate people so that they are involved in their jobs and give their best? Several studies examining management styles and levels of individual and team output have shown that telling people what and how to do their jobs might not be the best technique to get them going and that in the majority of cases, collaboration, motivation and involvement in decision making are vital to engage others.

What works best for engaged employees?

In 1939, a group of researchers led by psychologist Kurt Lewin[1] set out to identify the impact of different leadership styles on team productivity and morale. They examined three different leader styles – authoritarian, laissez-faire and democratic. The individual and group outputs as well as general group atmosphere were then compared between the groups.

They found that both individual and group performance as well as the group atmosphere (engaged and motivated) was highest in teams led by democratic leaders – where people were consulted about the goals of the group and the approaches to take and where their opinions were valued.

The results led the researchers to believe that the observed differences could not be explained in terms of individual differences of particular team members but was directly related to the style with which these groups were managed.

This tool can help

Since that seminal study, it has been shown time and again that if managers consult staff and include them in the decision-making process, their level of engagement and individual output increases. This tool is about how to engage others to deliver and will help you understand your role in recognising the qualities of individual team members, delegating tasks appropriately and engaging people to take ownership of their roles and deliver to the best of their abilities.

● INTRODUCTION TO ENGAGING OTHERS

Whether you're a line manager, a project manager or have no managerial responsibilities at all, we all sometimes need to engage others to ensure we can fulfil our own responsibilities.

How do you go about it?

- Do you delegate to others?
- Do you set others tasks?
- Do you ask colleagues to pick up on things for you that you need assistance with?
- When you do this, what are the results?

Most of us have asked and relied on someone to do something but been left thinking we'd have been better off doing it ourselves!

Or, we find ourselves picking up the trail of a colleague who hasn't done things the way we asked and find ourselves with as much work, if not more than we began with.

Maybe, if you've managed a project, you gave most of the more mundane tasks to a particular individual to free up others' time. Can you remember how that individual performed or reacted?

Delivering high quality work is, of course, enough of a challenge without the added burden of thinking about more than monitoring people's progress against deadlines.

Understandable as this is, in order to get the best out of the people you work with, you need to recognise that the process of thinking and planning how to fully engage them (instead of merely instructing them) is critical to interim and eventual success.

We'll show you how to recognise the strengths of those you work with and how to engage, and motivate them to deliver — at all costs.

● RECOGNISING THE STRENGTHS OF OTHERS

As a manager, you're accustomed to assessing people's skills and knowledge according to particular roles, but we'll give you a structured and more sophisticated method of considering how to optimise resources.

This model describes a process of identifying the strengths of others. However, you don't have to stick to it rigidly — identify or adapt those parts of it that are most helpful to you:

Strengths Identification and Matching Process

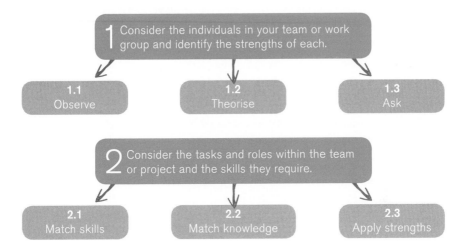

Stage One

Consider the individuals in your team or work group and identify the strengths of each.

1.1 Observe	• What is it that energises this person?
	• What is it that makes this person feel under pressure?
	• When have you seen this person absorbed in a task?
	• How do others most commonly describe this person?
1.2 Theorise	Which of these team roles are represented in your team[2]:
	• **Coordinator** – clarifies goals, promotes decision making
	• **Shaper** – challenging, dynamic, drives to overcome obstacles
	• **Plant** – creative, imaginative, solves difficult problems
	• **Monitor-Evaluator** – strategic, sees all options, judges accurately
	• **Implementer** – disciplined, reliable, turns ideas into practical actions
	• **Resource Investigator** – extrovert, explores opportunities, develops contacts
	• **Team Worker** – co-operative, perceptive, diplomatic, listens and builds
	• **Specialist** – single-minded, dedicated, provides knowledge and skills in rare supply
	• **Completer Finisher** – conscientious, searches out errors, delivers on time.
	Consider this person's preferences, e.g. how do they make decisions? How do they gather information? How do they organise their 'outer world?' Do they get their energy from within or from others?
1.3 Ask	• Ask them to describe what most energises, absorbs and motivates them.
	• Ask them about the work they've been doing in the last month and notice which roles they talk about excitedly and fluently and those they have little to say about.
	• Ask them when they've felt under pressure.
	• Ask them when they've felt comfortable – and when challenged. Notice which challenges have been enjoyable and which they found stressful.

2.1 Match skills	● Consider the tasks that need to be completed and the roles that need to be played and write down the skills that are required for each. Consider which individuals have the necessary skills and enjoy using them.
2.2. Match knowledge	● Are there any areas of specific knowledge or experience that are required to complete the tasks and play the roles?
2.3 Apply strengths	● Consider which tasks and roles would benefit from the strengths of team members that you identified at stage one.
	● Bear in mind that variety in a role is important and to engage others you'll need to help them use more than just one of their strengths!
	● Consider the strengths of each individual in the team and consider how you can bring their strengths to life in completing the task or in the role that you are giving them.
	● If you're not sure about how you can best use an individual's strengths, be sure to ask them.

● ENGAGING DIFFERENT TYPES

Here are examples of how to use team members' strengths, which will help increase their desire and ability to deliver.

How to engage an achiever

An 'achiever' is someone who is motivated by their progress and completion of tasks, and tends to be very goal- and time-orientated.

- Recognise that they like to be busy and sitting in meetings may bore them. Ask them to attend crucial meetings only, where they'll be more fully engaged.

- Help them recognise their simpler achievements so they're aware of their productivity as well as the time they contribute, such as the number of customers served, phone calls made, reports reviewed, etc.

- Reward them for achieving difficult tasks and set further challenges immediately rather than giving a rest or an easy assignment.

How to engage someone strong in input

Someone strong in input tends to want to influence decisions and output by providing information and expertise and also offering constructive criticism. They tend to be very analytical in their approach.

- Engage their natural inquisitiveness by asking them to undertake associated research for a project, before work begins on it.

- Give them a role in which they'll be doing research. Keep them informed of any news that influences the team or project. Pass on journals, articles and books to stimulate their interest.

- Encourage them to organise all the information they collect, so others in the team can benefit from it.

How to engage someone high in idea generation

People high in idea generation tend to be very creative and imaginative. They will drive the early theoretical stages of a project and provide constant inspiration throughout.

- Position this person where they can produce creative ideas which will be valued.

- Whatever their field, make the most of their ability to design. Use these skills at the beginning of a project where concepts and project outlines are being created.

- Ask others to come to them to 'bounce around' ideas. They'll love the thrill of helping others think things through and the ideas will be of better quality as a result.

- They need to know how everything fits together. Take the time to explain how decisions are arrived at.

Use the grid below to help you engage those around you more effectively and confidently. Consider how you can:

- Observe and talk to team members to identify motivations, strengths and development needs

- Match team members' skills and knowledge to the tasks in hand to ensure each individual has an opportunity to work to his or her strengths

- Use the tips given to help you engage the different characters in your team.

Use the grid to systematically work through the previous steps:

Tasks	Skills	Name	Knowledge Management

● NEXT STEPS

Here are some practical suggestions that may help to improve your ability to engage others to deliver:

Use the grid template with your team

Use the template to record observations and conversations regarding team member characteristics. Use the data recorded in the template to delegate tasks. Having delegated tasks set SMART goals and realistic deadlines. Agree plans with each team member. Monitor progress against the agreed action plans and review on a regular basis.

Use the exercises in this tool

Use the process described in this tool to uncover and explore the individual characteristics of your team members and how they affect the ability of each to deliver.

Write a development plan

Make 'engaging others to deliver' part of your personal development plan, or create one using this topic as a starting point. Ensure you clarify your objectives and give yourself practical things to do to make real progress.

Gain feedback

Ask for comments from your team about how they perceive you. Encourage them to be honest – assure confidentiality, if necessary – to get a realistic and objective overview.

● FURTHER INFORMATION

If you found this tool useful then you are likely to find the following tools both insightful and relevant:

- How to direct people
- How to motivate others
- How to influence others
- How to gain buy-in and commitment
- How to make reasoned judgements
- How to deliver every time
- How to maintain momentum
- How to delegate
- How to use optimism to achieve.

● REFERENCES

1   Lewin, K., Lippit, R. & White, R. (1939). Patterns of aggressive behavior in experimentally created social climates. Journal of Social Psychology, 10, 271-301.

2   van Dierendonck, D., & Groen, R. (2011). Belbin revisited: A multitrait–multimethod investigation of a team role instrument. European Journal of Work and Organizational Psychology, 20(3), 345-366.

3   Adapted from Buckingham, M., & Clifton, D. (2001). Now Discover your Strengths: How to Develop Your Talents and Those of the People You Manage. London: Pocket Books.

SUSTAINING

HOW TO BUILD RESILIENCE

Overcome obstacles and explore what resilience means. Understand how you can deal with difficult situations more effectively.

● ISN'T IT INTERESTING?

We all know how resilient weeds can be. They just keep coming back regardless of how hard we dig.

Deliver every time

This 'bouncebackability' is proof that nature shows resilience to even some of the toughest conditions. In the same way, work can be tough, drain our energy and occasionally leave us feeling demotivated and tired. The pace and nature of the contemporary workplace is such that we all need to understand how to take care of ourselves to deal with demanding workloads. A psychologist named Hans Selye[1] nicely captured people's responses to work pressures as capacity, demand, adaptation. As humans, we are very adaptable and some of us cope better than others with stress and pressure. The study below explored our perceptions of how hardy we are:

The power of positive thought

Jason Riis and his colleagues[2] investigated how resilient we are likely to feel if faced with a life threatening situation, such as having a terminal illness. They asked patients who had end stage kidney illnesses and some 'healthy' people to record their mood every 90 minutes by pocket computer for a week.

Surprisingly, the average ratings for both groups were equally positive but when interviewed, the healthy participants predicted that their mood would be negative most of the time if they had chronic kidney illness. Conversely, the patients predicted that they would feel much more positive if they had never had a kidney illness. So both groups appeared to underestimate the resilience of people's mood to illness.

This tool can help

Like weeds in a garden, there are many occasions in life where we experience setbacks and have to bounce back in the face of adversity. This tool is all about **how to build and maintain resilience** in order to overcome these obstacles and helps to explore what resilience means and help you to understand how you can deal with difficult situations more effectively.

● WHAT IS RESILIENCE?

- When something goes wrong, do you bounce back or fall apart?
- When faced with challenges, do you bury your head in the sand or tackle them head on?
- When circumstances change, do you feel powerless or think of it as an opportunity?

Resilience is the ability to adapt to or withstand adversity, trauma, tragedy, threats and other stress causers. It is the process of embracing challenges and 'bouncing back' from difficult experiences.

Resilience has always been admired, as this quote from Horace, the Roman poet, describes:

'Adversity has the effect of eliciting talents, which in prosperous circumstances would have lain dormant'.

Alongside this century's achievements – globalisation, ever increasing amounts of and access to information and continual change – causes of stress proliferate.

The key to surviving today is resilience. It's our skills and attitude which help us overcome adversity, turn challenging events to our advantage and determine whether we win or lose.

● ARE YOU RESILIENT?

So, do you consider yourself resilient?

Use this short quiz[3] to get a general idea of how resilient you think you are. Remember, your results will not be seen by anyone (unless you want them to be), so be honest. In fact, that's the starting point to becoming resilient – 'be true to yourself!'

Statement	Response
I embrace change and adapt well.	Yes/No
I feel in control of my life.	Yes/No
I tend to bounce back after hard times.	Yes/No
I find support in others.	Yes/No
I always look on the bright side of life.	Yes/No
I can think clearly and logically under pressure.	Yes/No
I can always see the lighter side of stressful situations.	Yes/No
I have real strength of character.	Yes/No
I know where to turn for help.	Yes/No
I seek out fresh challenges.	Yes/No
I can cope with ambiguity and uncertainty.	Yes/No

If you answered 'yes' most often, congratulations – you're clearly a hardy individual and probably deal with most ups and downs successfully. If, however, you didn't have as many as you hoped for, don't worry, it's not too late!

Whether you had more 'yes's' or 'no's' in the quiz, make a note of the 'no's' which you feel are important for you to revisit and, as you work through this tool, relate them to the exercises and advice to get what you need most from it.

Resilience is not something you either have or don't have. It's not fixed and it is important you don't fall into the trap of thinking that once you reach adult life, you are what you are and nothing's going to change. Resilience is something that can be learned and developed.

In this tool, we'll help you understand the three attitudes needed to build resilience and teach you a coping strategy to maintain it.

● BUILDING RESILIENCE – THREE RESILIENT ATTITUDES

Over the course of twelve years, psychologists in the US studied resilience in the workplace, identifying its three foremost characteristics – the 3 Cs.[4] Significantly, each of these can be nurtured and developed.

Commitment

Commitment helps you engage fully in events around you. During stressful circumstances, you do your best to remain an active participant and don't fade into the background. You find meaning and fulfilment through playing an active role in life.

Control

Control allows you to take direct, hands-on action to manage change and the problems it may cause. You firmly believe you can influence the outcome of a stressful situation and are, as a result, better able to cope with it.

Challenge

Challenge helps you embrace change and adversity as normal processes. You can identify opportunity in every difficulty and think of change as a challenge.[5]

● BUILDING RESILIENCE – A PRACTICAL GUIDE

Use a paper and pencil to work through the following steps:

Step One

Think about people you work with, in relation to the three attitudes of commitment, control and challenge.

Identify one person you consider to be highly resilient; that is, the person who demonstrates strength and courage to overcome adversity.

Identify one person who you think lacks resilience; i.e. the person who was withdrawn and felt powerless and threatened under stress.

Step Two

Ask yourself the following of each of the people you identified:

- What stressful circumstances did he or she encounter?
- What problem-solving actions did the person take? Did they work?
- Did the person's coping efforts include getting support from others?
- How did his or her coping efforts express attitudes of commitment, control and challenge?

Step Three

Reflect on your findings and try to compare them with your own reactions to stressful situations. Do you see any similarities? Which attitudes do you display well? Which do you need to work on?

Apply your understanding of those around you to your own behaviours – that means borrow the good stuff and actively avoid the bad stuff! Practise demonstrating the three building blocks of resilience.

● MAINTAINING RESILIENCE – TRANSFORMATIONAL COPING

Understanding the nature of resilience to build your own hardiness in the face of adversity is only the beginning – you need to adopt those characteristics and maintain them, which is where transformational coping comes into play.

Transformational coping is a 'proactive mental and behavioural coping style' necessary to staying resilient. It's about turning stressful situations into opportunities and has three stages:

Broadening your perspective

The first stage is to make the cause of stress more tolerable by putting it in perspective. Many 'stressors' at work happen at an organisational level and are not specifically targeting you. For example, if your company has significantly increased your targets for the new financial year, you might put this in perspective by realising that it's reacting to internal and external pressures, not singling you out as an under-performer. In adjusting your attitude, you gain a more balanced perspective and can start developing those resilient characteristics needed for the challenges ahead.

Deepening your understanding

Next, get a better understanding of what's stressing you and why. You, your problems, those around you and the situation itself all co-exist. Transformational coping helps you understand how separate elements interact to create and increase the stress you feel. Exploring the causes produces insights and opportunities to make yourself feel and cope better.

Taking decisive action

Now, sitting around, mulling over what's making you stressed is pointless unless you decide to do something about it. Taking decisive action can take a little courage – there are times when we'd all rather collapse under the duvet and shut the world out. Instead, take a few deep breaths and 'map out' a strategy. Using this third element of transformational coping helps you turn stressful circumstances around and bring the 3 Cs to the fore.

● MAINTAINING RESILIENCE – A PRACTICAL GUIDE

Step One – Estimate the impact of the stressful event

A useful way of gauging this is to use the 'ABCs of Human Needs' – ask yourself if whatever situation's worrying you now violates any of these:

Accomplishment – The need to achieve worthwhile goals.

Belonging – The need to define oneself through relationships with others.

Comfort – The need for calm and security in life.

Dependability – The need for predictability and stability.

Esteem – The need to feel good about ourselves.

Finances – The need for enough funds to live a fulfilling life.

Step Two – Broaden and deepen your understanding

- Reflect on the situation, then **describe it** as fully and comprehensively as you can.
- Identify ways in which the situation **could be worse** and ways in which it **could be better**.
- Explore ways in which the worst of those two versions could really happen, to **understand how bad things** happen and what can be done to avoid them.
- Explore ways in which the better version could occur, to **understand what can be done** to bring about a good result.
- Try to use the knowledge you have learned to **put the event into perspective** and to consider ways of resolving it.

Step Three – Take decisive action

Hopefully, by now you've got an idea of the shape and size of your problem and understand it a little better. However, although you probably feel a bit relieved about it all, don't stop there.

- Now, you must resolve it. Put together an action plan, using the following guide:
- Identify the goals of your action plan, working from your newly gained understanding of the problem.
- Explore, identify and document the actions you need to take to achieve your goals.
- Set out SMART* objectives: **S** pecific **M** easurable **A** greed **R** ealistic **T** imed
- Stick to your plan and do it (Remember, though, to revise it if necessary).

*For further information on how to create an action plan see the tool 'How to formulate action plans'.

● SIX TOP TIPS

In addition to building the 3 Cs and developing your transformational coping skills, try some of these tips[6] as well, because they really work!

Seek and accept the help of others

Develop strong, open and honest relationships with colleagues, friends and family. They are a valuable source of support, feedback and help; make use of them.

Make yourself laugh

As the good doctor said, '**laughter is the best medicine**'. Use laughter and humour to defuse the stress.

Be proud of yourself

This doesn't mean shouting to the world about how great you are. It is about nurturing your self-confidence and self-esteem.

Use determined language

Change 'If I can...', 'I hope...', 'Maybe...' to 'I can...', 'I will...', 'I must...'.

Take care of yourself

Be good to yourself, both physically and mentally. Take up a hobby, work on that exercise regime, read a good book and get enough sleep. All of these build mental resilience.

Accept change as an important part of life

Change is good. It revitalises and energises. Risking an overused catchphrase: it refreshes the parts other things can't reach.

● FURTHER INFORMATION

If you found this tool useful then you are likely to find the following tools both insightful and relevant:

- How to formulate action plans
- How to be assertive
- How to manage your impact
- How to take control
- How to maintain momentum
- How to cope with setbacks.

● REFERENCES

1 Selye, H. (1956). **The Stress of Life.** New York: McGraw-Hill.

2 Riis, J., Loewenstein, G., Baron, J., Jepson, C., Fagerlin, A., & Ubel, P. A. (2005). Ignorance of hedonic adaptation to hemodialysis: A study using ecological momentary assessment. **Journal of Experimental Psychology: General,** 134, 3–9.

3 Adapted from the Mayo Clinic website: **Resilience: Build Skills to Endure Hardship.** MayoClinic.com http://www.mayoclinic.com/health/resilience/MH00078

4 Adapted from Maddi, S. & Khoshaba, D. (2005). **Resilience at Work: How to succeed no matter what life throws at you.** New York: Amacom.

5 For further reading see – **10 Tips to Build Resilience.** American Psychological Association http://psychcentral.com/lib/2007/10-tips-to-build-resilience/

6 Adapted from Reivich, K. & Shatte, A. (2002). **The Resilience Factor: Seven essential skills for overcoming life's inevitable obstacles.** New York: Broadway Books.

HOW TO USE OPTIMISM TO ACHIEVE

Find out how taking a more positive approach can help you to realise your goals.

● ISN'T IT INTERESTING?

Are you a 'glass half empty' or a 'glass half full' kind of person?

Can you see the positives in what you do?

Optimism has been defined as 'an inclination to anticipate the best possible outcome'. How you see situations can have a profound effect on how you think you are going to be able to cope with challenges or take opportunities. The study below outlines some very good reasons to be optimistic.

Is optimism the key to Olympic success?

In 1995, three researchers[1] illustrated the power of optimism in a study of Olympic medallists. They found that those athletes who achieved silver medals were often less happy than those who achieved bronze medals.

This may seem counterintuitive – the higher an athlete places in the medals table, the happier we would assume them to be. However, the research shows that a person's actual achievement often mattered less than how they perceived that feat.

Those who achieved second-place success appeared to base their feelings on the context of 'failing to be the best'. However, those who achieved third-place positions were more likely to make downward comparisons, being pleased to have achieved a medal position.

Interestingly, those athletes who felt more satisfied with their position (i.e. the bronze medallists) were, in turn, more motivated to maintain their efforts and engage in further training to sustain such feelings. That is to say, those athletes who framed their achievement in a positive manner – glass half full – were more likely to succeed in the future compared to those athletes who saw the result unfavourably – glass half empty.

4. Can you reframe your belief based on this information?
I gave a bad presentation on this occasion for various reasons, but I have shown in the past that I can give good presentations.

5. Visualise the situation going better next time. What does this look like?
I would be better prepared and more able to deal with PowerPoint if it crashed. I would remain calm.

6. What small step can I take right now to move towards this?
I can enrol on the in-house PowerPoint course. I can ensure that I go to bed early before a big presentation and give myself more time for preparation and potential last-minute changes.

● HOW TO COUNTER NEGATIVE SELF-TALK

As we go about our lives, we all 'self-talk', which is our inner voice saying such things as, 'I'm really looking forward to that game'. However, sometimes that self-talk can be negative and hamper us, such as when a test is coming up and we say to ourselves 'I'm going to fail for sure', thereby sowing the seeds of our own downfall.

The most effective way to resist persistent negative self-talk is to challenge it with positive, realistic analysis. The tool below is designed to help you analyse and challenge negative self-talk by looking at it objectively and giving you the platform to challenge and defeat it, preventing it from bringing down your natural potential.

Tool to analyse your self-talk

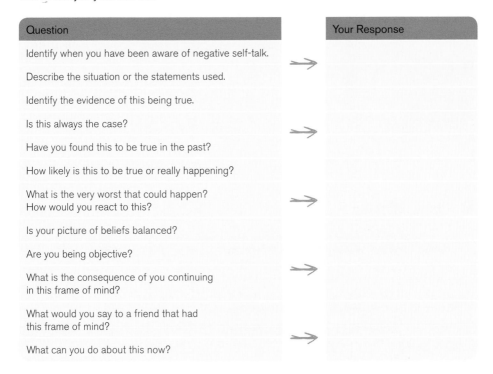

Question	Your Response
Identify when you have been aware of negative self-talk.	
Describe the situation or the statements used.	
Identify the evidence of this being true.	
Is this always the case?	
Have you found this to be true in the past?	
How likely is this to be true or really happening?	
What is the very worst that could happen? How would you react to this?	
Is your picture of beliefs balanced?	
Are you being objective?	
What is the consequence of you continuing in this frame of mind?	
What would you say to a friend that had this frame of mind?	
What can you do about this now?	

Seek inspiration

Find something that inspires you (such as a book of quotations or autobiographies of successful people in your field) and use it daily.

● HINTS AND TIPS TO REMAIN OPTIMISTIC

Avoid negativity

Spend time with people who have a positive outlook.

Focus on strengths

Olympic athletes didn't focus on the sports they couldn't do, but on becoming experts in the ones they were better at. Try doing the same. Acknowledge and manage your development areas – but concentrate most of your energy in developing your strengths even further.

If you can't change it, manage it or ignore it

Identify what you can change and forget the rest.

Look for the hidden positives in situations

Explore the potential benefits of the situation.

Use positive language

Eradicate 'Yes, but' from your vocabulary.

Summary

Remaining optimistic can simply be a case of reframing negative points to consider the more positive angles. Try to focus as much as possible on a solution-oriented view, especially when dealing with important, high pressure situations at work.

● FURTHER INFORMATION

If you found this tool useful then you are likely to find the following tools both insightful and relevant:

- How to reframe problems
- How to be confident in making judgement calls
- How to balance risk with potential benefits.

● REFERENCES

1   Medvec, V. Madey, S. & Gilovich, T. (1995). When less is more: Counterfactual thinking among Olympic medalists, Journal of Personality and Social Psychology, 4.

2   Seligman, M. E., & Csikszentmihalyi, M. (2000). Positive psychology. The science of optimism and hope: Research essays in honor of Martin EP Seligman, 415-429.

3   Segerstrom, S., et al. (1998). Optimism is Associated With Mood, Coping, and Immune Change in Response to Stress. Journal of Personality and Social Psychology, 74, 6.

4   Seligman, M. (1990). Learned Optimism. New York: Knopf. Free Press.

5   PK500 Mood and Emotion at Work. June 2006, Survey 3. Pearn Kandola.

6   Glass, C. (2007). Solution Focussed Coaching: A Method for Applying Positive Psychology in the Workplace. Special Group in Coaching Psychology One Day Workshop.

HOW TO GET THE MOST OUT OF YOURSELF

Make the most of your potential, by thinking about how best to align your motives with your abilities.

● ISN'T IT INTERESTING?

We only use 10% of our brain…

Maximising our mental ability

This common saying has been exposed as largely a myth by contemporary research. Instead, it has been shown that our brains tend to work in bursts which can be using a wide array of different sections at any one time. These bursts become more coordinated as we repeat certain tasks and actions. This is the basis for what psychologists call the 'practice effect'. This explains how practising tasks gets the best out of our brains. As well as our experience, understanding our motivations and talents is vital to unleashing our full potential at work. Psychologists who study people at work have consistently found that if people feel that their motives line up with the type of work they are doing, then they are both happier and more successful in their careers. This is called the actualising tendency.

Believe you can do it

In a recent study, Hoffman and Spatariu[3] tested the impact of ability and self belief on problem-solving success. They tested 81 students in mental multiplication, as well as recording their confidence levels. They gave the participants a number of calculations, each one becoming more difficult. In a twist, they gave half the students so-called 'metacognitive prompts' during the testing; for example, the computer screen would flash up prompts like 'What steps are you using to solve these problems?'.

They found that the highest-performing students were those who had higher ability and self belief. The metacognitive prompting helped with speed and accuracy only with the harder sums.

The main implication of this study is that it is a combination of both self-belief and ability which aids effective problem solving.

This tool can help

Taking time to think about the kind of person you are, your thinking style, and what drives you will help to ensure that you perform to your highest ability at work. This tool is all about **how to get the most out of yourself** and will help you to make the most of your potential, by guiding you to think about how to identify your strengths and weaknesses and match this up with your motivations at work.

● GETTING THE BEST OUT OF YOURSELF

This may seem a broadly sweeping title for a development tool. The simple truth (supported by copious amounts of research) is that while there are techniques for becoming proficient at whatever you think you don't do well, the way to really get the best out of yourself is to do those things for which you have an affinity or enjoy more often!

At work, do you have the opportunity to do what you do best every day?

Out of 198,000 people asked that question, those who said they did were 50% more likely to work where there was lower staff turnover, 38% more likely to work in more productive businesses, and 44% more likely to work for organisations whose customers offered praise more often than complaint.

When we are given opportunities to do what we do well, or able to incorporate our strengths in our jobs, a positive cycle begins. That is, our resulting success builds confidence and motivation to do more of the same. There is evidence that this also positively impacts our performance generally, for example in our approach to problem solving and decision making.

● CAREER ANALYSIS CHART

It's surprising how many of us doggedly continue doing what neither inspires us nor makes use of our strengths, and then end up persuading ourselves that we have no choice – or even any talents. Here, we'll show you how to identify your own talents and where you'll find opportunity to use them in your job.

Throughout your career there will have been 'highs' and 'lows'. Try to remember what you were doing and which skills were required of you during those experiences. You'll find this easier than it sounds if you fill in the Career Analysis Chart on page 102 (we've also given you a completed one on page 101, to show you how yours might look). Follow the step-by-step guide below:

Step 1

Create a timescale on the chart which covers the whole of your career, along the middle horizontal line (this depends on the length of your career). Then fill in the time interval along the axis.

Step 2

For each 'time point', think about where you were in your career and how you felt then: Was it a career high? Did you feel happy, successful and engaged in your job? Or, was it a career low; did you feel disengaged, unmotivated, bored or restless? Or were you neutral, coasting along with no strong feelings either way? For each time interval, plot where you remember being on this scale of job satisfaction. It might help to sum up with a notable event during that time, as shown in the example chart.

Step 3

Once you've done that, join the dots so you can see where the peaks and troughs are.

Step 4

Now, for each of the peaks think about what made it particularly positive. If you're stuck, ask yourself the following questions:

- What was the environment like?
- What was motivating you?
- What skills were you using?
- What did you enjoy most?
- What were you really good at?
- What did you get rewarded/recognised for?
- What were you proud of?

Step 5

Look at the peaks and see what they have in common. Are there any skills or types of activity which are common to all the high points of your career? This should give an indication of the types of skills you could consider to be your strengths. Once you have identified the commonalities, make a list and use it in the next task, 'uncovering signature strengths'.

● CAREER ANALYSIS CHART EXAMPLE

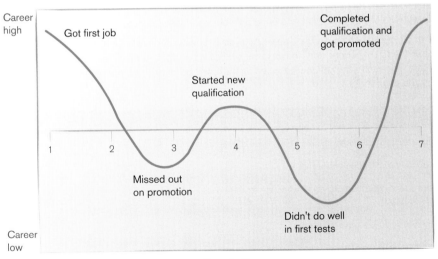

● YOUR CAREER ANALYSIS CHART

Years in Career

● UNCOVERING SIGNATURE STRENGTHS

The last task should have helped you identify some of your most inspirational and not-so-inspirational moments at work. Hopefully you will have noticed some trends of what it is that you feel that you excel at, and what you might struggle with. Also, the kind of work that you enjoy and spurs you on, and what drains you and leaves you feeling unsatisfied.

We will now start focusing on the positives. Being aware of your strengths means you can take on tasks with the ball in your court and bring out your best performance.

First of all, decide which, on the Career Analysis list below, are really your key strengths, and then number them 1-6. There don't have to be 6 – pick the right number for you based on the last exercise. For each strength you've listed, tick off any or all of the statements that were relevant when you used them.[4]

	1	2	3	4	5	6
I feel a sense of authenticity, like this is the real me.						
I feel excitement while displaying it.						
There was a rapid learning curve when my strength was first practised.						
I yearn to find new ways to use it.						
I feel that using my strength is inevitable, just try and stop me!						
I feel invigorated rather than exhausted while using my strength.						
I tend to pursue personal projects that revolve around my strength.						
I feel joy, zest, enthusiasm, and maybe even ecstasy while using my strength.						

Now, choose the one (or more) for which you've ticked the most boxes – these are your 'signature' strengths!

The next stage is to consider how you can leverage these strengths and use them more. The next section will help you.

● CAPITALISING ON SIGNATURE STRENGTHS

Asking yourself the following questions will help you discover whether you use your strengths currently and how you could capitalise on them, using them more often and in different ways. Use the table on page 104/105 to help you work through this.

What are the areas in which I currently use my signature strengths at work?

> You could review your diary over the past month, or just think through the work you've been involved in, and identify where you have used your signature strengths.

Example: One of my signature strengths is meeting and building relationships with new people. I currently use this when I work with new clients.

How often do I currently use my signature strengths at work?

> Again, use your diary to gauge how much you actually use your signature strength at work. Is it every day? Every week? A few times per month? Or less?

Example: I tend to meet new clients about twice a month, mostly when I work on new projects.

Is there potential for me to do more of this within my role? If yes, how?

> Are there opportunities to use your signature strength more?

Example: I can try to work on more new projects.

Are there any other areas of work where I can use my signature strength?

> What do you need to do in order to a) do more of the things you currently do, and b) get involved more in them?

Example: I can speak to the project managers about new projects and ask to be included in the team. I can also speak to the business development department and ask them if I can attend pitches for new business in my areas.

Are there any barriers which might stop you or slow you down? If so, what actions will you take to overcome these?

> Think about how this might impact the rest of your daily role. Are they things you could do as well? Are the 'signature strength' activities ones you could do instead of others? If so, who would you need to speak to about that? Do you have the other skills required for these activities? (be realistic here!)

Example: I can speak to my manager and ask that I be put on more projects less often, rather than the same project all the time. I might not be skilled in going to sales pitches, so I will start off by shadowing other people. The business is unlikely to pay for me to attend a conference without a clear business benefit, so I will put that option on hold for now.

By when will you have done this?

> You will have a list by now of actions which will help you use your signature strengths more, and how you can overcome any barriers. Now, set yourself a date by which you will have completed these actions, so that you have something to work towards and use to review your progress.

Example:

- Speak to the manager about which projects I work on by...
- Speak to the project managers about new projects – ongoing but aim to be on two new projects by...
- Shadow sales pitches – shadow two by...
- Attend sales pitch as part of team by...

When setting timescales, be realistic and allow slightly more time than you think you need to allow for the unexpected. When you feel under pressure, development can be one of the first things to fall off your 'to do' list, and if you keep extending your timescales you are less likely to stick to them.

● CREATING THE BEST ACTION PLAN

Strength	1. Where do I currently use it?	2. How often?	3. Can I do more?

Above and below is a set of tables into which you should enter up to 6 of the strengths that you have identified so far. From this you will be prompted with 6 questions that will get you to think about these strengths, what you are doing at the moment, and what you can do in the future, in order to get the most out of them.

Strength	4. Other areas I can use it?	5. What actions can I take to do this?	6. Barriers & how I will overcome them

Reach your ambition

It is better to reach a slightly less ambitious goal than not reach it at all!

● FURTHER INFORMATION

If you found this tool useful then you are likely to find the following tools both insightful and relevant:

- How to motivate others
- How to be assertive
- How to give feedback
- How to support and challenge in tandem
- How to deliver every time.

● REFERENCES

1 Robertson, I. (2003). The Mind's Eye: An Essential Guide to Boosting your Mental Power. London: Bantam.

2 Rogers, C. (1967). On Becoming a Person: A Therapist's View of Psychotherapy. London: Constable.

3 Hoffmann, B. & Spatariu, A. (2008). The influence of self-efficacy and metacognitive prompting on math problem-solving efficiency Contemporary Educational Psychology, 33 (4), 875-893.

4 Criteria for signature strengths taken from Peterson, C. & Seligman, M. (2004). Character strengths and virtues: A handbook and classification. Washington, DC: American Psychological Association.

INDEX

● INDEX

Page numbers in *italic* indicate a graphic or illustration